A Still, Small Voice

Healing from Abuse

Diane K. Lavett

iUniverse, Inc.
New York Bloomington

A Still, Small Voice
Healing from Abuse

iUniverse books may be ordered through booksellers or by contacting:

iUniverse
1663 Liberty Drive
Bloomington, IN 47403
www.iuniverse.com
1-800-Authors (1-800-288-4677)

Because of the dynamic nature of the Internet, any Web addresses or links contained in this book may have changed since publication and may no longer be valid. The views expressed in this work are solely those of the author and do not necessarily reflect the views of the publisher, and the publisher hereby disclaims any responsibility for them.

ISBN: 978-1-4502-1937-2 (sc)
ISBN: 978-1-4502-1938-9 (ebook)

Printed in the United States of America

iUniverse rev. date: 4/01/2010

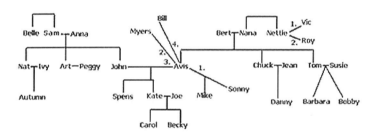

This is dedicated with hope to my children. This is also dedicated to Jessie and Sadie, who went out, and to my grandchildren, who came in.

Author's Note

The following pages tell a story that is true in all aspects except for names and locations. If you think that you recognize a neighbor, undoubtedly you are wrong.

There are two typographical anomalies in this text. First, because of the material, flashbacks occurred that were, at the time of the narration, outside the conscious awareness of the main character. Italics are used to indicate these flashbacks. The flashbacks only developed into conscious awareness later. Italics are also used to indicate flash memories that occurred during conversations. Second, current time in the manuscript is 1976-1980. Material that is written about the past, from the perspective of the characters at that time, is presented in a different type.

Additionally, there are times, especially in the beginning, when the main character dissociates and refers to herself in the third person. This has been preserved.

The therapy described in this book took place between 1976 and 1980. At that time there was little or no training for the treatment of adult survivors of physical and sexual abuse and the posttraumatic stress disorder (PTSD) that accompanies them. Most student therapists were still being taught that reports of child physical and sexual abuse by patients were the products of an hysterical personality, rather than being true. Kate Dubose and Renee Rocklin were pioneers traveling into uncharted territory, uncertain as to what they would discover or how to deal with it. The therapy used was far from the traditional therapy of the period. Renee creatively adapted methods available to her. She used terms that have since been redefined and clarified in the literature as many more professionals have done research in, and begun to treat, child abuse patients.

"And after the fire a still, small voice."

I Kings XIX, 12

Table of Contents

Prologue

We walk towards the pine woods together. He carries the fishing poles and tackle. I skip and run, trying to keep up with his gigantic strides. It is early May. The wind puffs, a crow raucously celebrates surviving until yet another time of plenty, the pine trees fill the air with fine, yellow pollen. We are alone together, and no brothers compete for his attention. I feel so very special to be alone with him.

Later I look down through the railing of the bridge and see a crayfish start climbing up my line. It is silvery in color, huge, coming at me. Its eyes stare at me, focus in on me, look at its next meal. "Daddy, there's a crayfish climbing my line." He reaches down and plucks a hook out of his tackle box.

Nervously, I look down again. Still climbing. Closer and closer. "Daddy, help me! A crayfish is coming!" He ties a firm knot, then reaches down to get his knife to cut the excess line.

"Daddy, please help me! It's getting closer and closer. It's going to pinch me and never let go. Daddy, help me!" He closes his knife and puts it in his back pocket. Then he reaches down for a worm.

The crayfish continues his deliberate climb towards me. He begins to thread the worm on the hook. Closer it climbs, closer and closer. Why doesn't he do something?

I back as far away from the crayfish as I can, holding the long pole by its very end. The crayfish appears on the fishing line in the space between the railing and the tip of the pole, and my fear takes over. I flip the butt of the pole towards the river as I wheel about and begin running to him for protection. I need, with a three-year-old's desperate intensity, to be held tightly and told that the world is safe.

He lets out a yell of surprise as the pole slides over the railing and tumbles slowly into the creek below. Reaching down, he grasps me under my armpits and begins to raise me into his arms, so I think. But he raises me and raises me until he holds me as high as his arms will allow. Then he pivots toward the railing, and he throws me off the bridge.

Like the pole moments before, I go into a slow, lazy tumble towards the spring-swollen creek. Only afterwards, as I first get my head out of the water that has held me under for so long and then try to fight towards the bank through the current, is there time enough to begin to know what has happened. Only then does fear catch up with me, chilling me far more than the water could have done.

I stop fighting against the current, stand buffeted by roiling chest-high water and turn to look up at him, bright against the dark of the pines. He leans on the rail, looking down at me curiously, wondering, it seems, how I came to be where I am.

He says nothing.

I struggle out of the water, slipping several times on the muddy bank. Then I begin trudging along the path leading towards the house where I will get a spanking from my mother for falling into the creek. Dry, soundless sobs shake me.

Part I : Discovery

Chapter 1

One day I sent my girls off to school and realized that I didn't have enough energy to send me off to school, too. I walked into the bathroom and stared into the mirror. I looked haggard and worn. I had lost over ten pounds. As I stared at myself, I remembered Mom's depression when my father was hospitalized and its effect on my brothers and me. No, I couldn't do that to my girls. They needed and deserved a fully functional mother. I would have to find a better way to cope with the situation. Most of the day I sat on the couch and gazed out of the picture window at the Long Island Sound, seeing nothing, thinking of Joe.

Since I had left him three weeks ago, Joe had been writing letters filled with anger. They arrived nearly everyday from Atlanta, ten to twenty pages long. They minutely dissected our thirteen years together and catalogued my every failure and fault. What had happened to our mutual promise to work on our relationship long distance? His letters beat at me, driving me further and further from him.

When I went out to get yet another letter from Joe in the mail box, however, a letter in different handwriting was there. It was from my father. Why now after a full five years of silence from him? When my resources were at the lowest that they had ever been, why did he have to write me now? Why couldn't he stay out of my life permanently? I wanted nothing to do with him, I had told him that so many times in the last twenty years. Why couldn't he simply leave me alone?

His letter was the proverbial last straw. I had reached the end of my ability to cope by myself, and I needed help if I were to get the girls and me through this terrible time. I called and got the name of a therapist from the Yale Health Plan. The use of Yale stationery and the Yale Health Plan were the only two tangible benefits of being a postdoctoral student at Yale. I called the therapist for an appointment. When I hung up, I felt a little hope; maybe I wouldn't have to be totally alone.

. . .

Renee's office was in an old house on Trumbull Street, just off the Yale campus and about four blocks from my lab in Kline Tower. I was terrified as I walked there that first time. All my life I had avoided therapy because I didn't want anyone to know that I was just like my father. If I could successfully hide the fact that I was like him, for all intents and purposes that meant I was not like him. I was more than willing to settle for that and had tried so hard to keep tight control of myself. Now the inevitable was happening: I had been doomed all along. I had known since I was sixteen that I had a 12.5% risk of developing paranoid schizophrenia, and I had foolishly hoped that I had won the genetic dice toss. I hadn't. I was on my way to see a therapist, and soon she would know that I was crazy.

Renee greeted me in the waiting room, then silently led me upstairs and into her office. She was young, probably too inexperienced to handle someone as difficult as me. She wasn't even a psychiatrist, just one of those "do-gooding, meddling social workers" that I had occasionally heard about. I had made a mistake in choosing her.

I looked around the office. There was a desk, a low couch, two comfortable chairs and a coffee table. There was a rather odd picture on the wall that looked like an airplane cockpit. The golden fall afternoon light shone through the window. It was a spacious, cheery room, very peaceful. It would be nice just to sit and talk quietly in it. Today I would do it, because I was there already. Later, if I still felt as if I were going crazy, I could see someone else.

Renee asked me to take a seat and, as I sat down on the couch, she sat directly opposite in one of the chairs. She really was far too young. She had big dark eyes and long raven-black hair. Slender, almost too thin, she radiated an intensity that I found uncomfortable. I had a hard time looking at her and had to keep forcing my eyes back to her face. I was having trouble breathing, and my glasses actually steamed up in the rush of pure panic that I felt.

Renee asked what brought me in. "M-my husband and I are separated, but we don't know if we are going to divorce," I stuttered. "I'm feeling very confused. I've, I've begun to stutter. I have to make a major career decision soon, and I'm in no shape to make it. Th-the kids are very angry at me. I'm afraid I'm depressed, and I know what it's like to have a depressed mother. I can't do that to them."

Renee nodded slowly as I talked. When I was through she asked, "Is there anything else?"

"No, nothing," I answered. (I am terrified!) "Why did you ask?"

"Usually," responded Renee pleasantly, "people feel some nervousness about coming to see a therapist for the first time. So I thought that perhaps you were feeling that way."

"I am. I don't want to be here at all. It's the last thing in the world that I want to do." My vehemence startled us both.

"Then why are you here?" she asked.

I shifted in my seat, so that I didn't have to face her directly. Her eyes seemed to be boring into me. "I guess because I-I feel that my kids need a mother in better shape than I am right now. I could tough this out if I were b-b-by myself. But I'm not, and I have the obligation to get better as fast as I can for their sakes."

"What about for your sake?" asked Renee.

"My sake?" I asked, somewhat confused.

"Yes, your sake. Don't you deserve to be as happy as you can be?"

(What is she talking about?) "I-I guess so. I never thought about that."

Renee smiled then. "Everyone, even you, has a right to as much happiness as their life allows, Kate. Right now your life doesn't seem to contain much of it. If we can work on some of your problems, you'll be able to find ways to add more happiness to your life."

I nodded, not knowing what to say. Renee looked at me as if she were waiting for an answer. When my silence had gone on for an uncomfortable length of time, she asked, "Of all the things that you've listed, which is the most urgent?"

"It's really something else," I answered, surprising myself. "I-I no longer trust my perceptions." (I think that I'm crazy!) "It's kind of hard to explain. I wonder if, if what I think I detect is really occurring." At Renee's raised eyebrow, I tried to tell her what I meant by that. "Joe tells me that he loves me, for instance, but I don't feel that his behavior is very loving. So I wonder if I'm so mixed up that I no longer can detect the love that he says is there." (Maybe being crazy means that you no longer can feel what is real.) "Does that make sense?"

Renee nodded yes then asked, "Can you give me an example?"

"Yes, I can," I answered, then stopped talking. Each example running through my mind made me feel increasingly ashamed. Why had I even begun talking about this? Finally, I chose the most innocuous seeming example that I could remember at the moment.

"A couple of years ago I had surgery on my left wrist. Although it was considered major surgery and took over two hours, I had it done on an outpatient basis. That was a mistake because I really wasn't able to take care of myself, let alone everyone else in the family. The pain afterwards was terrible. Joe took the girls - we have two of them - out to supper the first night, a Friday.

"At noon the next day, he said that he had to go to his office. I asked him to do the dishes first. He did, but he told me in all sorts of non-verbal ways that he was thoroughly disgusted. I was lying on the couch as he was doing them. I wanted the window open but decided to do it myself rather than ask him for anything else for a while. So I stood on the couch and pushed up with my right hand. The window gave suddenly, my hand flew up, and I smashed a finger against the top of the window frame. Immediately, I knew that I had broken it. I started screaming and jumping around the room, not really from the pain, though, because I wasn't feeling anything. Anyway, Joe rushed in just as I began to be extremely dizzy. He caught me as I started to fall and carried me back to the couch." Remembering what came next, I couldn't go any further.

"And?" prompted Renee.

"And then, then he got me some ice, finished the dishes and went to the office," I said in a rush.

"What about your finger?"

"Two days later I had an X-ray and it was broken."

"Why did you wait so long?"

"Big deal, a broken finger," I answered evasively.

"Why did you wait so long?" Renee persisted.

I felt a flush of anger at her for having to detail my humiliation. "I waited so long because Joe wouldn't take me to the hospital and I couldn't drive with a broken finger on one hand, a cast from the operation on the other and two babies to care for. That's why. Also, I didn't have any money to pay for a taxi, and I was too ashamed to ask a friend."

"Kate," Renee asked gently, "why are you feeling shame?"

(My mother must have been ashamed of her injuries from my father!) "It was my fault." (She must have thought that it was her fault that he beat her!) "If I hadn't been so stupid, I wouldn't have tried to do what I couldn't. Joe had a right to be disgusted with me." (Was my father disgusted with her? Is that why he beat her? Is that why he beat me?) "It was his way of getting back at me for being so stupid."

"And it made you feel unloved," concluded Renee.

"Yes," I sighed. "I didn't ask anyone for help because I didn't want anyone to know that Joe didn't love me enough." (Is that why my mother never asked for any help?)

"You're shaking," Renee said. "What's going on?"

"Nothing, I'm just cold, it's nothing more than that. I'm okay." (Liar! Will you ever stop?) "I remember thinking that my problem was that I no longer could recognize love when it was there. I don't know what it is anymore."

"Do you think Joe loves you now?" Renee asked.

"He says that he does."

"Do you feel loved?"

"No, but then I no longer know how love feels. I'm horribly confused about it, to tell the truth. I may never have known how love feels. I used to ask Joe if he loved me when we were first married, and he always said yes. But I didn't feel loved. One time, in our third year of marriage, I asked him and he said no. I was so devastated by his answer that I never asked again. I was afraid to hear his answer. At the time, I didn't respond for what seemed about five minutes. I lay next to him in the bed fighting against panic. When finally I could talk, I calmly asked him what had changed his feelings for me. Calmly, because I was so close to screaming in pain that I was afraid to let any emotion show. He responded that he was so very proud of me for not freaking out at that news that he loved me. I was totally confused. 'What is love?' was the only thing running through my mind. I fell asleep pondering that question, and I still don't have an answer. So anyway, I now no longer trust my perceptions. It's like there's such a huge disparity between what Joe says and what I feel that I can't trust either his words or my feelings. One is wrong but I don't know which." I took a deep breath, surprised at the conflicting emotions I was feeling as I talked. At Renee's raised eyebrow, I continued.

"I feel paralyzed by indecision because of that. If he loves me, as he says, then I'll stay with him. If he doesn't love me, as I feel, then I'll leave. But which is real?" I asked, almost in tears.

"Maybe both are, Kate," answered Renee.

"How could that be? Either he loves me, or he doesn't. Both can't be true, simultaneously." I was really irritated by the lack of logic in her statement.

"It's possible that Joe loves you but can't translate that feeling into behavior that would make you feel loved. Also, it's possible that you won't allow the feelings of love to penetrate to awareness. It's even possible that Joe is confused enough about love that he's mislabeled what he is feeling. But for us, here, what's important is that you feel unloved. That's real. Do you love Joe, Kate?" she asked.

"I don't know," I said in despair. "I care about what happens to him. If he's unhappy, I want to take the unhappiness away. Last night I was setting the table and pulled out enough silverware for the four of us. When I realized that we are only three now, I felt a bit sick to my stomach."

"You must really miss him," Renee said with sympathy in her voice.

"I do, that I know. But how much of that missing is simply habit?"

"We'll find out eventually, Kate."

"I hope so. I can't keep all four of us in suspended animation for too much longer. It's ripping us to pieces. I have got to come to a decision and act on it."

"You will, when the time is right."

Renee shifted in her chair, which caused a shift in my thoughts. I realized that I was feeling relief at being able to discuss my confusions with her. Maybe my problem was simple confusion, not craziness. If we could keep our talks on this level, then the whole issue of craziness could be avoided. (But, I feel crazy!)

The hour went quickly, amazingly so. I felt so much better as I kicked through the fall leaves on my way back to the lab that I decided to keep the appointment for next week. I liked Renee. She asked good questions, ones that helped me clarify what I felt as I answered them. If I could figure out how I felt, I could make the decisions that I needed to make. I could get loose from this terrible paralysis that I had been feeling.

. . .

Over the next several weeks I kept each appointment. I was anxious beforehand but almost euphoric with relief afterwards. The good feelings never lasted long, but they were the only ones I had all week so I looked forward to them. Renee wasn't a Freudian and my childhood had never been mentioned. We didn't need to talk about that, anyway. My problem was what to do about Joe.

He was still writing me long angry letters, attacking everything about me from my sleepiness in the morning to the type of socks I wore. I spent long hours each night defending myself in letters to him. The girls continued to be angry, but Becky was beginning to settle down and accept our new life. Carole, however, vowed to make me so angry at her that I would eventually let her go back to our house in Atlanta with Joe. Never. I wasn't going to let my family be split the way Mom had. I was a much better parent than Joe; she was going to stay with me.

Chapter 2

One day about a month later I went to see Renee feeling as if a slight knock on my head would cause me to shatter into a thousand fragments. My father had written me yet another letter that I had received the night before. His ostensible reason was that he was revising his will and needed the girls' birth dates in order to include them. His real reason was that he had been trying for twenty years to establish a relationship with me. Although a part of me had always wanted to have him in my life again, each time that I had responded to his attempt I had been ultimately forced to reject his overtures.

Still, he was the only one in the world who was reaching out to me at that moment. Everyone else seemed to be pushing me away. I longed to be able to trust him but didn't dare. Maybe later I could, but not now. But if I told him no yet one more time, he might say no later when I said yes. I couldn't handle him now, but I didn't want to tell him to leave me alone. Forgetting that I had promised myself to keep my childhood out of therapy, I started talking about the letter.

Renee began asking questions, each one more scary than the last. I started shaking. Would the hour never end? Finally I couldn't stand it anymore and got up to leave fifteen minutes early. Renee looked startled, then jumped up. She took me by the hand and asked me to explain why I was leaving early. I almost pulled away and continued out, but she had been very nice to me. She deserved some sort of explanation.

"Your questions scared me. My stomach is hurting so badly that I may vomit. I don't want to talk about her family. You'll hate me, then."

"Why would I hate you, Kate?"

"I'm so bad."

"I don't understand, you're not bad. How are you bad?"

"She's like my father. I always hurt the ones closest to me. Always."

"Who told you that?"

"My m-m-mother. Besides, it should be obvious. Everyone has left. They wouldn't have done that if I weren't so bad."

Renee looked thoughtful for a moment before asking, "Will anything you say hurt me?"

"It might. I don't want to do that, Renee. Please, let her go. Thanks for the help. I think that she'll be fine now. Please, let go of her hand."

Renee let go, but she took hold of both of my shoulders and stared into my eyes with a frightful intensity. "Kate, I can protect myself from you. I can't be hurt by you."

"You don't know me," I almost screamed at her. "If you did, you'd run away as fast as you could."

"The way your father did?" she asked.

"My father, my brothers, Joe, my kids. They all did. You will, too," I said in despair.

"Look at me for a moment, Katie. Come on, look at me. Good. I promise to stay with you as long as you need me. I won't let you hurt me, you don't have to protect me from you or anything you want to say. I will be here for you and will help you as much as I can. I promise. Will you try to believe me?"

I looked at Renee. She was leaning forward, staring intently at me, waiting for an answer. Dare I take the risk and find out for sure whether or not I am crazy? If I start talking, there will be no way out except by going forward. It will be a point of no return. Can I take whatever I might find out about myself? I can still back off, but I have been miserable for thirty-two years. It will continue unless I do something to change it. Is it better to know that I am crazy or to fear it? The girls, what about the girls? They deserve something better than divorced parents. If I straighten myself out, maybe Joe and I have a chance.

Renee was still waiting for an answer. I nodded yes, then felt her arms go around me in a tight hug. I cried for the first time since I had started seeing her, long racking sobs that shook us both. Later, as I slowly walked back to the lab, I felt drained yet strangely peaceful.

Chapter 3

"Renee, I'm scared," I began. "I almost didn't come today. I, I feel as if . . . as if the whole world is about to crash down on me." My hyperventilation made it almost impossible for me to talk. "All weekend I've had this picture flashing through my mind. I don't know what it means."

"Maybe we can figure it out together, Kate," she encouraged.

I shook my head no. There was no way in hell that I was going to let her see how crazy I was. Only someone crazy would be haunted by pictures. (Why did I even tell her about it? Am I into self-destruction now, also?)

"Katie," she said gently, "last Friday you showed me that you are very upset about your childhood. You're going to remain that way until you deal with the emotional issues from it. It's hard, I know, to start talking about what happened, but that's the only way that I can help you."

"But . . . I feel as if I have very successfully kept the lid on a box that contains horrors, except I'm not sure that they are horrible. Now you're asking me to open it up and find out what's inside," I said in near panic.

"We don't have to open that box right away." She was smiling just a little. "What we could do is take a look at the picture that's bothering you. That's right now, not something from the past."

The tension in my body had reached the point that every part of me ached as I thought about what she had said. Past or present, which is it going to be, I asked myself. Taking a deep breath, I began.

"I'm playing by myself about ten feet from a cliff. I'm really quite happy and content to be fooling around with some stones." Now that I had started, I could feel the tension easing. "I'm peaceful, actually. Suddenly you come along and ask me to leap off the cliff. You tell me that there's a beautiful country on the other side and ask me to go there with you. The way you describe it, it's so attractive. I know that I would really like it, that I would be even happier there. But when I look towards that other country, all I see is a cloud bank right at the edge of the cliff." I stopped talking, preoccupied by the choice presented to me.

"And?" Renee encouraged.

"And I'm scared." My anger at Renee surprised me. "How can I believe you? You sound very sure of yourself, but I see no indication of safety on the other side. There may be no other side. Maybe it's a deep abyss and I'll be destroyed by following you. All I see is clouds."

Both of us were silent then. I was busy being surprised at how angry I was with Renee when she began talking.

"Kate, what you are feeling is anxiety." (Is that what anxiety is? I've felt like this many times. Me? Anxious? Am I?) "You're feeling like that because we're about to start something that scares you very much. It's common at this stage of therapy, but it will pass," she reassured me.

"I feel so silly. All you're asking me to do is talk. What's scary about that?"

"It's something new, and each new experience is frightening at the beginning."

"Not for me."

"Sure, not for you. Your anxiety daydream doesn't come from you. It just wandered in and sat down in your head," she said with a faint smile. I had to start laughing at that.

"Okay, okay, I'm being silly," I said with more laughter. "I'm scared, anxious you say. Let's begin."

She smiled again, and I realized that we already had. Even while I continued to laugh at myself, I could feel the anxiety rising again. I started talking quickly, before it could reach intolerable levels once more.

"All w-w-weekend I've been trying to figure out how I can explain my childhood in a coherent way. But I get confused so rapidly when I think about it. Nothing makes sense to me. How can I explain it in a sensible way to you?"

"It doesn't have to make sense right now, Kate. If it did, there would be no reason for you to tell me about it. The confusion is a sign that you need help with what you're remembering."

"Okay, but it's going to be a mess," I predicted. "Where do you want to start?"

"You know the best place."

"I don't," I protested.

She smiled again. "Who knows better than you?"

"Okay. Sorry that I'm being so stupid today. We'll start with my mother." Once I had said that, I could go no further. As the silence grew between us, I could feel anxiety beginning to pound at me again. Taking a deep breath to control the hyperventilation I was once more beginning to experience, I started.

"My mother. My mother . . . she made a room feel good when she entered it. I've always wished that I could be as nice as she was. I'm not, though."

When my silence had gone on for an unknown time, Renee asked, "What are you thinking, Kate?"

"I was just remembering."

"What?"

"Nothing," I said with irritation. "I was just remembering. I was remembering . . . well, I was remembering something very weird. I don't know why it came to me. It's nothing."

"Kate, it's very important that you learn to pay attention to those flash memories that I suspect you're having. They are called flashbacks. Can you get back to the one that you just had?"

"Okay, but first, what's a flashback, exactly?"

"Flashbacks are memories that may be too painful to remember consciously. Sometimes a person can have a flashback and be fully aware of it at that moment. Mostly, a person cannot remember the flashback at the time and cannot convey the information to anyone else. You can be unaware of a flashback but it can still affect your behavior and feelings. Flashbacks can happen when you are very busy or very quiet or at any point between. As you become less afraid of your memories, you will remember more and more of your flashbacks. Do you think you can you get back to the one you just had?

"Leaves. Fall leaves. Crying. I can't go any farther, Renee," I pleaded even as the memory came rushing back with its' full impact. I remembered all right, but there was no way I was going to tell Renee about that.

"Leaves and dirt, Mom. I've got them in my eye! Where are you?" I shout into the silence. "It hurts bad!" Tears streaming down my face, both eyes squeezed shut in pain, I rub at my right eye even as I tell myself not to. "Mom, help!" I scream again into the silence of the living room.

From upstairs this time I hear her voice faintly. No words, just the sound of her answering. I grope my way to the stairs, then run up them as I often do, using my hands and feet much like my dog does. At the top I straighten up and call for her again, "Mom? I need help. Please."

"I'm taking a nap. What's the problem?" she yells from the bedroom.

"A bunch of us were playing in the leaves, and I got some in my eye," I answer, trying not to cry.

"Why did you wake me up for that? You know how to get something out of your eye. Pull the upper lid down, then let go slowly."

She sounds very angry because I woke her. I grope my way into the bathroom, climb from the toilet onto the sink, then sit with my feet in it while trying to look through tears into the mirror.

Frantically I try to remove the burning fire from my eye but my hands are shaking, my lid is slippery from tears and the pain is terrible. Twice I almost lose my balance. "Mom, please help. I can't do it!"

"Try a cold wet wash cloth. Your eye is probably just irritated," she yells back at me.

With both eyes closed, tears pouring down my face, I climb down from the sink and make my way to the closet where the clean wash cloths are stored. Managing to open my left eye for a fraction of an inch briefly, I find one and then make my way back to the sink. God, how it hurts! Cold water doesn't help at all. I sit on the closed toilet holding the wash cloth to my eye. Something is seriously wrong. Maybe I will lose my sight or even my eye. Then I will have to get a white cane and a seeing eye dog. They are nice dogs but awfully big. And it might fight with Taffy. How can I play baseball and go to school and stuff if I can't see? Everybody will laugh at me because of my black eye patch. I wish Mom would get up. She probably isn't even asleep because she's so mad at me. If I yell for help again, she might spank me. It hurts! Please, Mom, please, I need your help. I can't take care of this by myself. Please get up. Please. I want you to hold me. I'm scared. "Mom, this isn't working and my eye really hurts. Couldn't you please get up?"

"Dammit, Kate! Your eye's just irritated, there's nothing in it any longer. Hold the wash cloth on it until it feels better and don't wake me again," *she yells back.*

"But, Mom . . .," *I begin, but she interrupts me.*

"Do what I say! There is absolutely nothing wrong with your eye, it's just irritated. I've about had it with you, Kathryn Ann. If you wake me one more time, I'll spank you."

So I sit. I sit on the toilet for at least thirty minutes with the wash cloth held to my eye. Now and again I blindly rinse out the washcloth. The tears continue to flow, the burning gets worse. I sit.

My fear gradually turns to anger. My anger gradually turns to rebelliousness. Each sharp stab of pain pushes at my self-control until suddenly I am on my feet, crying and shouting. "I hate you. I hope you die. I'm going to run away tomorrow and never see you again. You'll be sorry you were so mean to me. You're as bad as Daddy, maybe worse because you pretend to be nice. I hate you, hate you to my guts!"

I am still yelling as Mom races out of her room and into the bathroom. She grabs me by my left arm and spins me around. Even before she begins spanking me, she is yelling at me for awakening her one time too many. She hits me lots of times, then spins me around facing her again. She is still yelling but ends suddenly as, I guess, she gets a good look at me. "Oh, my god! You're eye is all swollen. Let me see."

I shrug off her hands, put the wash cloth on my eye again and try to walk past her blindly. I don't want her to touch me now. I am crying from pain and fear and anger. Mucus is all over my face, and I hate her so badly that I shake from rage.

She grabs me again and slams me down onto the toilet seat. Then tilting my head up, she pulls my upper lid down over the lower, releasing it slowly. "Does that feel better?"

"No," I growl.

Trying several more times with no results, asking anxiously each time if she had gotten it out, she eventually straightens up and says, "You'll have to go to the eye doctor. I'll go call a cab. You wash your face, then come downstairs."

Numbly I stand up, wash and dry my face with my eyes closed, then slowly make my way down the stairs, one hand holding the wash cloth to my eye, the other tightly grasping the railing.

At the bottom, I sit on the last stair until I hear the cab honk. Mom runs up and down the stairs a couple of times, first to change her clothes, then to get me a clean wash cloth. At the honk, she pulls me up and walks me out the door to the cab, guiding me by my arm. I shrink away from her as best I can.

All the way to the eye doctor's, she apologizes. I refuse to answer her, except to shake my head "no" when she asks if I'll forgive her. Never. I hate her, hope she will die or get hit by a train or something.

Once in the doctor's office, we go straight in to see him. "Dr. Whitesides," says Mom, "Kate has dirt and leaf fragments in her eye. I tried washing them out, but couldn't," she said in a funny voice.

"Let's see," he rumbles in his deep voice. Strong hands grasp me about the waist and lift me gently into the examining chair. Gently, he forces my head back and rolls up my lid. "This will feel good, Kate," he says as a cool liquid floods my eye. It does, too, even though the burning continues some. I blink several times, then find that I can keep my eye open now. He turns out the light and asks me to look through a machine.

"Will her eye be okay?" Mom asks anxiously.

"It sure will," he answers. "She's got a number of scratches on her cornea, but they heal rapidly. I'm going to bandage her eye to

*prevent her from blinking because that hurts. Take the bandage off
in 24 hours." Then he puts a cool salve in my eye that stops all the
pain and gently tapes a soft gauze pad over my eyelid. "There, you
look just like a pirate princess," he says.*

*I look up at him with my left eye and try to smile back. Without
looking at my mother, I get up and walk into the waiting room. Behind
me, my mother thanks him over and over again. She comes out too
soon for me to have a chance to find any pictures of naked people
in the National Geographic magazines that he keeps in the waiting
room.*

*On the way home and for the rest of the day, I refuse to talk to
my mother. Even the next day, I say as little as possible before going
off to school. That afternoon, I won't let her take off my bandage
either. It makes her feel so bad that I insist on wearing it for two
extra days, until a baseball game starts up on the corner. Then I rip
off the bandage and run inside to get my glove.*

"Nothing's wrong," I said as I quickly wiped away a few tears.
"I just had a brief flash of something that I've forgotten already. I'm
cold, that's all. Really. That's why I'm shaking. It was nothing. Right
now, the only thing I'm feeling is kind of low."

"Depression?"

"Yes, I guess you could call it depression. Whatever it was that
flashed through for a moment left me feeling badly about myself, I
guess. Reminded me that I was such a rotten kid. Rotten in all ways.
I was impatient and rather vindictive. She was always making a big
deal out of everything, demanding attention. I still feel that way
about myself. If I had been better, some of the bad things wouldn't
have happened, maybe. I tried hard, but I was always in trouble about
something. It was like there was no way she could keep me from
doing something wrong."

"Kate, please let me in," Renee pleaded with me. "Maybe I can
help."

"Dammit! I said that there's nothing wrong. Why don't you
believe me?"

"Your behavior tells me differently." (Now she knows that I lie!)
"I see you crying some, very scared, feeling very, very badly about

yourself. I can't ignore that. You've remembered something that's important. What is it?"

"Nothing!" I yelled at her. The shock of my voice echoing in the room slapped me to awareness. "Okay, Renee," I said in a much subdued tone, "you're right. I remember but I can't talk about it right now. Please don't make me."

"Kate, I can't make you talk about anything. Surely you understand that," she said with a hint of sadness in her voice.

"I do." Even I could hear the regret in my answer. It would be so much easier if it weren't me who had to decide to say what needed to be said. "I was remembering something about my mother, that's all. And there's something else. All my life I've told myself that she was nice, very nice, that everyone loved her. Everyone told me she was nice. It was always like that. But some of my memories don't square with that. Do you know what I mean?"

"It reminds me of your problem with Joe," Renee answered. "He says that he loves you, but you don't feel loved by him."

"Yah." I could feel myself sinking into gloom.

"Your feelings are real, Kate, even if they don't square with what other people say."

"I know, I guess." The sigh came from deep within me. "Except, it's so hard to know what's real. Was she nice or wasn't she? Does he love me or doesn't he? I don't trust myself enough to decide between the alternatives."

Renee waited until she was sure that I had stopped talking before asking me, "Do you suppose that you could tell me something about your mother?"

"I guess," I said, then was silent. I stared at the floor remembering, remembering the memories that I had always not allowed to register before. The room was quiet as Renee waited for me to find some words.

"I remember . . . I remember when I was sixteen. I spent the summer at the University of Chicago in a National Science Foundation program. I was studying genetics. There were ninety of us, all kids in high school. It was a great summer. One evening I was in a friend's room. Her name was Carla. Somehow or other she and I started talking about our mothers. I said something - I don't remember what, maybe something about promises never kept - and she said that I sounded very angry at my mother. It surprised me, but I knew she was right. Right then I had a flash memory of when I was eleven. My brothers, Spens and Mike, and I were on a week's vacation at a cottage with our father. The people next door were curious. Instead of telling them that my parents were divorced, I told them that my mother had died."

"You did?" Renee asked, very surprised.

"Yes," I said with shame.

"But why?"

"That's what my mother asked when Mike, my older brother, told her. I didn't know how to answer. She cried and accused me of wanting her dead. I felt terrible. Can you imagine how I felt then?"

"Not really."

"Well, it was horrible. I didn't want to make her cry. I didn't want to hurt her, Renee. I didn't want her dead. Except now, I think that I really did want her dead." I was horrified at my words.

"Why, Kate," Renee asked gently.

"I don't know, Renee, I really don't." And I didn't. I had no idea at all of the source of my anger. I didn't even feel angry at that moment, just defeated and ashamed.

Perhaps for the first time in my life I let myself simply feel for a while. The silence extended into many minutes as wave after wave of emotion washed over me. I was vaguely aware of Renee in the room but felt no pressure to pay any attention to her right then. Finally, though, she broke into my thought with a request. "Tell me, Kate." When I didn't respond, she spoke again. "Kate, the first day here you spoke about your broken finger. Do you remember?" I nodded yes. "It was the example you chose when you wanted to explain your confusion over Joe and love. He clearly did not take care of you when you broke your finger. I'm wondering if your confusion over your mother also concerns her taking care of you. Did she?"

I began to answer her very carefully, for we were on dangerous ground. I simply could not tell her some things. I couldn't say them about my mother to someone who had not known her. She wouldn't understand and would get the wrong impression. I couldn't lie that way about my mother. "I had good medical attention when I was a kid. Doctors, dentists, the usual. Remember, we were firmly middle class. But routine hygiene was not taught in our house, as far as I remember. No one checked to see if a child brushed his teeth. If I needed to go to the dentist for a check-up it was up to me to remember it, to make the appointment and to get myself there from the time I was about seven. I must have had earlier training, though, or I wouldn't have known to see dentists. I could have learned it at school, I guess, because hygiene was part of the elementary school curriculum. Maybe, with so much going on in the house, the non-essentials were simply forgotten.

Although I have been able to force myself to walk the half mile to the dentist's office, I am stopped now from crossing Main Street and entering the low, red brick building. Running through my mind is my mother's voice, telling me about her trips to the dentist in pre-Novocain days. Her father had had to spank her with his shoe to keep her in the chair. Sometimes our dentist doesn't use Novocain. Then, he tells me to be brave. But it reminds me of when my father hurts me. Why should I sit still and let someone hurt me? Maybe this time he won't use Novocain because Mom isn't here. Darn! Why did Mom tell me about her father hitting her to keep her in the chair? She's giving me her fears, I don't want them.

Maybe the dentist will hit me if I complain too much. I don't like him. He always makes my gums bleed, and he tells me not to be such a baby when I spit in the bowl and see the blood. And I feel like I'm dying when he has his fingers in my mouth. If I don't cross the street right this minute I'll be like Mom, who's so scared to go to the dentist that her teeth are rotting in her mouth. I don't want to be like her.

But I'm scared. Maybe I'll call his office later today and tell him that I forgot the appointment. I can make another one, for later. A couple days or a week won't make any difference. But, if I don't go today, I'll feel like a coward, a baby, and it will be harder to go next time. Mom, why aren't you here with me? Little kids shouldn't have to supply their own courage.

"It was no big thing. My mother was busy, why should she have to do what I could do without her? It would waste her time. Look, by the time I was nine I was taking care of herself because there was no r-r-reason at all why I couldn't. I was big enough. I took myself to the pediatrician, after making the appointment, from about seven also. The polio vaccine became available when I was eleven; I was the one who called the doctor and found out the schedule for immunization. When I got sick, I put myself to bed. I was my own mother because I didn't need anyone else to be. I could take care of myself."

"Were you neglected, Katie?"

"That's a dumb question. No, she didn't neglect her. Her mother wouldn't do that. Her mother loved me. If I had really needed help, she would have been there. But those kinds of things, doctors and dentists, who needed help with them? I didn't."

My mother and I get out of the taxi cab. She hands me a dollar and tells me to go to the Little Store and get two bottles of Vernor's Ginger Ale for my throat. The Little Store is not too far away, just a little over a block, and I have been going there on errands since I turned four last month. I proudly walk to the store all by myself. When I tell Ken, the owner, that I need to get two bottles of Coke, because I like it better than Vernor's, he gets them for me. When I get home with the Coke, my mother is very mad at me and sends me back to the store. I am embarrassed when I tell Ken that I was really supposed to get ginger ale. He asks me who is sick. "No one," I answer. "I just had my tonsils out this morning and the doctor said it would help with my throat."

"Did you take care of your mother when she was sick?"

"Sure, I took care of her. What kind of kid wouldn't help when it was needed? I wanted to help her. It was like I was her mother, sort of. She didn't have anyone else to help her. What would have happened to her if I didn't care enough to help?"

"Why are you shaking, Kate?"

"It's just getting colder in here, that's all." (Why didn't she care enough about me to take care of me?) "Can't you feel it?" (I must have been a horrible kid.) "Do you mind if I put on my coat?" (What was wrong with me?) "My mother was a good mother." (If she didn't take care of me, it is because deep down I am very bad.) "I'm sure that she loved me."

Chapter 4

"Kate, I think that I need to give you some homework." Renee broke into gentle laughter at the face I made at her suggestion. Almost, I laughed with her. "For the last month or so you have come to every session so filled with anxiety that I have been spending all our time together trying to reduce it. It's okay, Kate, I don't mean to criticize you for being anxious. I expect anxiety at this stage of therapy." How she guessed at the rush of guilt I had felt at her words, I didn't know, but her knowing without my telling raised a momentary hope that maybe she cared a little about me. "The problem is, however, that I am not learning anything about your past this way. Every time I ask a question that could lead you backward in time, your anxiety goes up another notch and . . ."

"I don't think we need to talk about my past. It's done and gone, over, finished," I interrupted.

"Yes, it's done and gone, but it is not over and finished, Kate. It's with you every moment of every day, as far as I can tell. Your response to my questions tells me that. Every time that I ask a question about your past, you go mute on me. There are things that I must know about you in order to help you; only you know what those things are," Renee said patiently.

I stared out the window, not acknowledging her words in any way. She was right, of course, even I could see that. I did not want to admit that she was right, though, because then I would have to start talking. What she did not realize was that I literally could not talk. There were no words when it came to describing the past.

The silence between us went on and on, and I was content to let it be forever. Renee wasn't, however, and eventually she started talking again. "What I have in mind is this, Kate. I want you to start writing about your childhood. Each session, I want you to bring a minimum of five pages to me. More would be all right, but five is the minimum. I will read what you wrote between sessions. In here, we can either talk about what you have written since the last time I saw you, or we can talk about what you wrote that I read since the last session. Or we can talk about any topic of your choosing. The important part is that you keep writing. Do you think that you could do that?"

I nodded my head yes in reply, although I was not at all sure that I could do the writing.

"Okay, Kate, bring five pages in tomorrow. We're through for today."

"What do you mean 'we're through!' We just started five minutes ago." The surge of anger I felt was incredibly strong.

"Yes, we just started, and you have barely said five words. It's not good for you to be doing this. This room and this time are for talking. We'll meet again tomorrow, when you have written at least five pages. Maybe then you will have something to say."

When I slammed out of her office, that was it, I was never going to see her again. All the way back to work, I kicked viciously at the leaves which were now a dry and brittle brown. To hell with her, I didn't need her help at all! I didn't need anyone's help. I could go it alone, just like I've always been alone. No one could help, anyway.

The seething anger remained with me through the rest of the day, on my drive home, throughout the evening. When the girls were finally asleep, I sat for a long time in the deathly quiet house without thought. Then I dragged myself over to my briefcase and pulled out the yellow pad of paper I had tossed into it at the last moment before leaving the lab. My task was impossible. For an unknown time I looked into space and then, without real self-awareness, slowly and tentatively, I began to write.

. . .

Before a tornado ripped through the area, tall old oaks lined all the streets in the neighborhood. There were eight in our yard, three in the front and five in the back of the lot that stretched down

Hawthorne Street. In the summer they fully shaded the yard so that grass struggled to grow. Every spring my father dug up the grass in the front and reseeded it with hope. He made a string fence to keep off kids who would cut across the grass instead of walking around the corner on the sidewalk. He spread straw over the newly-seeded dirt until the tender green shoots were several inches high. Then he raked up the straw and hoped that this year his grass would take root. It never did. Despite his careful tending of it, it turned brown and died in large patches.

In the fall, those lovely old oaks would let go of their leaves. By then my father must have tired of hoping about his yard, because he never raked them. Instead, Mike and I had to do it. I always found it exciting. We raked piles taller than my head and sometimes ten to fifteen feet long. Invariably we had a leaf fight. We whooped and shouted, throwing armfuls of leaves and diving headfirst into the pile in order to escape from each other in the mock fight. Friends frequently joined us, and we formed teams and did battle.

By late afternoon we would have the leaves down as far as the sidewalk. Then it was time to start the fire. In the front of the house, on Alexander, the grass on the other side of the sidewalk merged into the street with no curb. It was there that we set the fire going.

I ran into the house and got newspaper. Mike and I balled it up, then piled leaves onto it. Our mother came out of the house, walked slowly down the front sidewalk and ceremoniously lit the fire. She smiled softly, then went inside to finish supper. As the flames rose and the heavy smoke spread in a deliciously smelling pall out from the fire and through the neighborhood, friends gathered again. I felt so very important as the only one allowed to dump on more leaves. Mike stood with the rake next to the fire and told me when to add them. He kept all the other kids away and let only me close. It was exciting to run up and dump on new leaves, ducking through the eye-stinging smoke.

We ate our supper on the lawn, watching to make sure that the fire didn't spread. As night descended, the glowing red became the total focus of our attention. I looked into the fire, imagining whole cities and forests going up in flame. Often Mike and I sat cross-legged on the grass, watching the fire and singing softly. Somehow both of us knew many songs from the twenties, thirties and forties, and we crooned such tunes as "Sentimental Journey" and "Begin the Beguine" together. My favorite was "Melancholy Baby."

Other nights we had to come in when the streetlights turned on. Until then we played such games as "Red Light, Green Light" and "Snail" with the many kids on our street. My favorite was "Kick the Can," a form of hide-and-seek that surged back and forth through the neighborhood, driving childless couples to distraction.

The corner of Hawthorne and Alexander was the center of the neighborhood for some reason. That's where we played softball during the summer and football during the fall. When it was time to choose up teams, Mike and Jimmy Quin were always the captains because they were biggest and oldest. I was never chosen first because I was too small, but Mike made sure that I never had to endure being chosen last. He would pass over bigger and better players for me, and my heart used to feel as if it were bursting with pride because my brother Mike, the captain, took care of me. Jimmy would do the same for Danny, his brother who was a year younger than I.

If we weren't playing games, we were climbing trees, trying to catch bees in glass jars, hopping fences, climbing on someone's garage roof or riding bikes. Marble games occupied us in early spring. When the Duncan Yo-yo man came around to demonstrate tricks and hold a contest after school each year, we were inspired to long hours of practice, which resulted in the entire neighborhood wearing a band-aid on their middle finger.

Sometimes a gang of us walked the mile to the furniture store on Main and dragged back huge furniture boxes that we used to build vast interconnecting bunks. We put them together close to the dining room window, and Mike ran an extension cord out of the house. Then we plugged in his radio and the bunker became home in which we played Monopoly, read comic books and ate our lunch. After it rained we sadly tore down the bunker and dragged the soggy boxes out to the curb on Hawthorne for the garbage men.

When we moved into the house on Alexander there were a number of vacant lots in the area. One, everyone's favorite, was actually three big city lots completely covered in trees. It was the "Small Forest." Mike and Jimmy dug a huge hole back in the woods and covered it over with branches. The only ones they allowed inside were Danny and me, but only on special occasions. The rest of the time they acted as if the "Small Forest" was their hunting grounds and they were Indians. Anyone who entered the woods was liable to be attacked by them. They made Indian calls, threw rocks and, if necessary, swung sticks to chase off all intruders.

The summer I was six, Danny and I were invited into their bunks, as they called it. We read comic books by candlelight, which of course was forbidden, and ate peanut butter sandwiches from supplies our older brothers had stolen from Jimmy's house. When it was time to leave, I slipped trying to crawl out and cut my arm in several places. I tried not to cry because Mike would taunt me with "Baby, baby" and never let me come back again, but the tears ran silently down my face anyway. Instead of teasing me, though, Mike helped me out and took me home, telling me how brave I was, that I would get a Purple Heart if only I were in the army. I was both surprised and not at all surprised at the same time. Like all older brothers, Mike capriciously wielded his power. Always, I expected the worst from him; often I was pleasantly surprised.

The "Big Forest" was the cemetery woods. A block from my house, down across Gardenia, was the extra property owned by the local cemetery. It was a heavily wooded area, about a half square mile in size. It was surrounded by a ten- foot fence that ceased to be a barrier to me by the time I was six. There, too, we built bunks. It was there that we hid out when we skipped school. Danny and I made bows and arrows and hunted for hours for deer. Stories of ghosts seen lurking in the woods only added to the fun since all of us weren't absolutely sure that ghosts weren't real.

The "Little Store" was a block away also. Ken, the owner, always smiled and said "hi" when we came in. He would leave any adults with whom he might be talking and go stand behind the candy counter while we deliberated as to how we would spend the deposits from empty pop bottles begged from childless neighbors. He had only one rule for us in his store: we had to put the candy wrappers in the trash can. None of us would dare throw them on the street because, if Ken saw, we could not go into his store for a week. When I started collecting pennies, Ken let me take home overnight two cigar boxes filled with rolled coins so that I could sort through them. I sat on my bed for hours looking especially for a "1909-VDB."

On my street, across Hawthorne and five houses down the block was the 'Idiot.' He lived with his gray-haired mother, who walked him to the corner and back each day while he sat strapped into his wheelchair and made animal grunts at us. We always crossed the street to safety when he was out.

Three houses closer lived the 'Witch.' She had a son, Georgy, who went to some private school and was never allowed to play with us. His mother was called the witch because she always came out on the porch and yelled at us if we stepped on her grass. Often, she had a broom in her hand.

The 'Old Ladies' lived down Hawthorne, next to Jimmy and Danny. There were two of them. If kids quietly went up and knocked on their door, the 'Old Ladies' would give them a piece of candy even when it wasn't Halloween. Mike and Jimmy dug under their front porch, where they had their clubhouse. They lit candles under there and one day set the porch on fire. All of us were terrified when the fire engines roared up to put out the flames. Our parents were furious at having to pay the damages.

There were other neighbors, of course. Buddy, who was eighteen and enlisted in the marines, came back two weeks after his neighborhood going away party and cut his throat. He died. Dick, who lived right next door to me and was my age, was always crying. Paul, whose parents spoke with a German accent, was a regular kid who was forced to practice violin every day for three hours. Bobby had a tumor removed from his big toe. No one knew the Germans because they kept so much to themselves. The Hahn family had eight kids - three girls and five boys. Mrs. Hahn didn't know how to read a thermometer so their son, yet another Jimmy, had heart damage from a strep infection before she took him to the doctor. He was in the hospital for a long time. Later he became a priest because his heart "wouldn't stand the strain of married life." Mr. Hahn was a mailman who had a nervous breakdown each time the two sets of twins were born. Doris became a nun. Johnny was disowned by his parents because the woman he married wasn't Catholic. My mother and Ken, the owner of the "Little Store," pretended to be his parents at the wedding. There were many neighbors, and I know stories about each one of them.

Chapter 5

"Kate! How many pages did you write? That's amazing!" Renee looked shocked but pleased as I handed her over ten pages from my yellow pad.

"Writing felt good, so I continued until I fell asleep around three this morning. It was like I was back in my neighborhood for a while. I really loved my neighborhood as a child, you can see it in those pages."

"How did you feel while you were writing?"

"Like a child, sort of. In fact, I think that I became the child I was while I was writing."

"Did any problems crop up?"

"Yes. A number of times something would occur to me, and then immediately I wouldn't be able to remember what it was."

"You were probably having flashbacks, Kate. Try to catch them next time if you can. Anything else?"

"Yes, sometimes I referred to myself in the third person. I don't understand that at all."

"Kate, you also do that when you are talking at times. I think that it indicates dissociation, which I don't want to go into for now. We'll talk about it at a later time, but don't worry about it for now. Leave it in when it happens. Any other problems?"

"Yes, there was one. The problem is that that kid from so long ago who turned out to be me, doesn't feel connected in any way to who I am now. I can look at her, remember exactly what she was wearing, the place where she was, who was there. I can even remember what she felt and thought as she made angels in the snow or played with her friends, but there's no emotional connection to her. For example, I can still feel the snow creeping down my collar and up my wrist from the slight opening between my mittens and the cuffs on my coat, I remember thinking that the chill was worth the beautiful angel that I was making, I remember hoping that this time I could get up and away from the angel without marring it with my footprints, but that kid is not me. She's someone else whom I observe thinking and feeling all those things. It's always been that way. I'm on the outside, watching what she was doing. When I think about her, it's as if I'm telling myself a story about her. I don't know how to bring her closer or make her me. Besides, she's not really me at all."

"That's dissociation, again, Kate. Eventually it will disappear, I promise."

"Whatever you say. This was a wonderful idea, Renee. Thank you for giving me back my streets for a while. There's nothing that I feel like talking about, however, so what I would like to do is go now, write until my next appointment, and then talk. Is that okay?"

"If it's what you want, Kate, that would be fine with me. Next Tuesday at four?"

"Sure, fine, see you then," I said and rushed out the door. Earlier in the week I had planned a three-day experiment, starting first thing in the morning. Now, however, I postponed that work for the entire week so that I could continue writing about the time that had been. The log jam had broken, and I had to take immediate advantage of the hole.

. . .

My house was an old colonial, red brick on bottom and white wood on top. Entering from the front porch, stairs leading up were on the left and the living room was on the right. The floor of the living room was covered with a red oriental rug whose patterns I traced over and over as I was growing up.

Behind the living room was an open arch that led to the dining room. If, as soon as you entered the dining room, you turned left, you would be in the kitchen. You could get out the side door of the kitchen, which opened onto Hawthorne. There were three stairs leading down from the kitchen to a small landing where the door to outside was. Also leading off the landing were the steps to the basement. Down there was a huge coal-burning furnace and a coal bin with an outside opening of its own. Each fall the coal truck would arrive and unload tons of coal with its chute. Black dust and an incredible racket rose into the air.

At the top of the stairs that were next to the living room was the bathroom. There was a short L-shaped hallway off of which were three bedrooms. *(the bedroom door slowly opens and light from the bathroom draws his silhouette he stands without moving i lie without breathing a cord of tension connects us each knows that the other is aware)*

Mike was my favorite brother even though he got to stay up a half hour later than I because he was more than four years older. Mike liked to play war at night with little figures he made from clay. He messed up his blankets to make the battlefield then would hide the two armies - one red and one green - in the hills he had formed. The scouts stabbed their enemies with toothpick knives or bayonets. He used toothpicks for rifles and pistols, too. Sometimes Mike let me play, but I always had to be the Germans so it wasn't much fun to know I had lost before I had begun.

Other nights Mike listened to the radio: "The Shadow," "The Fat Man," "Baby Snooks." Sometimes he let me hide under his covers or bed, depending on his mood, so that I could stay up and listen, too. When I was eight we heard the broadcast that said Fanny Brice had died, and we cried together. I remember one story, I think it was on "The Shadow," that involved a rattlesnake which came back to get the man who killed its mate. I had nightmares about that one for several years, and it wasn't until I was in graduate school that I learned snakes don't behave that way.

Mike had black, curly hair and big dark eyes. I thought he was very handsome. He laughed a lot and hardly ever was really mean to me. Mike hated school.

My younger brother Spens was a real pain. He was blond-haired and had big blue eyes. He looked just like an angel my mother said, but he was very bad. He told lies, stole things, had wild temper tantrums and swore a lot. My mother didn't know what to do with him. He looked like our mother but acted like our father. Spens was three-and-a-half years younger than me, a real baby.

I looked like my father but acted like my mother, except when I was angry. Then I acted just like him. I had brown straight hair, big brown eyes. I was small and skinny as a kid. My mother never had my hair cut from the time I was born. I wore it in heavy braids and hated having it combed every morning. I had to stand very still and ignore the sharp pains as my mother jerked through the tangles. Sometimes I would cry and move my head; then she would slap my bare legs with the comb and tell me to stand still. When I was six I was in a braid contest at the Michigan State Fair. The judge never saw me though because the big kids pushed me to the back. My mother got mad at me for letting them do it. The platform was so crowded that I fell off and skinned my knee.

I loved school, except for spelling. Both Mike and I couldn't learn to spell at all. Even though I could read long before I entered kindergarten, I always wore my shirt that had my name written in candy cane letters on days that I knew we were going to have to write our names.

Everybody said I was a tomboy because all those friends I told you about were boys. I learned to throw baseballs and footballs like a boy, Mike taught me to fix my bike all by myself, and I could run faster than anyone my age, so I was a tomboy. I hated that name, 'tomboy.' It meant that people thought I was really a boy, but I wasn't. I was just like all the other girls except that I didn't like to do girl things. Playing with paper dolls could never be as good as what I was doing every day.

My mother said that she had been a tomboy, too, but it was hard to believe. She always wore dresses and spent hours putting on her make-up. I used to lie on her bed and watch her, and sometimes she let me play with her jewelry box. Everyone told me that my mother was very nice. *(don't leave please i promise to be good please mom)* She was, too. Every year she invited my teacher and Mike's home for lunch, and she was president of the PTA when I was in second grade. She was also pack leader when Mike was in Cub Scouts. She even organized the first March of Dimes canvass of the neighborhood and let me go out collecting with her that night.

I got to hold the money. Mom wanted to be a doctor but her father wouldn't let her, so she got married.

My mother was really tall, five feet six. She said that she had always felt like a horse, but I thought that she was beautiful. She had blond hair that she wore long, sometimes on top of her head, and blue eyes. All my relatives said that when she was a teenager she had had a perfect figure and that the boys were always after her. Mom used to talk to me some about her old boyfriends, but she said that I shouldn't tell Daddy about them all. It was just between us.

My dad was a salesman for Crosse and Blackwell and had been hurt in the war. That's why he acted so mean, it wasn't his fault. His back was covered with all sorts of scars. He showed them to me and told me all about his tank. He'd painted my name on it when I was born, but it was blown up by a mine and he was the only one who lived. He should have gotten a Silver Star, but he only got a bronze one because he got hurt. But he was a real hero anyway. When he was in France he bought some records made by Edith Piaf, which he kept upstairs under the sheets in the linen closet. He told me that his father was from France. My dad was a Methodist but he didn't like to go to church.

My mother liked to go to church all the time, but she never went to the same one. I thought that she should go to the Episcopalian church where her uncle had been a minister, but she didn't like it. Every Sunday my dad drove Mom and me to a different church, and the two of us would go inside. He always seemed angry about it. She never made Spens or Mike go with her, but I always had to. Once I asked her why we went to a different church each week. She answered that she was looking for something and I wouldn't understand it. When we were through, we'd have to stand outside waiting for my father, and my mother was always sad.

During the summer I used to go to vacation Bible school with my friends. Usually I went to three or four different churches. We played games, sang songs and had good snacks. In return, I had to learn some Bible verses, but that was easy. When I was seven I brought home a picture of Jesus and put it in the glass-enclosed bookcase that stood in the dining room. I was looking at it that evening, enjoying the very first picture in a frame that was all mine, when my dad came up to me. With a strange intensity he asked me if I loved Jesus. I had never thought about loving Jesus before and didn't know how to answer. He was acting like it was very important, so I tried hard to guess the right answer. I told him yes, after thinking that he wouldn't have asked me if he didn't want me to love Jesus. He looked at her for a few moments, nodded his head twice and relaxed. She did, too.

There was a lot of talk in our neighborhood and in our family about Jews. Royal Oak was restricted, I knew, and Mom said that meant that Jews couldn't live there. She didn't say why. I also knew that something bad had happened to them during the war, but no one ever told me what. Mom used to say that I looked like a 'DP' when I came in at night from playing, and I knew that meant I looked like a Jew after the war. Nana, my grandmother, said they brought down property values; first comes the Jews, then comes the niggers. Every time she said that, Daddy would get really mad and maybe a little bit scared; he didn't say anything, but I could tell. I used to say someone had 'jewed' me, until Mike told me what it meant. Once I asked Mom's friend Con what the difference was between Jews and other people. She said Jews were still waiting for the Messiah and Christians thought the Messiah had already come. I decided that the Jews were right because people were still fighting a lot.

(We walked up the steps of the huge Shrine of the Little Flower. Daddy said to be quiet and to keep his handkerchief on my head. It was all gray stone, and our footsteps echoed as we walked into the lobby and entered a big room with a very high ceiling. Right next to the door of the room there was a bowl attached to the wall. It had water in it. From the ceiling of the big room distant lamps hung from chains, swaying slightly. Far up in front was a stage and behind it, a huge cross with Jesus dying on it. It was scary. On the side walls were big windows, 'way up high, that had pictures made from colored glass. Below them there were lots of tables that had their tops covered with candles in jars. Some of the candles were lit, and the flickering flames threw orange dancing shadows on the wall.

Daddy clamped his hand on my shoulder and steered me to the closest table on the right. With his other hand he reached into his pants pocket and pulled out a lot of money. He put it in a bowl that already had money, even dollars, in it. Then he said that he would light a candle for me and I should pray for my dead. He didn't tell me who they were.)

We didn't always live in Royal Oak. Before we lived there, we stayed at Mom's parents' house in Detroit. Mike and I slept in their basement even though both of us were scared of the big picture of the tiger on the wall. I could have slept on the couch in the living room, but it felt safer to be with Mike. Before we lived with them, we lived out in the country near Flint.

In Flint, we had a blizzard and Mom said we would have to eat Blackie's dog food if the roads didn't get cleared soon. She put it right on the table, just in case. We made popcorn one night just before Christmas, but then I wasn't allowed to eat it. *(damn you kate i told you to watch out for the pan now you've got the burn you deserve for being such a bad girl)*

Spens was born while we lived there, when I was three-and-a-half. I remember waking up one morning and being surprised to see my grandmother Nana. She said that I had a new brother. I was mad at Mom for not telling me she was going away, and I got even madder when we went to visit her. Mike and I couldn't go into the room, so Nana held us up to the window. It was a huge room, filled with beds. Mike said he could see her, but I couldn't. Mom said that I had had another brother named Spens, also. He died right away when he was born, so I didn't ever get to see him. I was in the hospital a couple of times when we lived in Flint.

Before we lived in Flint, Mom, Mike and I lived in a house on Westmoreland in Detroit. Dad was in the war then. You probably think that I can't remember that far back, because I was only two, but I can. I can remember many things: I got worms from eating dirt, and Mom said if only I had obeyed her she would not be so embarrassed by having to buy the medicine for me. Grandpa Bert had an accident in his car on Christmas Eve, and I bumped my head. *(gregg the boy next door kept biting me mom and his mother tied him into his high chair taped his mouth closed and tried to make me bite him even when they spanked her i refused i didn't want to teach him a lesson)* Bert held me one day while I was having my temperature taken, and I bit off the end of the thermometer. Everyone yelled at him, but I said that I didn't swallow the piece. Mike was locked in the backyard for a whole month because he pulled down someone's pants. I remember lots more than this, but I don't want to write about it now. Maybe some other day I will.

We moved into our house on Alexander when I was four. Mike had his own room. Spens, who was just one, had his crib in my room. Sometimes I had trouble sleeping. (*i hear him walking down the hall towards my door when the bedroom door slowly opens i can see him outlined by the hall light at his back through half-closed eyes maybe this time he will only stand watching me for a while*) Then, I would get up and move his arms and legs. I was fascinated that he wouldn't wake up even though they were moving. I wanted to have a horse. I told Mom that there was plenty of room in my closet for one, that he wouldn't be in the way at all, but she laughed and said no.

I didn't spend much time in my room because mostly I lived with Nana and Bert, Mom's parents. I was the favorite grandchild, although Mike had been before I was born. Bert taught me to play solitaire. In the evenings I would sit on his lap on the back porch until I fell asleep. He would yell "Yak, I need a cigar," and my grandmother would come running with one. She'd take off the cellophane and hand it to him. Then he'd give me the ring while she lit a match for him. He said he called her 'Yak' because she always yakked at him.

Nana was from England. She was the oldest of nine kids, and they'd all sailed together to Hamilton, Ontario. All of them lived on top of the Mountain in Hamilton. Only Nana and Nettie and Dolly had come to the United States.

I went with Bert and Nana to Hamilton a couple of times a year. Sometimes we took the train. Sometimes we drove. Once we took the boat and got to sleep on it overnight. We always stayed with Jackie and Cecil, who was Nana's brother. He turned Catholic to marry Jackie. In Canada I had all sorts of relatives.

Bert was make-up editor of the Detroit News. That meant he had to get up at three in the morning to go to work. Nana would get up with him and fix his breakfast while he shaved. Then she would tie his tie and do up his cuff links for him. Since I always slept with Nana in her room when I was there, I usually got up when she did. Later, I would go back to bed. Bert slept in a nightgown, which was pretty funny for a man to do.

Every afternoon Nana and I took the bus to the Grandmont Bar where we met Bert and his friends from work. I got to play one game of table shuffleboard. Then I sat beside Bert while he opened pistachio nuts with his knife for me and talked with his friends about the news. Sometimes Nana's sister Nettie, who also worked on the paper, was there too. We'd stay until it was five o'clock and then go home.

Sometimes on Saturday night Bert would have all his friends over for a poker game. They stayed until it was time for the Catholics to go to mass. Bert taught Mike and me how to play poker, and we played for toothpicks, popcorn or even sometimes money. Mike always tried to talk me into playing on allowance day, but I didn't like to because he cheated.

I liked staying with Nana and Bert. Although Nana yelled at me a lot, I was never spanked by either of them. At home I got spanked all the time.

Mostly my father spanked me, but sometimes Mom did after she explained that she was doing it so she could tell my dad that I had already been spanked. She said that she was protecting me from him, and I always had to thank her. *(you dumb stupid kid no one not anyone I ever met has an elephant's trunk in his pants i don't want to hear about it again god I'm so sick of you and your stories)* Once when Mom was at a PTA meeting he came into my bedroom. I woke up when he turned on the light, so he spanked me with his slipper for being awake that late. Another time, he spanked me very hard for falling down and skinning my knee. When we lived in Flint she got spanked because I caught a crayfish while fishing. It scared me, so I threw the pole into the water and went back home.

The only time I can remember him being nice to me was when we lived in Flint. One night he taught me not to be afraid of thunder and lightning. He turned out all the lights in the house. *(the elephant's trunk waves in front of my face it hits me on the nose moves up toward my eye slides down my cheek leaving a trail of wetness it caresses my neck i hold my breath hoping that it will go away instead of eating me i try to move my head from side to side both ways are blocked it pushes hard under my chin and now I can't breathe even if I want to i gasp for air as my mouth opens the elephant's trunk dives into it)* He showed me how pretty it was in the sky. After we moved to Royal Oak, he was never nice.

Chapter 6

"I don't know why. Suddenly I was feeling very scared and I had to stop writing. My hands were shaking and I couldn't think clearly. I was hyperventilating, also. It just came in on me, from nowhere."

"Like your anxiety cloud?"

"Yes, it was that quick."

"How are you now, Kate?"

"Still feeling shaky. I haven't really slept for a couple of days, since I stopped writing. Renee, I don't want to continue, it's making me dizzy. I can't see any connection between what happened so long ago and my problems now. What I've been writing about is so remote from who I am that there's a dream-like quality for me in everything I've been saying. Maybe I made it all up to justify my anger. It's possible, you know. Maybe none of it happened or it happened but it simply wasn't as bad as I remember that it was. Maybe the only thing that was truly wrong was my reaction to what happened. Maybe someone else wouldn't have been bothered by it at all. I get so confused when I think about all this. It's as if I lose all ability to judge, to evaluate. I feel lost, the world is spinning because I don't know if I even have a right to feel angry if what I remember did actually happen."

"That confusion you're feeling, Kate, is massive anxiety. Something happened, or you would not be feeling so very anxious. Maybe you are off on the details a little, or maybe you are off on the details a lot. It really doesn't matter if what you remember is absolutely accurate."

"It does, though. If I am making up something instead of remembering it, then I am actually telling lies about my parents and I am getting angry with them for no reason. My father has always said that there is no basis for my anger at him. Maybe he is right."

"You were a child when whatever happened, happened. It was a long time ago, and you were very upset at the time. When adults are confronted with a shocking, sudden event, very frequently they report inaccurately. They do that with virtually no time separating them from the event. The inaccuracy doesn't mean that they did not experience something extremely disturbing. The inaccuracy is a function of how disturbed they were at the time the event took place. So what's important is that you are remembering events, in a very hazy sort of way, that are very disturbing."

What Renee said made sense, but I still felt very confused. Renee must have sensed that because she soon resumed talking.

"There's something else, Kate. You are probably also having continuous flashbacks as you write. You wouldn't remember them, of course, but they can and do have an effect on how you feel. I imagine that it will be difficult for you for a while to sort out your response to a new memory from your response to a flashback that is triggered by your partial new memory."

"But how am I ever going to get to the flashbacks, Renee? If I can't, how am I ever going to reduce my anxiety level?"

"It's a slow process, but it does happen," Renee reassured me. "When it is time, when you are ready to deal with a flashback, then it will become a memory instead of a flashback. It will happen, but you have to remain patient and be gentle with yourself while you are waiting."

As I allowed her comforting words to sink in, Renee asked, "Have you been able to work?"

"Not really. Yale is losing money on me this week."

"I would like to try something with you that may help us understand what is going on. I'm just going to ask you questions, and all you have to do is answer with the first thing that comes to mind. Are you willing?"

"Sort of, I guess. Yah, I think I can do that." I got myself set to play the old word association game that I'd read so many jokes about, wondering if Renee was going to turn into a Freudian after all. Fortunately, she surprised me with her first question.

"How do you feel when you are scared, Kate?"

"Scared." (What else?)

"When you are scared, where do you feel it?"

"In my stomach," I answered, much to my surprise that scared had a location.

"And when you are scared and feel it in your stomach, what does it feel like, Kate?"

"It feels hollow."

"When your stomach feels hollow, what do you want to do?"

I could feel myself slipping into a trance-like state with the repetition of her questions. The pattern was clear, she was going to follow up everything I said with my own words. "Are you putting me into a trance, Renee?"

"No, you are putting yourself into a trance, Kate. I provide the words, you use them. Are you okay with this?"

"I guess so."

"Then, when your stomach feels hollow, what do you want to do?"

"Disappear."

"When you want to disappear, where do you want to go?"

"To the ocean. I will take a walk along the shore and listen to the sea gulls."

"When you disappear to the ocean, what are you running from, Kate?"

I couldn't answer. I knew the answer, but I couldn't say the words.

"When you disappear to the ocean, what are you running from, Kate?"

I decided to ignore Renee. It was peaceful where I was. I began to body surf in my mind, and I was only vaguely aware that Renee was speaking.

Finally, her words got through to me, however. "Kate, I need you to start speaking to me. Come back, Kate. If you need to grow up in order to speak, then it's time to grow up again."

After a few false starts, I managed to croak out, "What?"

"Do you know the answer to my question?"

"Which question? You asked me a lot of them," I said irritably.

"When you disappear to the ocean, what are you running from, Kate?"

"I don't know."

"How old were you, Kate?"

"Five, five-and-a-half, somewhere in there."

"Were you running from someone?" I shook my head no as I felt myself drifting back to childhood.

"Were you hiding?" This time I nodded my head yes as my trance got deeper.

"From someone?" Again, I nodded my head yes.

"Kate, do you know who you are hiding from?" Although I suddenly could see my father, I was unable to answer Renee's question.

"Kate, do you know where you are hiding?" With her question, I saw myself in my parents' bedroom, peeking over the bed. Again, though, I could tell Renee nothing.

"Kate, you have got to tell me what is going on."

I couldn't respond.

"Okay, Kate, you're not ready for this yet. Come back, now. That's it, start growing up again."

I opened my eyes slowly, feeling calm and peaceful. In answer to her question, I eventually told Renee that my anxiety level was down. Because the hour was long since passed, we said a quick good-bye, and I promised to try to resume writing as I left.

. . .

Back then, I didn't really understand why my father wasn't nice. Mom said his brain got injured in the war, when he was in a coma for six weeks. The control mechanism for making adrenalin got messed up and he made too much. That's why he got so mean, she said. I didn't understand that at all. It didn't make sense that a whack on the head would cause his adrenal glands on his kidneys to make too much of something. Besides, he only had one of those glands because the other was wrecked in the tank accident. What I did understand, though, was her saying that it wasn't his fault. We shouldn't be angry at him because he was out of control.

I tried not to be angry at him, but sometimes I just couldn't control it. I would start yelling at him that he wasn't fair before I realized what I was doing. When I'd realize, I stopped immediately. Mom's face would be all pinched-looking, because she'd be afraid. Daddy's eyes would get bigger and bigger as he opened and closed his hands rapidly. I would stare at his eyes and always knew when he was about to come after me because they looked like they were about to burst. Sometimes Mike would 'accidentally on purpose' get in the way, and I would try to run. Mostly I stood and waited for the punishment. Once he surprised me though and, instead of getting mad, burst into laughter. Mom's face relaxed and I nervously laughed, too. But I walked away shaking.

Mom washed my mouth out with soap once. My friend Gerald Hahn had told me about the secret missing line to "Butcher, baker, candlestick maker." It was "Son of a butcher." Mom got mad at me when I told her and made me stick out my tongue while she scrubbed it with the bar of soap. She said it would clean all the filthy words. I didn't talk to Gerald for a full week after that. He didn't tell me it was so secret that I could never say it without getting into trouble.

Mom said I was a secretive little kid, never let anyone know what I was thinking. That's true. When I was four I taught myself how to read, but I didn't tell anyone until a year-and-a-half later, when the kindergarten teacher caught me. The next year I had an abscessed tooth but no one knew for five days, until my teacher discovered that I had a temperature. I hardly ever cried when I was little, except when I was hurt, and stopped completely when I was seven. *(my father is choking me he hits me in the right eye it stings bad as his thing goes into my poop-place my mother walks into the bedroom she is wearing a house dress with a snowflake pattern it is gray with white snowflakes on it the collar lies flat with rounded ends she has her left arm the one with the watch wrapped around her body her right hand covers her mouth there is a funny look on her face she slowly sits down on the bed her right side toward me up near the headboard she watches i think she is happy that she is not being hurt i hate her)*

Mom had lots of secrets, too. She was always saying that I should not talk about what happened at home. It was private. Sometimes she wouldn't go to Nana's and Bert's because of her bruises. She said I should just not say anything because the bruises made them unhappy. I was very good at keeping my mother's secrets for her.

I think my daddy had secrets, too. I don't know what, but I think there were some. He hardly ever talked about his family and he never talked about when he was a boy the way my mother told me about being little. I asked him questions, but he didn't answer.

Even when I was scared I didn't cry. It was dangerous, even worse than getting angry. Daddy loved to play a game with me called "being a cigar." I had to remain as stiff as I could. He picked me up, held me lying on my back parallel to the floor and threw her into the air. The first time we played, she got scared and yelled out. He threw her across the room against the wall. We played that game many times in the next four years. Each time I was terrified; each time I laughed. That's why I didn't cry when I was scared.

They all got scared every night, at supper time. On the good nights Dad didn't get home until after we ate. Then we would be laughing and talking, having a good time. When his car would drive up, the fun ended. I could feel the tension climbing long before he entered the house. Spens would get sullen looking, Mike and Mom would look sort of pinched tight, and I wouldn't feel like eating anymore. Often I'd leave the table and run upstairs while Mom hurriedly carried my plate into the kitchen and scraped the food into the garbage. On nights when Daddy started eating with us it was worse.

There were hundreds of meals that I couldn't eat because my stomach hurt. My father was a brooding presence, waiting to be triggered. Mom always had a rolling pin beside her at the table. Although she never used it, all of us knew that she kept it with her for protection. My father used to joke about it and ask me if I thought it would stop him. I laughed and said no, but I felt like I was betraying Mom. Spens frequently broke the tension from his high chair by throwing his glass at the wall. It was a relief when that happened because it signaled that Daddy would be good that night.

Meal after meal I sat playing with my food, unable to eat. It was a family rule when Daddy was there that I, and only I, could not leave the table until I cleaned my plate. Often I sat for what was literally hours facing down cold mashed potatoes, shrunken peas and meat coated with congealed grease. I was reprieved only if I vomited. Beginning at age two, in Flint, I went to the hospital lots of times because I couldn't stop vomiting. (*gazing up at the stars i saw them moving too rapidly they made me dizzy and I let my head fall again onto my mother's shoulder she held me tightly wrapped in a blanket with an urgency that I knew came from fear of my vomiting again "oh god he's stuck in the mud why can't he do anything right" she said and i wanted to tell her but didn't that my daddy was trying as hard as he could to get the car through the sea of mud to the porch she didn't understand him and there was no reason to be so afraid for me*

"calm down mommy" i wanted to say but i simply snuggled into her shoulder trying to burrow away from the nausea that was beginning to rise again

memory dissolves then brings me back to a hard table and a too-bright light shining into my face i know that i am in the emergency room of a hospital in flint but i don't know how i know i have just propped myself up on an elbow to vomit neatly into a basin now i'm flat again with eyes closed

a male voice nearby says "such a stoic child it's hard to believe that she's only three is she always like this" my mother's voice delighted by what she perceives as praise for her assures him that I always always try very hard not to make a mess and I never cry no matter what happens she adds she doesn't tell him that I get yelled at and spanked for making messes and crying i wish she would i want the doctor to hold me but he doesn't maybe if I'm very good he will let me stay in the hospital).

If my father went into the basement after supper, my mother let me get up from the table without finishing on most nights. I used to hold off from vomiting in hope that he would descend into that mysterious place where only he was allowed to go. At the same time, however, his descent served to heighten the tension in the house. Mom would hurriedly rush us upstairs, through our baths and into bed. The fear became palpable because, quite frequently, he emerged from the basement in a full-blown rage.

This went on for nearly four years, from the time that I was almost four until I was a bit more than eight. After he didn't live with us anymore, I made my first legal trip into that basement with Mom and Mike.

(i see the cot it is an army cot from the second world war olive green it has an olive green wool blanket on it folded back the blanket is scratchy it makes me itch there is a flat pillow on the cot it is at the head and the head is in the corner i hate flat pillows i am on the cot i can see the rafters above me there's a dusty musty smell to the blanket i am four five seven rapidly sequentially

i see my father's head above me i also see everything from above and behind my father he does not have his pants on and I can see his body moving up and down i can even see his scars is this real i feel nothing except boredom my father gets up then a hand comes out of nowhere it flies into my cheek sending my head rolling loosely to the right i feel nothing the cot i could draw it i know exactly how it looks folded up or opened folded it is menacing opened it has no emotional impact it's there in the corner waiting and I walk calmly to it I lie down on it

my father undoes my pants lifts my legs in the air as he pulls them off then he throws the pants on the floor they will get dusty he kneels as he does this fully clothed then he stands looking down on me while he slowly undoes his belt he very carefully takes off his pants so that they do not touch the floor he folds them by the creases carefully then lays them gently over a footlocker at the foot of the cot folded next he removes his underwear i see him in his nakedness with his shoes on he leaves his shoes on his thing is big but I refuse to see it momentarily I feel a piercing pain then I make it go away

outside the sun is bright there's dust on the window i see it over my father's shoulder as he pauses above me there's no sound upstairs but then no one is upstairs except my mother and Spens who is taking a nap my father fears women because they are unclean all but upper caste women from India who do not menstruate and little girls and all boys i am not unclean like my mother he does not fear me i fear him tremendous stomach pain comes and goes in a flash as I impose control except now I am taking huge breaths to control the pain that lurks just behind the fragile sheet I am barely able to draw over it it is bad this time but I can make it go away very soon on and off flick it comes flick it goes real unreal follow in merry progression tumbling over each other in their eagerness to be my father is on top of me i have my head turned to the left so that I can breath it is very dark i think i will go for a walk by the ocean)

We found a total of 276 empty liquor bottles down there. Mom said that she had not even known that he had been drinking. It took us about six months to get rid of all those bottles because she didn't want anyone to know about them. Each trash pick-up during that time had several bottles at the bottom of the bag.

Worse than vomiting, worse than his descent into the basement were those times when his rage erupted at the table. Yet, at the same time, the violence was a relief from the tension. It was no longer necessary to pretend that all was well, fear did not have to be hidden any longer. There would be yelling and screaming, there would be pain, but at least there was the release from tension. The waiting for the unknown was over, only reality had to be considered.

I cannot remember what happened whenever I was the target of my father's rage, but I do remember many scenes when Mom was. They have stuck with me over the years like photographs in the family album. There's my mother with orange juice dripping from her head and face, eyes big with shock, outrage and fear at what was coming next. There's the cut glass container with a pointed top filled with Mike's marbles caught midair as it flew towards my father. When it crashed into the wall, the marbles sounded like a hail storm as they bounced wildly in all directions throughout the room. There's my mother doubled over in pain from a blow, and the next shot of her head flying backwards from another blow. Then there's the one that haunts me still. Mike and I had run out the front door, on the way to Con's house. I stopped at the kitchen window and watched my father repeatedly smashing my mother's head into the refrigerator. Over and over he smashed her into it, without any emotion, and I don't remember hearing one sound.

Frequently, we ended up at Con's house after one of his rages. She was Danny's and Jimmy's mother and my mother's best friend. They lived four houses down Hawthorne and always left their house unlocked all night so that we could have a place to hide. Feeling returned once I had made it down there. Until then, it was safer not to feel. It was always the same. Mom would collapse into tears and sobs and Con comforted her. Mike and I would stand silently, watching. I can remember far too clearly how I felt as I watched that particular scene.

The fear came rolling over me, crushing in its impact. Mom talked and cried, and I was too scared to cry or ask for help. Con would hold Mom as my fear began to diminish. It never occurred to me to ask for help then, since there had been none when it was really needed. If I were to cry, I would be interrupting my mother who obviously needed help far more than I did. For some mysterious reason, it was all right for Mom to cry but it was not for me. When she cried, she got attention; when I cried I got beaten or yelled at. Or, it suddenly began to feel dangerous. Someone had to watch out for my father, just in case he came after us while Mom cried. Maybe that was why I couldn't cry, I had to be on guard. They would sit for hours, Con and Mom, talking about what had happened.

I began to relax when it was clear that my father was staying home, and then a sense of absolute aloneness would come over me. It was an aloneness so complete that I could do nothing but endure it. There was no possible source of relief anywhere. I saw myself as hollow. Little bits and pieces of her were breaking off inside and falling forever through that hollowness. If that continued long enough, I would be such a thin shell that the next piece that broke off might make a hole in the shell that was me. Then, I would be dead.

. . .

Saturdays were always bad. Daddy insisted on having kippers for breakfast and other special things to eat. Mom was always angry, mumbling under her breath while she cooked. "He gives me only twenty-five dollars a week for everything, then demands expensive food, the bastard." I tried to get outside before that began.

School and the streets became my refuge from home. I made friends with every teacher I met so that I could stay after school and talk about anything rather than go home. I watered plants, washed blackboards, graded papers, and ran errands, anything to postpone the time of leaving. Once home, I quickly changed my clothes and headed outside.

Winter was a hard time for me. It got dark so very early and the cold was so intense that I had to return home with long hours left until bedtime. Weekends in the winter were torture, unless I could talk someone into inviting me to their house. My transparent eagerness to be invited made me suspect to the other kids, and eventually I was forced by the weather to go home and try to be invisible. Spring would come just when I was sure that I could not stand one more day of freezing. On Saturdays I was out on the streets by seven most mornings, not to return until dark. It was lonely on the streets at that time in the morning, but at least I avoided the increased tension that was Saturday at our house.

These long hours away from home began when I was five. I never had to account for my time, I never had to ask permission, I was completely free to roam. Although I wandered as far as four or five miles from home, I never got into trouble. I did get hurt occasionally, but never seriously. I ran, I played, I fought and never once was I afraid of the world outside my house.

It wasn't always bad, though. You shouldn't think that. Mike and I couldn't stop laughing the day Daddy started washing the car in the rain. He filled his bucket with suds made from Tide, thinking that the rain would rinse the car. Instead, the car became one huge bubble as the pelting rain made even more suds. They flowed out the driveway and down the street. Mom was terribly upset, wondering what the neighbors would say, but Mike and I had to hold our sides from laughing so hard. Another time, he painted the fence in the rain, thinking that the cold water would set the paint. Again, Mom fretted about the neighbors while Mike and I roared with laughter.

Once Daddy came home with a magic trick that fascinated me. He said that the kid who was best for the next week would get it. That was going to be me, I vowed not to do a single thing wrong for the next seven days.

Mom spoiled it the next day for me. I was telling her how good I planned to be, and she swung around towards me with a bitter look on her face. She said I was a dope to think I would get it. Mike wouldn't because Daddy didn't like him. I wouldn't because I always did something wrong every day. Only Spens had a chance because Daddy doted on him. That night at supper when our father asked Mom who had been the best that day, I started screaming about how unfair he was. I repeated what Mom had said before I realized what I was doing. I stopped suddenly and looked around the table. Spens was gripping the arms of his high chair tightly. Mike was slumped down in his chair with a silly grin on his face. Mom looked scared. All three were staring intently at Daddy, who was looking at Mom with fury on his face.

Nothing happened then, but that night I could hear them fighting. Daddy hit Mom a couple of times. I heard the blows and her yelps of pain. The next morning she had a big bruise on her cheek, and it was all my fault.

Christmas was a strange time in our house, and eventually I grew to hate it. For at least a week before, the tension was close to unbearable because of Daddy. He didn't seem to understand about Christmas. There was always a fight about having a Christmas tree. He would never sing any of the songs, and I think it was because he didn't know the words. I offered once to teach him; he looked sort of scared when I said I would. And he didn't understand at all that I had to do my own shopping for Mom instead of him buying something for her and putting my name on the tag. I used to get pretty mad that I wasn't allowed to choose the presents I gave her.

On Christmas morning, everybody had to pretend that everything was perfect in our family: everyone loved everyone else; no one was ever hit; each present, even a dumb pair of slippers, was totally thrilling. I felt like a big liar, but I didn't dare do anything except behave like everyone else. But it made me sort of sick inside. Just as soon as all the presents were opened, Daddy took his and Spens's upstairs so that I wouldn't ruin them. I never understood that.

Likewise, I never understood about Easter. We were not allowed to have Easter baskets from anyone, Daddy wouldn't let us. When I was seven, though, Con's brother Tom felt sorry for me. He gave me a basket. At first I didn't want it, but then he said that I could keep it at Con's house.

We used to spend all the major holidays at Nana's and Bert's. But then Bert got very sick and so we stayed home. It wasn't any fun. None of the days seemed like holidays anymore, and I badly missed the gathering of the family.

Although I knew all of Mom's family, I never knew my father's family. We never saw them. I knew that he grew up with his two brothers, Nat and Art, in Chicago. His mother had died in the early thirties, and then the family moved to Buffalo. We drove there when I was five but stayed less than a day. My father fought with someone and we had to leave. I never met his father that I remember. No one exchanged cards or presents with us at Christmas the way Mom's family did. I knew of their existence but they weren't part of my life.

. . .

With time, my father's rages worsened. Mom was always bruised in some way. She hid the bruises if she could with long-sleeve blouses and high collars. If she couldn't, she stayed home until they faded. Her glasses were frequently broken in the struggles. She had a large wart removed from her knee and the wound was badly split open by my daddy before the stitches healed. The doctor put sulfur powder in it even though she told him she was allergic to it, and her knee swelled all up. That put her on crutches for two weeks and left a very bad scar. Her nose was broken. She had black eyes all the time.

Neither Mike nor I escaped the batterings. Our father took him into the basement one winter night and held him by his ankles in front of the opened furnace door. Each time he hit him, Mike swung towards the glowing coals. For a whole lot of nights after that Mike screamed while he was sleeping.

Kicks and slaps became routine around our house. I started having nightmares of being chased by German soldiers in the school yard and was spanked whenever I cried out in my sleep. To be jerked awake from a nightmare and roughly spanked is terrible. *(the sudden brilliance of the overhead light startles me out of my sleep with one eye open I watch my father go through a drawer of his desk that he keeps in my room he hears me groggily ask him what he is doing and stiffens turning around he crosses to my bed then jerks off his slipper tearing the sheet and blankets off of me he grabs me by the arm flips me over then starts whipping me with his slipper).*

Spens, whose temper tantrums got worse, was never spanked by our father. Furthermore, Mom was forbidden to punish him in any way. She was also forbidden to bathe him; Dad did that when he came home from work. If he found a bruise or cut on Spens's body, Mom was beaten. We became like two families under the same roof. There were Dad and Spens, who both ruled with their rages, and there were Mom and Mike and me, who were beaten.

My father seemed to be getting more and more strange. One night he came home and asked my mother if she had put poison in the food yet. She answered, "If you think that I'm going to poison your food, why do you come home to eat?"

He responded, "I'm trying to catch you at it."

He beat up the roasting pan one night, jumping up and down on it in the dark behind the house. Another night, he took a knife and cut up a sheet into precise squares about one inch by one inch. I suggested that scissors might make the job easier, but he glared at me in response. His speech became funny, too. In the middle of a sentence he might pause for up to a minute, staring blankly, then resume with the next word and no awareness that he had been silent. Mike and I called them "John-Pauses," because his name was John, and made a game of trying to guess with which word he would begin speaking again.

Always, always, Mom kept repeating that we should feel sorry for Daddy, not be angry at him, remember that he wasn't to blame. And she said so many times that I can today recall the exact tones, "You always hurt the ones you love best." That didn't make me feel very special to my daddy, though.

To tell the truth, I didn't feel very special to my mom, either. She never held Mike or me, just Spens. And she always seemed to be yelling at us or hitting us. She hit Mike more than she did me. I don't know why because I did at least as many bad things as Mike did. Both of us were always bad, Mom said. When she was very mad at Mike, she would get on the telephone and call the bad boys' school to come and get him. He always got very scared, but they never came. There must not have been a bad girls' school because she never called about me.

Meanwhile, my grandfather Bert was clearly dying. No longer could I go there to escape home. Mike and I spent every possible moment away from home. I was only seven and he was almost twelve, but he let me join his friends in play. He fought for me on the streets and he did his best to protect me at home. Often he got hurt as he stepped in the way to slow Daddy down as he was coming for me. I now ran out of the house and down to Con's whenever I could if a fight started. Mike ceased to be a direct target of Dad's for some reason, and only Mom and I were truly in danger. Mom said that Daddy hated females. I slept with a coat next to my bed at all times, and Mike had orders to get me out of the house whenever he heard a fight beginning. Many times we made wild dashes down the deserted street to Con's late at night. Sometimes during those flights it seemed as if my nightmare had come true and I ran, a Jewish child pursued by German soldiers.

. . .

Bert died early on April Fool's Day the year I was in second grade. I was eight. Mom told Mike and me when we got up. I remember sitting on the arm of the green couch, swinging my legs, and feeling overwhelmed with loss. Bert was the only person in my life with whom I felt totally relaxed inside. He made me feel good about myself. I felt safe with him. Who was going to protect me now? I could feel his gentle stroking of my face and his arms close around me as I sat there.

Lost in my sense of aloneness, I could barely hear Mike crying across the room. Suddenly he shocked me to awareness by screaming at Mom. "Look at her. She's not even crying. She's just sitting there with a dumb look on her face." I was bewildered by his attack as he turned to me and screamed with a contorted face. "You've never loved anyone. You don't care about anyone except your dog. Why aren't you crying? Don't you know that Bert is dead? You're never going to see him again, and you don't care." He went on and on, but I stopped listening. Mike didn't even begin to understand how I felt, and I hated him. If he wanted to think that I didn't care, let him. I got up and slowly walked upstairs to get dressed for school.

I sat through class in a fog, and the teacher yelled at me three different times to pay attention. Finally she sent me to the principal's office, where I was spanked then told to stand in the hall until school ended. I didn't cry.

When I got home Mom said that she had to go to the funeral in Hamilton. No, I couldn't go. I would be staying at Jean's house, the wife of Mom's brother Chuck. A sitter would stay with Mike and Spens each day until Dad got home from work. My dog couldn't come with me, either.

Oops, my dog, I forgot to write earlier about my dog. Taffy was a honey-colored Cocker Spaniel. I picked her out when she was five weeks old, and she quickly became my dog. I fed her every day and brushed her ears, which were long and soft and silky. She ran the streets with me. When I was sad I would lie on the floor and she licked away my tears. We became inseparable.

Taffy slept on the back stairs landing. Each time my dad went up or down the stairs, he kicked her. She was so afraid of him. When we let her into the house she would bounce through the front door into the living room. On weekends, though, she would see my father and scrabble to a halt. Then she would slink through the living room, keeping as far away from him as she could. I hated to see her so afraid. Mom said that Taffy wouldn't have had any trouble with Dad if she had been a boy dog.

Always when I went to Nana's and Bert's, Taffy had gone with me. I had never been separated from her, and the thought of going to Chuck's and Jean's without her was terrible. As Mom loaded up my belongings in the car, I held Taffy and told her that I would miss her. Mike promised to feed her and play with her for me.

Chuck was my favorite uncle. He was short and very thin and somewhat sickly looking. He got pneumonia almost every winter. He was a salesman. At that time he had only one child, Danny, who was three years younger than me. The only reason that Chuck was my favorite uncle was that he was very gentle with me. He never teased me. He laughed a lot and would hold me for long periods of time, until I got tired of it even. His wife, though, didn't like me.

Jean was tall and talked funny, through her nose. She was nice to me, but I knew she didn't approve of me. She thought that I was too wild and undisciplined. She made me feel like shrinking up into a tight, invisible ball. I told Mom that I wanted to stay home, not go stay with Jean, but she said that it wasn't safe for me at home.

So I went to Jean's and spent the entire time trying not to cry. I missed my mother desperately. On the last day I was there, I spent the full day looking out the window, waiting for her. I hid the tears that kept sliding quietly down my face. I had packed before breakfast and kept the suitcase beside me the entire time. When it got too heavy to hold, I would set it down for a while, one corner resting reassuringly on my foot. Jean left me alone, she didn't tell me to go play something as she had done the previous three days. She even brought lunch over to the window and let me eat standing up. I began to think that maybe Jean did like me, after all.

Mom and Chuck finally came back after dark. On the way home Mom told me all about the funeral. Tommy, her other brother, had fallen apart, sobbing uncontrollably. Nana had held up well. Surprisingly, Chuck had been the most strong. He had taken care of everyone and then had gotten uproariously drunk at Cecil's after the funeral. He had been so funny that he soon had everyone feeling much better. She said that it seemed like Chuck was relieved that Bert was dead.

When we got home, Taffy wasn't there. My dad said that she had run away. I remember blinking up at him, not saying a word, not believing him. I ignored his sympathy and went up to bed. The next day I learned the truth.

Mom had a friend named Shirley, who was the only friend that my father would tolerate in the house. Shirley lived three houses down Alexander towards the cemetery woods. She once was so afraid of polio that she kept herself and her three daughters inside the entire summer. That didn't work because she caught it and had to wear a back brace for a while. Mom said that she just scared herself into thinking she had it.

Shirley would come in without knocking all the time, and she was the only person who I ever saw teasing my father. She would even flirt with him. Well, one night while we were gone she came in about ten o'clock. Mike and Spens were obviously asleep, the lights were on downstairs but my father wasn't there. She heard strange sounds from the basement, as if a fight were going on. She went into the kitchen and listened at the door. She said she could hear what sounded like kicking and, once, a yelp of an animal. She ran out of the house and never came back until after my father left. I didn't know about that the next day, though, but I did learn something else.

My friend Doris Hahn was waiting across the street for me when I started off to school. She barely said hello, she was in such a rush to tell me what she had seen two days ago. My dad had come out of the house carrying Taffy by the scruff of the neck, and he jammed her into the garbage pail. When I heard that I knew Taffy was dead.

I got sent to the principal's office again that day, again she was spanked and again didn't cry. I had to take a note home this time, saying how bad she had been. I hadn't really done anything except not listen, though. When I got home I gave the note to Mom but she said not to worry, she would talk with my teacher. Then I told her what Doris said, and she told me what Shirley had said. That was it, Taffy was surely dead.

I wanted to report my dad to the police for murder, but Mom said that I should never, never say anything about it to anyone. Most especially I should not let my dad know that I knew what he had done. Even if I got very angry at him, she should not say anything.

I went out and sat on the front porch. I stared up at the clouds. Bert was dead, Taffy was dead, there wasn't anyone left for me. Taffy must have been very afraid. I hoped it didn't hurt too much and that she had bitten him lots of times. I felt all hollow again. I looked down and watched her hand shake. Both of them were shaking. Strange, they never did that before. When I looked up at the clouds again, I thought that I could see Bert's face in them. Yes, I could! I could even see his pipe sticking out of his mouth. Heaven really did exist, just like they said in church, and Bert was up there watching me! He hadn't left me! Maybe he had Taffy with him somewhere. I promised him that I would be very good from now on and that he would be proud of me when I grew up. I would try to do a better job of protecting Mom, too, since he couldn't anymore.

Later that afternoon Mom said that I was going to go stay with Nana for a while. She was missing Bert badly and needed my company. When I protested about school, she got mad at me. After all that Nana had done for me, this was very little to do in return for her. I was an ungrateful, spoiled child who only thought of her own pleasure. I would go, I would be nice to Nana, and I wasn't to complain about anything.

I went, but I couldn't help Nana be happy. I told her all my jokes, but she just sat and cried. The house was silent, almost spooky. The clock striking the quarter hours was the only sound to be heard. It measured away my days. Bert's door was closed, as if he were taking a nap. Towards the end of the second week, Nana and I opened the door and went in. We folded all his clothes carefully and put them in bags for the Salvation Army. As I sat on the bed and watched, she went through his papers at his desk and threw most everything away. When she was all through, it wasn't his room anymore. We closed the door, and I never entered that room again.

I went home and back to school. The first Saturday I was back, we were all having breakfast together. I couldn't eat. Daddy started yelling at me, Mom said leave her alone, and he threw his orange juice in her face. Then he threw the scrambled eggs at her. The plate hit her on the forehead and blood spurted out, ran down and got into her eyes. They were both shouting, Spens was crying, Mike jumped out of his chair and ran over to me. I sat and watched.

Mom started running towards the stairs, and Dad grabbed up a long chain of sausages and went after her. Mike yelled at me to get up and, as we headed for the front door, I could see Daddy whipping Mom with the sausages.

As Mike and I tore out the front door, we heard our parents running upstairs, Mom shrieking and Daddy swearing. We stopped outside on the grass, staring up at the house. Mom leaned out the window and shouted that we should run to Shirley's and have her call the police. Mike and I whirled around and started running but my father shouted my name twice and told me not to go. "Kate, Kate, don't go, come back here immediately." I stopped and watched Mike continue running. He shouted over his shoulder to come on. My father spoke again, quietly. "Kate, go sit on the porch. If you follow Mike, I will kill you."

I turned and looked up at the window. He was pulling Mom's head back by her hair. His other hand was around her throat. Neither was moving, although Mom was still telling me to go. My eyes locked with my father's, and we stared at each other for a very long time. It was as if there was nothing else in the world except his eyes. Then she put her head down and walked over to the porch.

Upstairs the battle resumed. She heard blows and curses and shrieks of pain from her mother. Mike had done the right thing, he'd not been too scared to obey. If Mom were killed it would be my fault. If I had eaten my breakfast, none of this would have happened. The whole fight was my fault, and she was such a baby that I couldn't do anything to save my mother. She must hate me now. I never did anything right, I always caused trouble.

A few minutes later a police car screamed up to the house and Joe, who lived across Alexander and down two houses, jumped out and ran up the walk, pulling his gun out of the holster. "Mr. DuBose, Mr. DuBose," he shouted. "Let Avis come downstairs. This is Joe Bruster. I'm a policeman and I have a gun." Joe looked down at me and winked.

"Let Avis come downstairs, Mr. DuBose." The noise upstairs stopped. Soon I could hear Mom weeping softly as she started down the stairs. She came out on the porch and fell into Joe's arms, sobbing uncontrollably. There was blood all over her face and down her blouse, which was torn. Her eye was swelling shut. She had scratches and beginnings of bruises all over her arms. "Avis, are you seriously hurt?" Mom shook her head no but continued crying.

Joe set Mom down next to me on the porch. Mike appeared from somewhere and held my hand. He startled me and when I looked up, he gave me his scared grin and squeezed my hand. Most of the neighbors were gathered on the sidewalk, staring, and I saw others down the street running towards our house.

Joe was talking to Mom, trying to get her to sign out a complaint so that he could arrest Daddy.

"Avis, Avis, you don't have to live this way. He could kill you or one of the kids. Please sign."

"And will you be here to protect me once he's released? No, you won't. He'll be even more angry and dangerous then. Do you actually think that I like living this way? Just go away, Joe."

Joe stood up and went to the screen door. "Mr. DuBose, come down here." He said it three or four times, but my father didn't respond. "My god, be a man and come down here this instant."

Daddy slowly walked down the stairs and stood on the other side of the screen, head hanging down. He looked like a little boy caught doing something bad.

"Mr. DuBose, I have no respect for someone who beats up on women and little kids. Do you see this gun? The next time I catch you doing it, I will shoot you. Your wife refused to sign a complaint or I'd take you to jail right this minute. Next time, I'll shoot you. Now come out here and apologize to Avis."

Daddy half stepped out the door and mumbled something. Then he went back upstairs. Joe asked Mom if he could take her to the doctor's but she told him just to go away. He walked down the walk and told the neighbors to leave. After they did, he drove away. Shirley put her arm around Mom and led her down to her house. Mike and I were left alone. Then he remembered Spens, and we rushed into the house to find him.

Spens was lying face down on the couch, holding his bear and quietly crying. His face was all white and pinched when he looked up, but Mike said something to make him laugh. Mike suggested that we make Dagwood sandwiches, then go down to the school playground and fly kites.

Mike invented the Dagwood sandwich game. We each took turns choosing one thing to go on the sandwiches. The person who refused to put on what someone else suggested lost. Our sandwiches would usually have meat, cheese, peanut butter, graham crackers, carrots, lettuce, mustard, ketchup, mayonnaise and many other things on them. I always lost when Mike put on pickles. Spens would lose if Mike put on horseradish. This time, though, Mike lost first when I chose sauerkraut. Then I let Spens win with soda crackers.

We spent the afternoon away from home. The kites soared like birds once we got them into the air. They dove toward each other in a mock fight that Mike and I staged. He told me about how the Chinese put powdered glass on their kite strings so that they could cut each others' lines while flying kites. He said we could try it someday.

Later we ate our sandwiches in the park across the street, sitting in the cool shade of the trees. We took turns pushing Spens on the swing. Towards late afternoon we headed home. As we got closer and closer, fear settled down on us once again, wiping away our smiles. Mike said to wait at the corner while he scouted the house. He sneaked up to the kitchen window, climbed on the sloping top of the door to the coal bin, and peeked through the window. Then he relaxed, turned and gave us a big smile, and waved us on. Mom was cooking supper, which meant that the fighting had stopped. When all five of us sat down at the table that night, the usual tension was gone. I ate my dinner completely, without having to be yelled at once.

Several days later, when we got up Mom was very upset and nervous. She said Daddy hadn't come home last night and she didn't know where he was. Maybe he had had an accident and was in the hospital somewhere. She cried and fretted, and I was happy to go off to school. But when I got home, there was a sitter there who said Mom had gone downtown, and then I got worried.

It was almost supper time before she drove up with Con. Daddy had stolen a gun from one of his customers, then gotten drunk in a bar. The bartender had been scared by his behavior so, when Daddy went to the bathroom, he had called the police. The police arrested him, found the gun which had been reported as missing, and had thrown him into jail. Tomorrow, Mike and I had to go talk to the judge.

I was really scared then. If I said anything against my father to the judge, Daddy might kill me. I told Mom that I didn't want to miss school, but she got mad at me and said I had to talk to the judge, there was a court order about it. That night I sneaked into Mike's bed and slept with him. He only pretended to be angry before he put his arms around her and held me tightly.

Con drove us to the courthouse in downtown Detroit the next morning. An old man, whom Mom introduced as Mr. Kessinger her lawyer, was waiting for us. I hadn't even known that she had a lawyer. *(the ceiling is very high but the heavily varnished oak walls seem to be pressing in on me there's a pressure on my chest that feels like someone is bouncing on it if i could only breathe i would be okay mr kessinger talks funny i can't understand him at all i see his mouth moving but i can't hear any words all I can hear is a roaring sound like a big wind he turns to mom and begins speaking so that i can understand him. ". . . can't possibly put these kids on the stand, avis they're so scared that they can't talk we'll have to try to do it with con's and your testimony" does that mean that i don't have to tell the judge about my daddy)* He told Mike and me to sit on the stairs, and then hurried off with Mom and Con. We sat there all morning, watching people go in and out of some big doors to what I was sure was the courtroom. I got up and tried to peek through them a couple of times, but I didn't see anything. Just before lunchtime, my principal walked down the hall and through the doors. What was he doing there? I was astounded to see him. I also didn't like to see him because he was the one who was always spanking me at school.

A little later Mom and Con came out. Both were furious about Mr. Strouthers, our principal. He had testified that Daddy was a very good father and husband, but he had never even been in our house. I didn't think a principal should lie like that.

After lunch, Mike and I went back to our watching on the stairs. Mr. Strouthers came out of the courtroom. When he saw us, he gave us a big smile and came over. "Don't worry, kids," he said. "We'll have your Daddy home tonight."

I couldn't help it, I really couldn't. I answered, "Did you see Mom's big black eye? It really looks terrible, doesn't it?" He gave me a weak smile and walked away, while Mike and I roared with laughter. He told me that I shouldn't have said it, I was a funny little kid, but all the time he was chuckling to himself. I was feeling pretty good again.

Next, Con came out and said that we weren't going to talk to the judge. The judge had decided that Daddy was crazy and would be sent to a jail for the criminally insane. After Con went back into the courtroom, I thought about what that meant.

Daddy wasn't going to be hitting us anymore. He wouldn't be hitting Mom, either. I wouldn't be scared anymore, and I wouldn't have to sleep with my coat next to the bed. I had never dreamed of the possibility that he would leave us, I thought that he would always have to be around. There would be just the four of us, and we could be happy all the time. The more I thought, the more excited and happy I got. I was confused, though, when Mom and Con came out of the courtroom. Instead of being happy, Mom was crying.

On the way home Mom said something that shocked Mike and me. "Mike, I want you to know that Daddy isn't your real father. I was married once before to a man named Sonny Giodano. He's your father. Daddy adopted you when you were four."

I got really mad. Mike was too my brother. She shouldn't say he wasn't. Then Mom explained that Mike was my half-brother and I was his half-sister. Half wasn't as good as whole, but it was better than nothing. When I told Mike he was a bit better than nothing, he smiled at me, but then he looked very serious again. Thinking about it some more, I decided that I was jealous of Mike. His daddy wasn't crazy and didn't beat him the way mine beat me. Maybe his daddy was nice, even.

I don't remember anything about the rest of that spring. Mom drove to Ionia a couple times to see Daddy, and each time she came back very upset. She was told that he had paranoid schizophrenia and probably would be locked up for the rest of his life. The injuries that he got in the war had nothing to do with his symptoms. He was just crazy. Once I overheard her talking to Con about it. "I asked the doctor about the kids. He said that it's inherited, but there's no way to tell if Kate or Spens have it until they get older."

When I heard that, my world fell apart. Someday she was going to be locked up like Daddy. First, though, she would probably hurt those closest to me, just like he did. Maybe, if I never let anyone be close to her, maybe that wouldn't happen. If I didn't marry and didn't have kids, nothing bad would happen. She wouldn't have anyone to hurt then. I would be very careful and not lose control the way he did. I would watch herself very carefully. No more getting angry for me, that's when I always lost control and acted just like him. I would count to ten about everything. I would become totally reasonable to make sure that she didn't go crazy.

Chapter 7

"When did you put what you wrote in my mailbox, Kate?"

"Sunday morning. Have, have you read it?"

"Yes. Now I know why you have been having so much trouble talking." Renee's face was a study in grimness. "How are you?"

"Okay, I guess. A bit numb, maybe. I, I have the feeling that I have broken many taboos. I wasn't supposed to tell any of that. Once I got started, I couldn't stop. You can see the fatigue in my handwriting towards the end; I wrote for something like fifteen hours straight. I must have been interacting with my girls during that time. I must have cooked meals, driven them to friends, tucked them in at night and read them a story, but I have no memory of anything that went on between us. It was like I was on automatic pilot."

Renee smiled in a gentle way. "How did it feel?"

"Bad, good, nothing. At times I was sobbing. Some of the worst parts, though, I wrote without feeling anything. It's like I clicked off the feeling switch."

"What does that feel like?"

(Damn, is she going to keep backing me up, using my words for yet another question? When does it end?) "When I stopped feeling, it was like I was all brain. I didn't have a body. I felt knife-sharp, but I don't really know what that means. Maybe it means that I felt a sense of clarity. I was very focused. There was no anxiety, no sinking sensation, no confusion, no nothing but words pouring out of my pen onto the paper."

"You lost all self-awareness?"

"Yes, that's how it was."

"And now, Kate?"

"Now, there's nothing. I don't feel focused, I feel nothing. Numb, like I said." I let myself go into silence again, it was better that way. Time passed. I heard Renee shift slightly but did not bother looking over at her. Eventually she spoke, and I dragged myself up out of the peace in order to answer her. "Yes, nothing is like not being, and I want to stay this way."

. . .

During the next several months Renee and I put my family under a microscope and minutely examined each detail. She asked me to stop writing, and then she refused to read what I had written when I did not stop. My anxiety got worse and worse, and soon I was back to seeing her twice a week, sometimes even three or four times a week. I kept writing, though, and used what I had written for our next time together.

Eventually I learned to say the words that needed to be said. When necessary I talked about Joe and the girls, but nearly all the time was spent on my family. I made a big diagram of my family tree so that Renee could keep the people straight, and she sat holding it while we talked, taking notes frequently.

When I was through I did not feel as if I had even begun to convey to her the essence of it. It turned out that my problem was that I had too many memories rather than not enough detail.

. . .

Fear and tension had disappeared after my father was hospitalized, to be replaced by depression. My mother did not smile for months. We had to sell the car, which meant a mile-long walk to the grocery store and back. At first I helped my mother carry the groceries. As her depression got worse and as the money got tighter and tighter, I gradually took over the shopping. I borrowed Danny's wagon and set off several times a week, clutching the list and money tightly in my hand. The lists soon disappeared to be replaced by verbal instructions that I desperately tried to remember. Then the instructions disappeared. Within a very short time, I was doing all the planning and shopping for meals. If I made a mistake, my mother cried.

My mother sat around all that first summer, looking sad and crying. We had so little money that we had to accept money from Aid to Dependent Children. It had been a shameful experience for Mom to go and apply for it, and I remember feeling guilty that she had to ask for that money because of me.

Mike said that we all should get jobs. He got a paper route, and I helped him sometimes with it. Mostly, though, I worked on my own business, which I started because I was only eight and too young to get a real job like him. I put signs up all over our neighborhood saying that I could do any kind of work. One woman hired me to soak wallpaper off her walls. I had regular customers for shoveling snow and cutting grass and raking leaves. Ken, the owner of "The Little Store," hired me to pick up candy wrappers that kids threw around. I also cut the grass and raked the yard around the store for him. I liked working for Ken. He always gave me a free bottle of pop when I finished and, if there were no customers, he would come out and sit under a tree with me while I drank it.

Some of my other customers also gave me snacks when I worked for them. Mostly, though, it was just hard work. The only thing that made it good was Mom's smile when I gave her all my earnings for the week every Friday after supper. Mike and I made a contest out of it, to see who could give her the most. He usually won, but I didn't really mind that. After all, he was four-and-a-half years older than I was and had a steady job. When I got bigger, I would be able to help her more.

When it was time for school to start again, we had a family conference. Mom didn't know what to do. Even though Mike could still keep his paper route, I wouldn't be able to work very much and Nana had run out of money to loan us. The doctors said that my daddy was in the hospital for life, so we couldn't count on him. If Mom got a job, she would lose the Aid to Dependent Children and have to pay a babysitter for Spens, at least until Mike and I got home from school.

The biggest part of the problem was that Mom didn't know how to do anything, she said. She'd been a typist a long time ago, before Mike was born, but she wasn't very good at it now. Mike said she could practice, but we didn't have a machine. I felt good when I remembered that Ken had a machine. Maybe he would loan it to Mom so that she could practice. Then she'd be able to get a really good job as soon as she found a babysitter for Spens.

The next day I borrowed Danny's wagon and went to see Ken. Mom said it made more sense for me to ask him since I knew him best. Well, even if it made sense, I still felt kind of funny asking him if I could borrow his typewriter so that Mom could practice. I was dragging my feet walking over there until I realized that if Mom got a job, we could pay back all the money we owed him. Mom had charged a lot of stuff at his store. I always had to ask him to put it on the bill, and it didn't feel good. But, if Mom got a job, she could pay him back and wouldn't have to charge anymore. I was sure that he would like his money and would be glad to loan me the machine as the first step in getting it. When I talked to Ken about it, I promised him that Mom would pay her entire bill with her first check, cross my heart and hope to die.

Ken laughed when I said that and carried the typewriter out to the wagon. Then he did something he had never done before. He squatted down in front of me, put his hands on my shoulders and looked straight in my eyes as he said, "Katie, you're a brave little person, and your parents don't deserve you. I'm loaning this machine to you, not your mother. Tell her that for me." Then Ken gave me a long hug and for some reason tears were coming out of my eyes. I didn't let Ken know, though; I kept my head down as I waved goodbye and walked off, pulling the wagon carefully.

I didn't tell Mom what Ken said, of course. It would just have made her cry. I didn't tell her about my promise to Ken, either. Instead, I told her that he wished her well in job hunting. She sat down and stared at the machine which I had put on the dining room table, and I went outside quietly to try to enjoy the last day of summer vacation.

After my mother had practiced for about a month, one day after school she announced that she had a job interview. The army was looking for typists and she had gone and taken their test. She scored 94 and then got 10 extra points because Daddy had been hurt in the war. That meant she had 104 points when 100 was a perfect score. She was sure to get a job.

We celebrated that night. Mike wrote a play about a woman typist and her mean boss, who wasn't really mean but was trying to hide the fact that he was in love with his secretary. Mom cried when the typist and boss got married. It was a really good story, even if Spens did act silly and start to tap dance in the middle of it.

The next step was to get a babysitter. It took two weeks but Mom found one just before she had to start work. Her name was Helen, and she was from Hungary.

Helen was old, with gray hair and wrinkles. Also, her breath smelled funny, like the way Daddy sometimes smelled. She moved into my room, and I had to move into Mom's. I didn't like Helen. She cooked good things, which was nice, but I still didn't like her. She was always yelling at us, sometimes even swearing at us, while Mom was at work. But when Mom was home, she never did any of that.

None of us said anything at first about Helen to our mother. We didn't want to worry her. Things were going so well that it seemed stupid to complain about an old lady who swore. During her first week at work, Mom's boss had come up to her and said that she was a terrible typist. She said that she was sure she was going to lose the job then. She didn't, though. Instead, he made her the supervisor of all the typists, and she even got a raise. She went from a G.S. 3 to a G.S. 4 in only three days of work. I was really proud of her.

When Mom got her first pay check, I did something pretty bad. She gave me a twenty dollar bill and told me to go get a loaf of bread at the "Little Store."

"Do you mean I should pay the bill with money, Mom?" I asked.

"Of course. That's why I gave you the money." Well, I knew she meant to pay for the bread only, but I pretended to misunderstand. I borrowed Danny's wagon again, loaded on the typewriter, then put the twenty dollar bill in the roller. At the store, I proudly told Ken that I was there to pay the bill in full. He smiled broadly and

made a big ceremony of canceling the debt of $19.24. I bought
the bread with the change and later held onto the memory of Ken's
smile while Mom cried and yelled at me for messing up her budget.
I didn't care, it was worth it to feel even with the world again.

Anyway, Helen swore at us a lot. Mike and I talked it over
and decided that maybe she was a bad influence on Spens, who
was only four. We knew she drank. That was no secret since every
Friday Mom drove her to the pharmacy to get a bottle of liquor. She
drank, she smoked, she swore, she yelled; who knew what she did
while she was home alone with Spens? It wasn't good, that was clear
since Spens absolutely hated Helen. He wouldn't say why, but he
hated her. So we decided to tell Mom how bad Helen was.

We told Mom, but she said to try to ignore it, it couldn't be that
bad. Well, it was. Mom didn't know what it was like to have Helen
yell at her. I don't think that she believed us when we told her. She
didn't do anything, she just said not to rock the boat.

So Helen lived in my room, never even coming out on weekends.
She sat in my room and drank her bottle. That went on for a long
time, until the start of Christmas vacation. On the first day that
there was no school, it rained all day. Helen yelled more and more
as the day went on, and I got more and more tired of being yelled
at for no reason. Just before Mom was supposed to get home, I
started yelling back.

Then Helen really let go. She was yelling at me and had
raised her hand to slap me when I saw Spens sneaking up behind
her. He had his bamboo walking stick in his hand, and he was
pointing it at Helen's back. I couldn't believe it, but it looked as
if it had been sharpened at the end to a fine point. I yelled no at
Spens and gave Helen a big push just as Spens started to run
towards Helen with a horrible look of hate on his face. Helen fell
backwards, Spens crashed into the wall with his stick and all three
of us started yelling as Mike pounded down the stairs. Mike tore
into the living room, looked at the situation and grabbed Spens,
who was screaming that he wanted to kill her. Helen was sitting
on the floor, hysterical I think. Mike was having a hard time
holding onto Spens, who was thrashing wildly, and all four of us

were yelling when Mom entered the house. Helen moved out that night.

Mom had to go to work the next day, so we held another family conference. Because Nana, who was living with her sister Nettie, was arriving the next evening, we only had to get through one day without a sitter. Then Nana, her sister Nettie and Nettie's husband Roy would be there for a week, and Mom would have time to look for another sitter. Mike and I volunteered to share watching Spens the next day.

The next afternoon I returned from playing for my turn with Spens. Danny came with me; we were going to play Monopoly all afternoon, make popcorn and have a good time. Mike took off and, before we'd even started the popcorn, there was a knock on the door. It was Gerald Hahn and two of his friends from Catholic school. They were carrying BB guns. Gerald got really mad when I told him he couldn't come in because he saw Danny in the living room. I tried telling him Mom had said only one friend inside, but it didn't help. He started pushing on the door, trying to open it further. Danny ran over to help me but by then Gerald had his friends helping him. They came right in.

I didn't know what to do except run upstairs. Danny followed me up, with Gerald and his friends right after us. All the screaming woke Spens up. I don't really remember what happened next. Suddenly, though, there was a shot and the sound of a breaking window. Then Gerald and his friends were running from room to room, all over the house, shooting at the windows. They pulled the beds apart, knocked books off shelves, emptied dresser drawers, and did all sorts of things that were bad. When they finally left, Danny called his mother and told her to hurry down.

Both of us were really scared. Spens was sitting big-eyed on his bed with a silly grin on his face, but at least he had stopped crying. I was sure Con would spank me because someone needed to be spanked for the mess and I was the sitter. She didn't, though. She said "My," and "Oh, my gosh" and "How horrible," but she didn't yell or anything. She just made us all come back to her house and called Mom.

And when Mom got home, boy, was she mad! She said it was disgraceful to have had a gang fight in the house, and it was all my fault. She spanked me, and then I had to go to bed without supper. I could hear her moving through the house, trying to clean up before everyone got there. She was crying while she worked. Horrible sounds came out of her, sounds that made me feel sick inside. When I had to vomit, I didn't know what to do. If I stayed in my room like she told me, I would make an even bigger mess. If I ran to the bathroom, I'd be disobeying some more.

I finally decided to go to the bathroom, but I decided too late. Running down the hall I started vomiting, and I made a terrible mess. It was all over the wall and floor and everything. I started screaming then. I don't know why, I just started screaming. I wasn't even saying anything, just making a lot of noise. It felt like it was going to go on forever and ever, it would never end. In fifty years I'd still be screaming.

Then someone, Mom I guess, slapped me in the face. It must have been her because right after I was hit, she was holding me and saying that Bert had died, my grandfather wasn't around to help anymore. She was crying.

Later, after my nose stopped bleeding and I had had a bath and was lying on the couch, covered with lots of blankets, Mom asked me why I had screamed Bert's name. She had finished up all the cleaning, patched the holes in the windows and was drinking a bottle of beer. Mike and Spens were playing cards in the dining room, and it was getting dark outside, as it does in winter. I was feeling kind of drowsy. Her question didn't make sense to me, I didn't scream Bert's name. No one did. Bert was dead, he couldn't help anyone anymore.

Just as I had almost found enough strength to tell her that, we heard Nana, her sister Nettie and Nettie's husband Roy coming up the front walk. Mike and Spens ran excitedly to the door and threw it open, welcoming them. Nana stepped inside and her big smile crumpled into a frown as she stared at Mom. Then she said, "Avis, if you drink alone, you'll become a drunkard!"

Chapter 8

I didn't know it at the time, but that Christmas was the last big family Christmas that we ever had. It wasn't much fun.

Before Bert died, we would gather for the holidays at Nana's and his house. There would be Chuck and Jean, with their son Danny. There would be Mom's other brother Tommy and his wife Susie. Eventually they ended up with six kids, but only three are in the photo that I still have of them. Susie used to say that the twins, Barbara and Bobby, were identical twins. Chuck was a salesman, but he wanted to be a writer. Mom was a housewife, but she wanted to be a doctor. Tom, the youngest, didn't want to be anything, but he was an auto mechanic. None of their marriages lasted.

Mom was married four times altogether. Between Mike's father and mine there was a man named Myers. I once asked her about him. She said that he asked her to marry him in front of her parents, and she didn't want to embarrass him by saying no. The marriage lasted six months. Later, when I was older, she married Bill.

Chuck and Jean, who ended up with four kids, also got divorced in the early seventies. Jean went off to college, then graduate school. When she was about to get her Ph.D., she told Chuck that she wanted a divorce after nearly thirty years of marriage.

The last two kids that Tom and Susie had were not Tom's. He knew that, but he didn't divorce her until the sixties, when she got gonorrhea and taunted him with the fact that she took money for sex. Tom remarried and settled down. Chuck remarried two or three times. But all of that happened long after Bert died.

Nettie, my grandmother Nana's sister, would also be there during the holidays with her husband Vic. He was an alcoholic who beat her, until she eventually left him and married Roy. She did not get re-married after her second divorce. Another of Nana's sisters, Dolly, would also be there. She, too, was an alcoholic. She had one daughter with her first husband and three children with her second.

This was my family. They had at least thirteen divorces among the older generation. No, it was at least fourteen because Bert had been divorced and had three daughters in Canada somewhere. There were three alcoholics, two beaten wives and one prostitute. Back then, though, before most of that happened, they were fun to be with. I liked everyone except Jean and Vic. Chuck was my favorite.

There was always teasing and laughing when we all gathered. I got hugs and kisses from nearly everyone. The food was delicious, the presents eye-dazzling, the goodwill reassuring. We kids went off to the basement to play noisy and fun-filled games while the adults drank their after-supper coffee. Later, we all gathered in the living room, people sitting everywhere with arms draped about each other. We sang for up to two hours, long after the youngest kids had drifted off to sleep on the floor. They were my family and I loved them.

The first Christmas after Bert died though, everyone gathered at my house, which was far too small. Bert wasn't there, of course, and my father was in the hospital. Nana cried almost continuously for Bert. My mother was mad at Nana for taking over her kitchen. Nana's sister Dolly and her sister-in-law Joan both got drunk. They just sat and laughed, except when they stumbled to the make-shift bar in the dining room to refill their glasses. Returning from one such trip, Dolly, who weighed over 200 pounds, dropped without warning into Roy's lap. He gasped, tried to smile, then tried to push her off of him. Dolly's husband Ken sheepishly hurried over and tugged Dolly into a standing position. Then she fell towards Ken, who tried to catch her. Both ended on the floor. Then several of the men got Dolly on her feet and back to her chair while the women fretted or laughed or made angry remarks, depending on their dispositions. Ken made Roy a strong drink and handed it to him silently, his head down and his face flaming.

All the babies cried through dinner, and all the adults kept yelling at the older kids to be quiet after dinner. We didn't sing that year for the first time. Everyone left early. When Dolly walked out onto the porch, she was so drunk that she missed the stairs and walked right off the porch into a bush. Joan, equally drunk, followed her and did a somersault in the air, landing in a snow drift. Only Mike and I thought that it was funny.

When everyone was gone but Nana, Nettie and Roy, my mother started talking bitterly about the family. No one had helped her when she had needed help. Everyone had more money than she did, but no one had offered to help with the Christmas dinner. She was sick of them all, and it would be a cold day in hell before she invited them again. Long after I had gone to bed I could hear her downstairs, complaining about the family.

Chapter 9

When school started again, we had a new sitter named Lani. Lani was black, so she didn't live with us. She couldn't cook very well, and she didn't clean at all, but she didn't yell either. Many days Lani talked Mike and me into skipping school to keep her company. Since she taught us card games and would joke and laugh with us, we loved to stay home. Mike wrote the notes to the school so well that we were never caught. But when our mother was called into school because both of us were close to flunking, she fired Lani.

Next Mike and I convinced our mother that we did not need a sitter even though our ages ranged from five to thirteen. I got my brothers up and fixed breakfast for them, then Mike was responsible for getting Spens to Con's house, where Con's housekeeper took care of him during school hours. After school I had to take care of Spens and cook supper while Mike did his paper route. Mike took over the shopping.

The situation got worse rapidly because of Spens. His temper tantrums became more frequent and more violent. Mike and I could not handle him, and each day was a major frustration as we tried to do what was expected of us.

Until then I had liked Spens despite the special treatment that my father had given him, despite his temper tantrums and despite his occasional destruction of my things. I felt sorry for him when he was tied to a tree like a dog because he would wander off as a toddler. I was horrified the day Mom had picked him up and thrown him into his bed from the doorway of his room, then tied his door shut, during one of his more spectacular tantrums. He could have gotten really hurt. I knew that he badly missed our father. He looked so sad as he had laid face down on the floor, not moving, for hours at a time. He had been so silly to think that he could safely use my umbrella to parachute from the second floor of a neighbor's house. I was furious that he broke the red umbrella that had my name, Katie, written on it with black letters, but I was also glad that he had not been seriously hurt. But now, I began to hate Spens for starting each day with a battle. He insisted on dressing himself, but didn't. He wouldn't eat his breakfast. He hid under his bed when it was time to take him to Con's. Mike and I had to drag him, screaming and kicking, down the street.

After several months of this, suddenly everything changed again. Mom went to visit Daddy, and the doctor told her that he definitely would be hospitalized for life. That meant that my mother could never marry again because it was against the law to divorce someone who was in a mental hospital. Two weeks later, he was released.

The story of why he was released, as I heard it, was confusing. During the war my father had saved the life of someone named Stephen. Stephen, who was very rich, went to visit my father a week after Mom had been there. Then Dad was released. Mother was sure that Stephen had bribed the doctors and spoke very bitterly about it. I didn't think that the doctors would lie just for money.

The divorce went through rapidly and Spens went to live with our father. That day is imprinted on my mind forever. Spens's things were all packed and waiting near the door. My mother and Mike went down the street to Con's. I stayed with Spens, waiting for our father. Nothing seemed real. I could not believe that our mother had actually agreed to give up Spens. Maybe someday she would give me up, too, if I didn't start behaving better. I felt guilty for having complained to her about Spens. He was scared. I was convinced that my father would kill me even though the doctor said that he was all better. And then, when he arrived, there was an incredible awkwardness. There was nothing to say to each other. He had had to shave off his mustache because of hospital rules and did not even look like our father. We stared at each other, said hello, then he walked past me into the house to hug Spens. I knew that he was very angry at me. While Spens helped pack our father's things, I sat on the porch and watched cloud formations. I could hear them inside but tried to ignore Spens's excited voice and our father's low replies.

I don't remember actually saying good-bye that day, but I do remember many other good-byes. Spens came to visit every second weekend for a while. He seemed to grow more fearful, more anxious with each visit. (Mom, you must realize that Spens is being beaten now, just like we were before!) Soon, he was asking to stay permanently with us. (How could you care so little to let him go when you know that he lives in terror?) When that did not work, he shifted to crying piteously when it was time for him to leave. (He might be killed, don't you understand?) Then, he began to fight getting into the car. (I take back everything I said about him, he wasn't too hard for me to handle. Give us another chance, please!) He would grab hold of someone, screaming fearfully. (How could you do this to us? He's my brother, your son, how can we live without him, how can we be happy knowing that he's living in danger?) As he was carried out the door, he would catch hold of the jamb and start kicking. (Someday, Spens, I will make up for this, I promise. I'm so sorry that you live like you do, I wish that you could be safe with us, I hate them for what they are doing to you!) They had to peel his fingers, one by one, from the jamb. (Nothing, nothing, justifies what you have done to Spens. You know what is happening to Spens, but you don't care enough to stop it. I hate you to the bottom of my being for what you are letting happen!) After one such fight that left me in awe of Spens, he was no longer permitted to visit us.

Thus, when Spens was six and I was ten nearly all contact between us was blocked. Although we lived less than ten miles from each other, weeks would go by without even a phone call between us. What haunted me was the memory of Spens quickly putting his forearm up to protect his head and face whenever he was startled. I knew that he was getting my beatings.

Chapter 10

"Hey, Sis. Let's skip school today. I've got three new comics I'll let you read if you'll stay home with me." Although I really want to go to school, Mike looks so sad that I decide to keep him company. We both get into Mom's bed, where I am still reluctantly sleeping every night even though one bedroom is totally unoccupied. Mike has brought the comics and a book with him. I read the comics first, snuggled close to him, then switch to a library book. We read the funny parts out loud to each other, giggle, talk about school, and share a peace and closeness that has been too long missing.

Then, the scary part starts again. As Mike reads, he puts his hand into his pajama opening and pulls out his thing. He pulls up and down on it slowly as he reads. "Mike, why are you doing that? I don't like you to do that."

"It feels good. Do you want to do it for me?" I don't answer him. "It really feels good, Sis. What feels even better is putting it inside a girl. Could I do that with you?"

This time, I feel that I have to answer but I can't talk because of the pictures shooting so rapidly through my brain. I know exactly what he wants me to do, but I don't know how I know how. "No," I growl at him. "You can't."

"Okay, don't get mad! You said exactly the right thing. Never, ever let someone put his penis in you. Promise me," Mike demands, as he pulls up and down on his thing.

"I already told you no. Why would I let someone else do what I won't let you do?"

"Well, it feels so good that you might."

"Not me. It sounds terrible. I don't want anyone inside me, ever!"

"If I can't put it inside you, will you please pull on it a little? Not for long, just a little? Please, Sis? Pretty please with sugar on top?"

Because the sugar part is our secret code for "it's very important to me," I agree. I reach over and pull his thing up and down as I turn back to my book. For a long time, I cannot see the words.

. . .

"Hey, Sis, do you want to skip school today?" I angrily answer no while I continue to dress. Mike stands watching me.

. . .

The fear settles in on me as I put the key into the back door lock. I enter the silent house, and search the downstairs thoroughly before I fix a toasted cream cheese and grape jelly sandwich, pour a glass of milk and carry them to the living room. I choose the chair in the corner, where I can watch both the front door and the entrance from the kitchen. My heart is pounding slightly, but I ignore that and start to eat. I hear footsteps upstairs where no one should be. Quietly I put down my plate and the glass, preparing to run. The footsteps move along the hall and start down the stairs. A paralysis takes hold of me, and I sit waiting for the attack, not feeling anything. The steps slowly descend. A foot appears, in slippers, followed by a pajama leg. "Hi, Sis. Did you fix me a sandwich, too? I decided to skip school today."

"I hate you, Mike! Why should I fix you anything but poison," I scream as I run out the back door and toward school.

Chapter 11

The next summer Mike was sent to a distant relative's farm, and I was sent to Columbus, Ohio, to live with my great aunt Nettie, Nettie's husband Roy, and Nana.

When Mike and I returned home, we were strangers to each other. We had been close to each other before, sharing, talking, always talking. But something had happened to him over the summer, he was no longer really the brother I knew. He did say that he had gone on strike, refusing to work on the farm for a while, but he would not talk about why. He just withdrew, would no longer talk about anything. He began to tease me in a way that made me feel that he was very angry at me, as if he didn't care at all about me anymore. He began to fail at school. All he did was eat, and soon he weighed 250 pounds.

Another change had occurred over the summer. My mother was dating a man named Ray, who had a wooden left leg and drank a lot. Ray worked with my mother. He was from Maine, close to the Canadian border, and had hurt his leg when he was a boy playing hockey. It still hurt him, he said, which was why he had to drink alcohol to kill the pain. Sometimes he said that he was trying to fill his hollow leg.

At first I liked Ray but then Mom and Ray began to fight a lot. The only difference in their fighting from what she used to do with Dad is that Ray didn't hit her as much and, when it got really bad, she would tell him to leave her house. And Ray never hit or yelled at Mike and me. I used to lie in bed at night, though, hearing them fight, and it made me feel both scared and angry.

I went back to the streets, but they weren't as nice as they used to be without Mike to protect me. My clothes were very shabby for our middle class existence, and I got into several fights that were started by teasing about them. I also got into fights for no real reason, with friends and with strangers who were passing by. One day, for instance, I was sitting on the porch when a boy I didn't know walked past the house. I yelled at him that he had funny ears and, when he yelled back that I was a creep, I dared him to fight me. Then there was Paul, a boy in my class who was in love with me, he said, and walked me home from school every day. I kicked him so many times in the shins that his mother said that he no longer could have anything to do with me.

There was an anger, a wildness in me that scared me, and after a while I realized that I was acting just like my father. That scared me even more, and I vowed to change completely. I made school and reading the focus of my life. Instead of joining the games on the street after school, I went to the library every day. I read there until it was time to go home. Then, after supper, I read in my room until it was time for bed.

Meanwhile, my non-relationship with my father began to change. Occasionally, he would take the three of us out to supper, for swimming, on a drive. I do not remember being scared of him during those outings. I remember that with him - but not when I was with my mother- I felt free to be a child. I did not have to make any decisions or do something that was far off from what could be expected of a child.

Most of all, I remember Spens during those occasional meetings. He was so delighted to be with Mike and me that he beamed. His eyes danced and sparkled, but he did not say much. He still became scared by any sudden movement.

The summer I was twelve, my father called me when I was home between camp sessions. He said that he was moving to California in two days. He wanted me to go with him to Spens's camp to get Spens. If I did not go, he said that I would never see Spens again.

As we drove to the camp, I worried all the way how Spens would feel at having to leave camp and move to California with no warning. Spens looked delighted to see me, then shocked at what I had to tell him. Again, I helped him pack. On the way home we sat in the back seat and whispered plans to keep in contact.

Once home, an incredible series of events began. My father said that he wanted to tell me some things before he left, things that I needed to know in order to grow up. Then, for what seemed like a half hour, he told me everything that he saw as wrong with me. I was stubborn (You bet!), lazy (Very wrong.), irresponsible (How can you possibly say that!), lacking in ambition (So what?), sullen (Only around you), too fat (Don't you like how I look?), selfish (Not with people I like.), unkempt (You can't stay neat and still have fun.), flippant (You don't really know me at all!), arrogant (What's that mean?), ungrateful (Do I owe you something?), disloyal (To you?), obnoxious (Am I?), immature (Am I?), dumb (But I get all A's!), ugly (Don't you like the way I look?), and doomed to get in serious trouble when I got older (I won't, I won't! I'm being very careful, I always control myself.) He called me every negative adjective that could be imagined. (Maybe he's right about me, maybe I'm just like he was when he was a kid.)

As he went on, his voice became louder and louder, and his eyes became very dilated (He's going to start beating me again!) His hands curled into fists. (No, never again. This is my house, not his. I could call the police and they would make him go away. I'm not a little kid anymore, I won't let him hurt me again.)

"Okay, Kate, I have to get home and finish packing. Think about what I said. Now, give me a hug and a kiss before I go. Spenser, too, since you won't see him for a very long time."

"No!" I screamed at him. "Get out of my house. You can't say things like that to me and expect me to be grateful to you. Do you really think that I could kiss you after what you just did to me? I never want to see you again in my whole life, and I won't, either. Leave or I'll call the police."

As I screamed at my father, I could see that he was getting more and more angry. But I wasn't afraid of him. He couldn't hurt me. I would kill him if he tried.

As his face got redder and redder he took several deep, shuddering breaths. His shoulders relaxed, his eyes returned to normal. I stared at him, waiting for his response. It came in a low, determined tone. "Kate, if you don't kiss me goodbye, you're no longer my daughter."

That stopped me cold. As I stared at him, all our years together roared through my mind. I remembered the many blows, the terror. I remembered his teaching me not to be afraid of lightning and how to swim. Once he taught me how to sit on the toilet so that I wouldn't get piles. He was always talking about piles, whatever they were. That was crazy, but it was motivated by caring. He did love me, even if his love was shown in crazy ways. His love was real in a way that my mother's wasn't. At least on some level he realized that I was still a kid, and she never did. But was his kind of love worth what went along with it? No! Nothing was worth being hurt and scared and feeling like the sky was going to fall down at any moment. Nothing was worth going to sleep being scared and waking up being scared and only feeling safe when he wasn't around. I took a deep breath and said, "It's a deal."

He stalked out of the house, yelling that I was no longer his child, and roared away in his car with Spens looking back at me fearfully. I collapsed in a sobbing heap on the floor.

I have never seen my father since that day; it was eleven years before I saw Spens again. My father allowed Spens and I to correspond for two years, then it was no longer permitted. On Christmas and my birthdays during those two years I received presents from him. Occasionally I would write my father, and occasionally he would answer. Then they disappeared. For a couple of years I sent letters to Spens in care of dozens of school districts selected from a map of California, but they were always returned.

The next time that I heard from my father was the day before my wedding. Mom had had his address all along, and she had written him that I was getting married. His letter forgot to say congratulations. Instead, it cataloged all my failings and closed with the conclusion that I must be pregnant. Otherwise, no man would be so foolish as to marry me.

Over the years that followed, my father wrote me about every two years. A fairly reasonable letter would come that I would politely answer, saying nothing. Next there would be an outrageous letter from him, full of self-pity or anger or recriminations. I would respond with anger and the correspondence would break off, to be resumed in a couple of years.

"Why, Renee? I kept hoping. That's why, but it's very hard to admit it. All my life I've denied that I wanted anything to do with him. My mother would have been horrified if she had known. She would have seen it as betrayal. In a way, I still do. Still, there's no denying that he is my father, as much as I'd like to, and there's no denying that a part of me wants him to act like a good father, still. Who wouldn't want something like that? But the reality is that it's impossible with him. Actually, I hate him."

Chapter 12

While I was still in junior high school, my mother stopped dating the abusive alcoholic Ray and then married Bill Edwards, a captain in the army. Mike lost fifty pounds and joined the marines. Outwardly, I became a normal teenager. I walled off the unrepaired damage and successfully kept it walled off for nearly twenty years. I was class president, president of the Girls' Athletic Association, involved with building a cyclotron and very popular at school. I started dating quite early for that time, at age thirteen. I worked on football floats for homecoming, sold bagels to raise money for school clubs, was the only non-Jew invited to join a Jewish sorority. I taught creative writing at the Y, tutored students in math and was a life guard. I went to camp every summer from the time I was eleven until I was fifteen, working very hard throughout the school year to earn enough money to ensure a complete summer away from home. I spent the summer after my sophomore year at the University of Chicago, studying genetics and mathematics, and the summer between my junior and senior years first at Girls' State and then living with Mike and his wife Michelle, who had just had a baby and needed help. I was in advanced placement courses, studied hard and gave the valedictory speech at graduation.

At night I kept awakening from nightmares of Germans trying to kill me. I daydreamed the death of my mother. I daydreamed a world war, featuring invasion of the United States. Under those circumstances violence would be permissible, and I daydreamed killing all sorts of faceless enemies. My fantasies were angry and violent, but I was never really that way. In actuality I was somewhat shy, soft-spoken, very serious and horrified by violence even as seen on TV and in the movies.

I wasn't very happy then. I felt isolated and alone despite all my activities and obvious popularity at school. I was scared, but I didn't know of what. I walked the quiet streets of our town late at night, and a feeling of total panic would often flow over me. I was sure that I was about to be attacked and that I would be killed. I was equally sure that, if I saw the attack coming, I would be unable to utter a sound or move in self-defense. At other times I walked the dark streets unafraid, frequently with tears quietly running down my cheeks as I looked into homes where people seemed to be enjoying each other. I didn't understand why I longed for a family. After all, I had Mom and Mike, before he went into the marines. I wouldn't let my mother touch me. I wouldn't let anyone touch me.

I had trouble sleeping. The nightmares of Germans chasing me were terrifying and made no sense to me. I experimented with religion but couldn't stand Christianity because of all its talk of love, turning the other cheek, forgiveness. It felt totally alien to me. I was very angry about nothing as far as I could tell.

I became fascinated by what had happened in Hitler's Germany after reading *Exodus* when I was twelve. I identified completely with the Jews, and thought repeatedly about converting to Judaism. I didn't because I felt myself capable of acting like the worst of the SS. I was confused. I feared that I was going crazy, like my father. There was a great and unfulfilled longing inside of me that I couldn't name.

My mother's marriage to Bill submerged much of my unhappiness. For five years, since I had been nine, I had longed for a new father. My only requirements were that he would relieve me of the burden of Mom and not be violent. Bill did and he wasn't, so I was very thankful to him. Slowly I grew to love him. He brought fun into our lives. He said things that hurt - I looked like a farmer walking behind a plow, my legs were like inverted bowling pins, I was a grind at school - but he thought that he was simply teasing me, so I tried to ignore them. He also said things that were important - that I could not be held responsible for my relatives, only my friends, and that I had the ability to become whatever I chose - and I loved him for them.

It took about two years before I thought of Bill as my father. During that time we fought a lot as we established the rules of our relationship. Each time that we fought, Mom tried to interfere. Finally, during a heated exchange over something Martin Luther King had done, her interference ended. The two of us were yelling at each other, Mom tried to intervene, and both of us turned toward her in unison and said "Stay out, this is our fight. You're not involved." We used almost identical words, it was totally unplanned. Mom started crying, but from that point on she left us alone to form our own relationship, independent of her, and he became my father in addition to being her husband.

There was one event in Bill's life about which he would not talk. During the war he was in the forerunner of what became the CIA, and he had been the official army photographer at the liberation of several concentration camps. He had hundreds of pictures of piled corpses, the ovens, walking skeletons that he kept in an album which he never opened. Only once did he mention his experiences. We were watching a Spencer Tracy movie on television called *Judgment at Nuremberg*. When they started showing pictures of the camps, Bill went into the bathroom and vomited. He said that the pictures brought back the smells for him. Other than that, he never said a word about what he had seen. It was a closed topic, never discussed, a horror that haunted him all his life.

As a child Bill had had a horrible family life. His father had deserted his family, he was put into an orphanage at the age of twelve when his mother remarried, and he stayed there until he joined the army. He married Mom when he was forty-nine; he had never been married before. When I think now about how rapidly he adjusted to married life, the joy that he got out of the holidays, the understanding that he showed to me, it's pretty clear that he shared my dream of a loving family. I responded to his delight. I put aside my anger and hurt and went off to conquer the world.

. . .

"Don't you understand, Renee? There is so much that I remember that I have not tried to capture with words, simply because I can't do it, Renee! I could use the word despair, but there would be no way to say what it is like at four or five or seven or nine and to be filled with despair. If I tell you that at age eight, I talked Mike out of hanging himself, there's no way that I can tell you what it meant to me to be doing that. I can say that that same year in music class I cried silently as the class sang *Toyland* because I decided that I had already passed the borders of childhood, never to return. There is no way, however, that I can convey what it was like to reach that realization and know that I was old without first having been young. I could tell of the shame of having divorced parents in a time and place where divorce tainted an entire family, but I can't convey the pounding heart and burning cheeks that accompanied my nonchalant response to any inquiries about my parents. Could you, could anyone possibly begin to know, even if I could find the right words, how it feels to be ten and helpless while your six-year-old brother is struggling against two adults with all his being because he fears returning to his home? Can anyone understand that he will be beaten as soon as he gets there for putting up such a struggle? Can anyone understand that he will be beaten with the closed fists and heavy feet of a man over six feet tall who is enraged? This man is crazy, he recognizes no limits, and he became the sole caretaker of a five-year-old child.

"No, there are no words for what it was like. The facts do not tell the tale. No one can understand, I don't know why I'm even trying with you, Renee. My father beat us, my mother did not do anything to stop him, one brother lived in terror until he was eighteen, daydreaming of murder and revenge, another brother essentially withdrew at fifteen from everyone. Never once did the feelings of anger, despair, fear, abandonment and guilt get discussed. I raised myself as best I could, and time did not heal the wounds."

Chapter 13

"Renee, I've been fighting against another flashback," I said fearfully. "It began when I saw a father spank a child in the grocery store this morning. That's why I called you for an extra appointment today."

"Do you want to go into it?" she asked.

"No! I want it to go away," I answered in almost panic.

"Do you think it will?"

"No, no it won't!" She let the ensuing silence tell me what I already knew. "Okay," I said with a sigh. "It's the only way that I can handle it, now that it's beating on the door of my mind. But when are these going to stop, Renee?" I could hear the child-like vulnerability in my plaintive question to her, but I was far beyond such concepts as dignity or embarrassment. I was four again, or maybe younger, needing above all to tell what had happened.

Renee moved next to me on the couch and took my hand. "Relax, Kate. Lean back and close your eyes." As she began talking in an hypnotic fashion, I could feel myself sinking down, down into the memory that had been hovering just below my conscious mind. I began to pant as some part of me continued to resist remembering. As the sound of my breathing grew louder and louder, I slipped in and out of a panic state repeatedly. I opened my mouth, but there were no words for it to say.

"What happened in the store?" Renee prompted.

"A-a man, a father, swooped down on his child and . . . and . . . and he picked her up and . . . he . . . he shook her. That's all I saw, except I-I only sort of saw it out of the corner of m-m-my eye. Almost

I didn't see. And then . . . suddenly I was having a flash-flashback," I panted out.

"And?" she led me on.

"I ran to him, Renee. I ran to my father. I was so happy to see him. I ran to him and he picked me up." The words were coming in a rush now. I was beyond fear, beyond panic, having stepped directly into the other time. "He picked me up. I felt like singing, a giggle was halfway between my stomach and throat. He picked me up but then he threw me," I screamed.

When my sobbing had begun to subside some, she asked, "Where did you land when your daddy threw you?"

"Don't say it was my daddy who threw me," I yelled at her as I jerked my shoulders out of her embrace. "My daddy wouldn't do that, not him. My daddy loves me. He wouldn't hurt me!"

"Then who was it who threw you, Katie?" she gently asked.

"It . . . it was someone who looked like my daddy. He looked just like him but it wasn't him. It was someone else, a bad man who pretended to be him. My daddy loves me. He wouldn't throw me. A bad man did it, not my daddy. My daddy loves me," I screamed at her before collapsing in sobs onto her lap.

After a while, Renee asked, "Who threw you, Katie?"

"My daddy," I wailed.

"Your daddy threw you?"

"Yes," I sobbed out. "He threw me. I don't know why he did. I ran to him because I was so happy to see him. I can see my braids streaming out behind me. My corduroy jacket is red. It's open and billowing out as I run. I leaped into his arms that he was holding out to me. I can feel my body hitting his. I thought he was going to hold me tight. BUT HE THREW ME! My daddy threw me."

A long time later Renee said, "Come back, Kate. It's time to come back." Slowly, I pulled myself into present time. I straightened into a sitting position, took the tissues she handed me and cleaned up my face. I could do nothing about the sweat that soaked my clothes. When I finished, she asked, "When you leaped into his arms, by any chance did your feet hit his genitals?"

"Maybe. They could have. Why? Do you think he threw me because I hurt him?" I asked. "I didn't mean to."

"I don't know, Kate," she sighed. "It's a possibility."

"I don't know either. But, Renee, would you throw a little kid just because of a mistake like that?"

"No, Kate. I would never throw a little kid no matter what she did. Never would I throw a child."

"But my daddy threw me," I said, beginning to slip back into other time.

"Stay with me for a moment, Kate." I forced myself to come back. "Do you know where you landed? Were you hurt?"

"I don't know," I almost wailed, beginning to pant again.

"Okay, go find out. You know."

Released, I was once again spinning through the air, falling, falling, tumbling out of control, wildly waving my arms and legs, coming to rest in the midst of a patch of tall, dried weeds. My breath temporarily knocked out of me by the force of the blow, I lay stunned, seeing nothing, hearing nothing. Gradually, sound and sight returned. Gradually, I began to roll painfully over onto my hands and knees. Gradually, I stood up and began to stagger towards home without a glance at my father.

When the memory was through, I laid with my head on Renee's lap resting. Occasional shudders and sobs rocked me, but her gentle stroking of my head and back eventually lulled me into a half-sleep state. I floated for a while, until I had the strength to begin again.

"Renee, the shock was terrible. From that point on, I could never trust him."

"You trusted him until then?"

"Yes. There's no doubt about it. The joy inside her was so complete, Renee. Never have I felt anything like that since then. I would like to feel it again, but I don't think I'm capable of being so totally joyful anymore. It's indescribable. But yes, I trusted him as I ran to him."

Her hands continued to stroke me as she asked, "Do you have any idea how old you were?"

"Not really. I can guess, though. It was fall. It was in Flint. That means either I was almost three or almost four. My guess is almost three, sometime around there."

"That's when your trust was shattered, when you were almost three."

"Yes," I said, feeling the tears start to roll slowly down my face again as I began to reclaim the child I once was.

Chapter 14

Between high school and college I wanted to go to Israel and work on a kibbutz, but my mother and Bill talked me out of that. My mother then had tried very hard to get me to attend school in the Detroit area so that I could remain at home, but I refused every bribe and stubbornly insisted on going away. The thought of remaining at home made me shudder, although I didn't know why. Instead of to Israel, I went to the University of Chicago.

The night before I left, Mike and I went out together for supper. He had married my science teacher's daughter, Michelle, whom I had introduced to him in a fit of matchmaking. They had a son, Sam, whom I adored. I had taken care of Sam for the first two weeks of his life while Michelle was recuperating, and I frequently babysat for him. Watching Mike care for Sam was healing in a fundamental way for me, even though I did not realize it at the time. Watching him with Sam, I think that I learned for the first time that a father could be gentle and loving.

Mike was doing very well at that point. After the marines he had ended up as a partner in a car wash chain. While in the marines he had been offered a chance to attend Annapolis and for a while he had contemplated going to college when he got out. In fact, I had tutored him in mathematics in preparation for the college entrance exam that he had been required to take at the University of Michigan. We had covered two years of algebra and both plane and solid geometry in three days, none of which had he studied while in school. Though Mike had been given a complete scholarship including spending money on the basis of the test, he seemed afraid of going back to school. It was as if, having flunked out in tenth grade, he had lost all self-confidence in his ability to learn.

In the restaurant, Mike asked me what I planned to study in college. I answered "genetics." I wanted to stop the birth of malformed and dead babies. Kids were so precious to me, I hated to see them suffer. Although I couldn't do anything about what might happen to them in their lives, at least I might be able to help ensure that each kid started his life in the best shape possible.

"Yah, I know what you mean, Kate," answered Mike. "We had it tough as kids."

"I've promised myself that I will never have any children unless I am absolutely sure that it wouldn't end the way it did with Mom and Dad. Do you know what I mean?"

"Me, too. Do you think that I would have married Michelle and had Sam if I thought it would end badly? I've had two fathers run out on me. I'm not going to do that to Sam. I love the little fellow so much, Kate."

When Mike hugged me in good-bye, he said, "So long, Sis. Don't lose your dream. Go save all those kids." I felt as if he were telling me to do it for him, too.

It was the fall of 1962, and I was eighteen. I planned to conquer the university in the same way as I had come out on top in high school. I was eager, ambitious and convinced that I was the best, except when I felt myself to be a fraud. Unfortunately, the university almost beat me.

That first week was one placement test after another and, as I discovered that I was not the smartest person in the world, I began to feel homesick. I couldn't believe it. I had spent all my time since I was eleven working to get away every summer. I had daydreamed for years of going to college. Now that I was finally away for good, I wanted to go home. It was as if all my self-confidence had been a fraud. As soon as it was put to the test, it evaporated and I was left feeling shaky and vulnerable. After two weeks I gave into the feelings and took the bus home for the weekend. I brushed away all questions as to why and returned feeling slightly better. My unexplainable homesickness continued, but I learned to live with it.

What I wasn't doing well was studying. I had received straight A's in high school and had never encountered anything that I couldn't understand immediately. I didn't know how to study and was close to flunking chemistry. During the first test I had panicked and spent the entire hour trying to decide which problem to answer first. I received a zero. On the second test I went into the classroom grimly determined not to lose control of myself again, and I received a hundred percent on it. I flunked the third test but received a ninety-eight percent on the fourth. I see-sawed back and forth, excelling and flunking, through that first quarter. My self-confidence was badly shaken in the one area of my life on which I had always been able to count, and I wondered if I were one of those teenagers who fell apart at the first real stress. I didn't understand at all what was happening to me. Was this the first sign of going crazy? Still, I survived the quarter at least, and the next two quarters were somewhat easier.

I made friends quickly and easily when I first arrived, and I dated a lot. One of my friends introduced me to a graduate student early in March. His name was Joe Slaboda. He smoked a pipe, and his sweater had leather patches on the elbows. He was a man, not a boy like the others I had dated. I fell in love, and I completely forgot that I was never going to get close to anyone.

Joe and I were married the next August, when I was three months pregnant. My father had been right in his guess. I dropped out of school and worked in a hospital genetics lab until Carole was born. Joe stayed in school and worked on his Ph.D. in economics.

The first time that Carole and I were alone together, I talked to her for quite a while. "Little girl, I feel so sorry for you. Your father and I have no money, we can't give you much of anything. I love him, but I'm not sure that he loves me. I will do my best to love you well, then let you go when it's time. I will try very hard to protect you. I will try very hard not to hurt you myself. I will make mistakes because I have no idea of how to raise a child, but I hope that they will not be serious." I went on and on in that vein, promising my beautiful daughter my love and my protection. I was determined to be a good mother.

I was, too. I surprised myself at how good I was as a mother to Carole. My love grew and blossomed in a fantastic way. When Becky came along two years later, I was the same for her.

In 1966, when the girls were six months and two years, we moved to Atlanta. Joe was teaching at a university there, and I started back to school as a sophomore. Mom and Bill, who were stationed in Germany for their third year, refused to help with my college expenses. This time, there was no panic during tests. I graduated in 1969, then began to work on a Ph.D. in genetics.

Mom and Bill returned to the States in 1967 and settled in Oakland, California. One night the next year, my brother Spens knocked on their door. He had gone to Detroit, tracked down Mom's brother Chuck who had moved to New Jersey, gone there and finally gotten her address. He lived in Berkeley, practically right next door to Mom in Oakland.

As soon as school was out for the summer, the girls and I flew to California. Bill greeted me at the airport, joy and delight sparkling in his eyes. Mom greeted me at the door to their house with a big hug and the information that I needed a haircut, her standard opening remark. Behind her stood Spens.

My baby brother had become a man.

Eleven years had gone by since my father had declared me not to be his child and had driven off to California with Spens. He was twenty now, and I could see the frightened little boy whom he had been peering out behind his charming adult smile. Hesitant, soft-spoken, Spens waited for my response to him. It was whole-hearted delight.

Mike flew up from Los Angeles, where he was living then, and joined us for the weekend. The three of us talked non-stop for two days.

Spens had had a terrible life after he left us and, once again, I felt a rush of guilt at how good my life had been compared to his. Our father had remarried. His wife, May, instead of being beaten, had beaten Daddy. Both of them had beaten Spens. May was a nurse specializing in terminal care, and most of her patients ended up adding her to their wills. Dad owned a mortgage company and was almost rich.

Spens said that he used to daydream of soaking their room with gasoline as they slept, then striking a match. During Spens's senior year in high school he had been beaten with a leather belt for reading *Catcher in The Rye* for an English assignment. He had moved into his girlfriend's home three houses down the street. Even though our father knew where he was, he reported Spens as a runaway. Spens spent several months in a detention home before returning to his girlfriend's house as a foster child. Now he was a physics student at Berkeley. On the financial aid form our dad had scrawled, "There is no way in hell that I would give this bastard anything!" In a very clever move, Spens had submitted that form and, as a result, he was given a full scholarship.

Talk turned to the earlier years, and Mom told us an astonishing fact. There never was a great tank battle and honorable wounds. Six weeks after I was born at Fort Benning, Dad had gotten drunk, stolen a jeep and crashed into a tree. There was a nurse in the jeep with him. His war ended in South Georgia. Another fact from her: she never once saw him naked during all their years of marriage. Late in her pregnancies he had joined her in the shower to make sure that she didn't fall, but even then he had worn his under shorts. Another: she thought he was a homosexual. Information that we all had needed while we were growing up came rolling out that day. Dad didn't start beating her after the war; it began during their first year of marriage. Dad had run away when he was eighteen, bumming around the U.S.; he hadn't sailed around the world as a merchant marine. His mother had died in an insane asylum. She, too, had paranoid schizophrenia. As a child our father had experienced the same sort of craziness as we had received from him. The revelations continued, and each prompted long discussion and speculation. None of us asked why we hadn't been told long ago and none of us asked if we were being told everything or even if what we were being told was true.

Spens and I corresponded and called each other after I went back to Atlanta. He was a regular visitor at our mother's. I felt that, finally, my family was back together again, complete again, even though we were scattered around the country. We hadn't talked about many of the sad events, there was still unexpressed anger, but we were on our way. Someday, the healing would happen.

Chapter 15

It all fell apart in September of 1968. My mother, who had been feeling run down, had a physical, and the eventual diagnosis was acute leukemia.

Bill refused to accept the fact, and for weeks he told people that she had anemia. My mother over-accepted it; she was content to be dying.

I had been waiting for the results of Mom's bone marrow biopsy for two weeks with increasing anxiety. Then Bill called and said that Mom had anemia. I was incredibly relieved. Mom called two hours later and said that she had acute leukemia. The two weeks of not knowing, followed by the relief from Bill's call, followed by the shock of Mom's call had me strung out. I felt as if I were vibrating.

I took the girls to a nearby park, and we cooked our lunch over a fire. After walking for a while in the woods, we went to the Children's Zoo so that the girls could pet animals and I could have a little time to absorb the information about Mom while they were busy.

I was furious at Bill. Okay, he told me what he did because he was unable to face the truth. But, I felt as though my emotions had been jerked back and forth because of his weakness. They had been, too. And then there was Mom: she was dying. My mother was dying, and there wasn't a damn thing I could do to protect her from this. In truth, I felt as though my child were dying.

I guess I was still in a state of shock over Mom, so I didn't react fast enough when I saw Carole begin to get in trouble. She was holding a rabbit as if she were cradling a doll. The rabbit began kicking. By the time I reached her, the rabbit had raked the entire right side of her face with his claws.

I got the rabbit away from her, called to Becky to follow, then rushed her to the car. Carole was screaming, Becky, who was only two, was scared and crying because her sister had been hurt and I was almost frantic because it looked as if Carole's eye had been scratched. I drove straight to the hospital, where they cleaned Carole's injuries then gave her a tetanus shot.

When we left, we got to the car to find that someone had parked us in so completely that I couldn't drive. I carried the two girls the half mile home, one on my back and one in my arms, feeling as if I were on my last legs, put them down for a nap and called Joe. He complained when I insisted that he come home and I blew up at him. But he came. I needed, just for a little while, to be free of responsibilities so that I could simply react to everything that had happened that day. I felt as if I were dying myself.

When Joe got there, he was in such a foul mood that he was the last person in the world with whom I wanted to talk. My mother was dying, and he was angry because I asked him for some help. He made it worse for me, instead of better. Carole was still sleeping so I took Becky with me for a walk in the neighborhood. Her sweetness and charm were so easy to be with that I melted into her activities and we watched a line of ants carrying food back to their nest. In the process, I relaxed and reached a level of peace again.

In California, Bill barred Spens from the house because he "hung out with hippies and was exposed to germs" that he could pass onto our mother. Spens got heavily involved with drugs and flunked out of Berkeley. Mike, our neighbor Con and my great aunt Nettie wrote me long letters and called continuously. I was the scientist and expected to interpret the meaning behind each blood cell differential. More, I was magically expected to disprove the diagnosis. I couldn't and felt that I was the cause of their hurt as I outlined the prognosis to each of them repeatedly. Often, they became angry with me for what I said.

My mother temporarily became convinced by Bill that there was a mistake in the diagnosis, that maybe she wasn't dying, maybe the doctors were lying to her, and she asked me to tell her the truth. I did, and Bill became furious with me. He told me not to write or call my mother anymore, but I ignored him. My mother decided not to tell her mother that she was dying; she couldn't stand the thought of a visit from her. So, until the week before she died, she wrote her long imaginary letters about her busy and fulfilling life. I protested the entire time. It was a crazy period, and it didn't end until July of the next year.

At the same time, my marriage began to fall apart. Until my mother had gotten sick, Joe and I were mostly happy together. But, when my need for emotional support increased, Joe wasn't there for me. Instead of helping me talk and cry, he pushed me away and forced me to be quiet. Sleep difficulties reappeared and, once more, Germans chased me through the night. As before, I turned to novels about Jews. And, as before, I toyed with the idea of converting. And finally, as before, I concluded that conversion required religious belief, not neurotic identification with victims.

I flew to Oakland during the week before Mom's fifty-first birthday in July. I got in on a Friday and, in response to the usual comments about my hair, proposed that we both go to the beauty parlor the next day.

Bill insisted on cooking supper that night. He said that I didn't understand Mom's special food requirements. In a practical way I didn't. By then she had developed gall bladder trouble and had to avoid all fats. The previous week she had been hospitalized by an attack, and the decision was not to operate. Still, that wasn't the real reason why Bill would not let me help. He was convinced that if he, and only he, took perfect care of Mom, she would not succumb to the leukemia.

As Bill cooked, Mom talked to me about her fear of becoming addicted to Demerol. Without thinking I laughed and told her that it wouldn't matter much in the time she had left. At first she looked stunned, but then she laughed with me. "You know, I am so tired of pretending for Bill and Nana that everything is just fine. Talking with you is refreshing because you're so firmly rooted in reality. Bill has been like a mother hen, fussing over me constantly. He's trying to drive away leukemia with fat-free food." We laughed together, and then she continued. "I hope that Bill marries Con after I die. They've become such good friends, and I've always suspected that she's half-way in love with him."

"Mom, as I see things you'll be leaving two tasks undone: Bill and Spens. I promise you that I'll watch over both for you. Bill and I long ago developed a relationship apart from you. That's going to continue after you die. Don't worry, I'll take care of him, he won't be alone. Spens will be harder, but I'll try to stick with him. As for Mike and me, we're both happily married so you don't have to worry about us."

"Thank you, Kate. I have been thinking about Bill and Spens, and I'm worried for both of them."

"I thought that you would be. They'll be okay," I promised.

An anxious look appeared on her face as she asked, "Will you explain to Nana when I die?"

"Why don't you call her now and explain yourself?" I suggested.

"No!" she almost screamed. "She'd want to come care for me and I couldn't stand that. It would be like being a child again, bossed by her continually."

"She does give a lot of orders," I agreed, "but she's going to feel betrayed after you die. So many people have been lying to her. Some secrets shouldn't be kept, Mom. They cause too much hurt."

"I keep hoping that she will die first."

"You really hate her, don't you," I said with amazed realization.

"Yes! No one should hate her mother, but I do. She made my life miserable when I was a child, and she always interfered when I was an adult. She never had any understanding of me. She was jealous of me. She resented the attention my father paid me, she resented my good looks, she deliberately was cruel to me. The only person that she ever loved unselfishly was you. She doted on you, and she still does. (Were you jealous of me, Mom?) You'll have to explain when I die."

"I'll tell her the truth, Mom." I quietly said. "I'll say that I feel she should have been told."

"No. Tell her that her doctor said it would upset her too much."

"I can't, Mom. I have no great love for Nana, but I do feel sorry for her. She trusts her doctor, and a lie like that would break the trust. She's dying, too, she needs to be able to trust him."

"You're just like your father, Kate." (No! Don't say that, please. Not again.) "Stubborn, selfish, you can't even tell a small lie because you're too self-righteous." (Mom! Please!)

"There was nothing I could say, don't you understand, Renee? She had told me so many times in the past that I was just like my father that I should have been able to shrug it off by now. But, like all the other times, I had a flash picture of how he had looked in a rage and fearfully wondered if Mom were right. She knew me better than anyone else."

Bill came bustling in with the food and saved the situation. As we ate, he talked about Con's visit the previous week. Right now she was in Los Angeles visiting her son Jimmy. She would be back soon, and I looked forward to her visit. She had made the soup we were eating, carefully freezing it and thawing it three times to remove all the fat from it.

We went to bed early, but I tossed all night in the separate basement apartment that I occupied. Running through my mind, over and over, was my feeble protest. "Mom is so much more frail than she was at Christmas. All of her tissues are disintegrating. She is starving to death. It won't be much longer now. Why did she have to say I am like Daddy? I'm not. I couldn't be. I keep my anger under control, I never hurt anyone or yell. I can't help it if I look like him. Does she hate me the same way that she hates my father and her mother?" Towards dawn I fell asleep, then staggered out of bed two hours later. We had a nine o'clock appointment at the beauty parlor. I didn't really want a hair cut, but it had been a good idea. Mom needed to get out a little, and maybe getting my hair cut would please her.

Mom had lost so much weight that she had also lost all her fat padding and had to sit on a pillow for comfort. With her pillow under one arm, I helped her into the shop and settled her. She complained continuously to the woman working on her, and I realized that her personality was also disintegrating. Never had she sounded so irritable and quarrelsome before. I would have to tip big to counteract all the guff that the woman was sweetly taking from her. I looked at Mom and decided, with horror, that she really wasn't very nice.

When we got back home, Mom took a nap. An hour later she awoke, moaning. She was having a gall bladder attack and wanted to go to the hospital. Bill and I carried her to the car, and I began to appreciate how much stress he had been living with for months. My hands were shaking, but he was cheerfully in charge, reassuring and supportive to her.

While she was being admitted, Bill sat next to me in the waiting room and said that this was all Con's fault. She hadn't removed all the fat from the soup. He sounded so rational that it scared me that he could be saying such a crazy thing. She was dying from leukemia, didn't he realize that yet?

When we could see her, she was so doped up from pain killers that she couldn't recognize us. There was no use staying around. Bill and I went home. He puttered in the garden and in his workshop. Spens called me and said that he'd be over that night. If he came to the basement apartment door, Bill wouldn't even know he was there.

About seven-thirty the phone rang. My mother had taken a turn for the worse, was in intensive care and maybe we should come quickly. I scribbled Spens a note, telling him to go home and that I would call him. Then we rushed back to the navy hospital.

Mom was in a coma now. She was hemorrhaging internally, and it was clear that she was dying. Bill and I sat out in the hall. He was cursing softly. I kept saying to myself, "Let go, Mom. Save yourself and us yet another crisis. It's time to die. Let go, give up. What you have now is not worth it."

A while later, I looked up and saw Spens and a woman approaching us. Bill growled, "What's he doing here?"

"She's his mother, too."

"Well get him out of here. I can't stand the sight of his dirty feet. If he's going to wear sandals, he should wear socks, too."

I jumped up and went to meet them, while Bill glared at Spens. Somehow, I had to keep those two separate. I hugged Spens, then took them downstairs. I explained what was going on and that he had to stay away from Bill. Kathy, Spens's girl friend, got angry. "Why have all of you always kept Spens outside the family?"

I looked at Spens and thought, "It's true. He has been outside, locked outside, all of his life."

"Upstairs there's a man whose whole life is dying. He's a bit crazy about some things, and one of them is Spens. But he's been the one who has devoted the entire last year to caring for Mom. Yes, he's excluded Spens. He almost did with me, too. He's been a tyrant, a dictator. But it's his life that is collapsing, dying, right now. If he says that he doesn't want to be around Spens, I think that we should honor it."

"What about when Spens was a kid? Bill wasn't around then," angrily demanded Kathy.

I went over the whole story for Kathy, really speaking to Spens about it for the first time, trying to explain as much as I understood of it. I gave her Mom's reasons for letting Spens go and said that they were terrible reasons. "She used to say that Spens had never been beaten by his father when we all lived together, so that he was safe with him. He wasn't, of course, and we all knew it. She used to say that she had sacrificed one child to save two, but I don't understand how she could sacrifice a child. She used to say that she couldn't have supported yet another child, which was why Spens had to go. We could have managed somehow, I think. I've thought about this for years, and I still can't make any sense out of that decision. Nothing justifies what she did. The only thing that I've come up with, and I have not one piece of evidence to support the idea, is that maybe our father held her hostage in some way. Maybe he threatened to kill some or all of us if he wasn't allowed to have Spens. He was capable of that, but I don't know if he did. What she did was horrible. I can't imagine me letting either of my children go and I don't understand how she could do it. The only thing I can tell you is what she said, I can't explain it. She was a very weak woman, something was missing in her. I don't know why."

And all the while that I was talking to them, my mind was on Bill and Mom upstairs. I had to get back to them. Throughout, Spens looked at the floor with a blank expression on his face. He didn't say anything.

All night I went up and down the stairs, worrying about Bill and Spens, silently urging Mom to die. I saw her twice, and each time she was murmuring, "No, no, no, no," in her coma. Once I held her rolled on her side while the nurse gave her a shot in her almost non-existent buttocks. I felt as if I were breaking a taboo by seeing her naked. The sheet underneath her was soaked with blood, but the color was pale pink rather than red. Her red blood cell count must have been approaching zero.

Later, Spens said that he wanted to see Mom. Kathy stayed in the cafeteria and, on the way upstairs, Spens told me that she was pregnant.

"With your child?" I asked.

"It could be. There's enough of a chance that I'm going to assume it is."

"Do you love her, Spens?"

"No, but I'm not going to desert my child."

Bill started to protest at the sight of Spens, but I firmly told him that Spens had a right to see his mother. Spens went in, and I sat holding Bill's hand. A while later I went into the room. Spens was standing and watching a doctor and two nurses working frantically over Mom. Then they stopped and I knew that she was dead. The doctor straightened up, looked at us and said that he would tell Bill. Spens and I trailed out after him. I gave Spens a long hug, told him to go home and let Kathy love him. I would call him later.

Bill stood up, looking frightened. "Colonel Edwards, your wife has died. Colonel Edwards, we did not do everything we could to save her because she would have died anyway. She was not in pain, Colonel Edwards. She died peacefully. We would like to do an autopsy and need your signature, sir. If you would sign here, Colonel Edwards, it might someday help another woman from dying like this. You can tell the funeral parlor that we'll be through by noon tomorrow. Would you like a sedative, Colonel Edwards?"

With each use of Bill's title, Bill stood a little straighter and gained a little more control. The doctor was doing it deliberately, reminding him of who he was and helping him to keep a check on his feelings. I thought about the years of discipline to which Bill was responding.

We went home. I called Mike, Con and Nana. Bill called Nettie and Chuck. Then I called Joe, who complained about being awakened. When he asked me if it couldn't have waited until the morning, I hung up on him. Bill ordered me not to cry around him because he couldn't take it, so I went down to the apartment and sobbed by myself for the rest of the night. It was Mom's birthday.

Early the next morning Bill and I made the funeral arrangements. Then we went to meet Con and Mike, who were coming in on the same plane from Los Angeles. All the way to the airport, Bill kept saying that Con had killed her, and he didn't want her to stay at the house. Finally, I blew up at him and what I said seemed to penetrate. Con was Mom's oldest friend, and he would be nice to her.

Bill greeted them with his no-crying rule, and both looked thoroughly puzzled while they agreed to it. Back home, we had lunch, then talked some about nothing. Every now and again, one of the three of us would slip downstairs to cry. Eventually all three of us were downstairs, and Bill was left alone. Spens knocked on the apartment door and came in. We passed the afternoon together, talking and crying.

After Spens left, Con and I were fixing supper when the phone rang. I answered it, and a strange man's voice asked for me.

"This is your father, Kate. Spens called me this morning and told me your mother died. How are you?" I stuttered out okay as a rush of fear went through me. He knows where I am! He lives only a short distance away, in Sacramento. He might kill me!

"I want to come to the funeral, but I felt I should ask you first." No, not that! He has no right!

"You beat her when you lived with her," I said, barely controlling my anger. "You don't deserve to be there. The idea is obscene. Of course you can't come."

He pleaded with me, and I kept saying no. Finally I hung up on him. Both Con and Bill were indignant about his call, Mike said that I should do what I thought best. I said no, he couldn't come, period.

A while later the phone rang again. I insisted on answering it, I didn't need anyone to buffer me from him. I was relieved, though, to hear a woman's voice until she introduced herself as Dad's wife May. She pleaded with me, said he had changed, but I said no, I didn't believe that, his letters told me otherwise, he could not come, I would not meet him anywhere, I refused to see him.

Later still, the phone rang again. It was my father. I said no to his every proposal, hung up and announced that I wanted to take a walk by myself.

The house was in the last row of houses surrounding Oakland. Above it were empty hills. I walked faster and faster, then started running up the hills. It was soon so steep that I was scrambling up on all fours, like a dog, as I had run up the stairs of our childhood home. I was crying wildly, "No, not him. Not now. I can't take this, too," as I ran. By the time I reached the top I had exhausted my panic. I cried quietly as I looked out over San Francisco Bay and at the sun setting beyond the hills on the other side. A long time later, I stumbled down in the dark and found Bill at the bottom sitting on a log, waiting for me. He put his arm around me and we walked home in silence.

During the funeral the next day, Spens sat out with the crowd, away from us at Bill's insistence. I went out to him, we talked and he promised to come see me the following day. Bill's fear of losing control kept us from crying during the service.

When we got home Bill, Con and Mike started drinking steadily. I stuck to lemonade, afraid to mix alcohol and grief. Soon all four of us were laughing at our favorite tales about Mom. Con and Bill eventually staggered off to bed. Mike got maudlin, then in the middle of his tears, he rushed into the bathroom. He never could drink. He fell asleep on the bathroom floor. When I could not rouse him, I covered him with a blanket and turned out the light. I cleaned up the kitchen, then sat in the dark looking out across to San Francisco. Later, I locked up and went to bed. Just before falling asleep, I remembered that Joe hadn't called me back.

The next day Con and Mike left. Spens didn't come, and I couldn't reach him by phone. Bill and I celebrated Mom's birthday belatedly by driving up the coast into Oregon. By the time I left for Atlanta, I still hadn't reached Spens.

Chapter 16

"I told you that he didn't throw me. Why don't you believe what I say?" I was so angry at Renee that I was ready to walk out on her.

"But, Kate! You also told me that he did throw you."

I turned around on the couch so that I could look out the window. Snow was falling, it was almost Christmas already. Joe would be arriving in three days. Big deal. At Thanksgiving he had brought his anger with him and, if his daily letters were any indication, he would be doing the same again. The girls, especially Carole, remained angry, their anger fueled by his. Both kids pulled away or ducked when I tried to touch them. Before, they had fought to sit on my lap and all my pants had worn out first on top of my thighs from their wiggling. As they watched television, they had always been in physical touch with me. Whatever we had done together, wherever we were, there had always been the constant physical connection between us. Now, each time that they pulled away from me, I had to fight to keep back the tears.

"Kate?"

"What?" I growled at her.

"What are you thinking about?" Her voice was low, so patient, so damn gentle. But it kept on and on at me, drawing out memories that I had hidden deep inside. She wouldn't let me get away with anything, dammit.

I had learned to trust her some during the past four months. She was totally predictable in one way: whenever I came in with a list of worries or complaints that included her or therapy, she would focus first on our relationship. That was clearly most important to her.

After I left each time, however, I no longer felt euphoric. Instead, I would shake uncontrollably for up to an hour. Sometimes that would begin while we were talking, and I had learned to realize it, then tell Renee about it. It was always a clue to buried emotions, my way of showing fear of the topic that we were skirting. Each time that I was brave enough to enter into my fear, Renee had seen at least one element in the memory that had changed my entire perception of it. That ability of hers was the only thing that kept me returning, day after day.

For instance, there was the time that I disobeyed and didn't go with Mike to call the police. When we went over that, I saw for the first time the terrible position in which I had been placed by my parents. No child, ever, should have to choose among being killed, letting her mother be killed or having her father arrested. No wonder I felt guilty and badly about myself. It was a normal response to an abnormal situation.

With each memory we dissected, I felt better and better about myself. Still, though, there was the fact that all those people, my family, the ones who should have cared most about me, had rejected me. Right now Joe and the girls were trying to. For every two steps forward that I made, I took at least one step back. Maybe I was crazy but Renee didn't have the heart to tell me. I was bad, deep down inside, she just had not acknowledged it yet.

Now she was at it again, forcing me to admit what I didn't want to. We both knew that I knew the truth about what had happened, but for some reason it was necessary for me to maintain the lie for a while. "Yah, I told you, but I was wrong. My father didn't throw me."

"Then who did, Kate?"

"I told you. Don't you ever listen? I told you already. It was someone who looked like him. My father wouldn't do that." New Haven in the winter was ugly, except when the snow was fresh. Maybe this snow would stay and cover the city's grime for more than just a few hours.

"Kate, could you please turn around and look at me? Thanks. If it was someone who looked like your father, where was your father?"

"Away."

"Did your father come back after the bad man threw you?"

"No, he never did, Renee. But he will someday, I know it. My daddy would come if he could."

It was quiet in the room for a while. I thought about what I had just said and realized that, yet again, I was about four. Apparently, that's where I needed to be.

"Then it was not your father who did those other things to you, Katie?"

"No! It wasn't him! It was that bad man who looked like him. My daddy wouldn't do that to me. He loved me." I was almost screaming in my frustration at getting her to understand.

"And it was the bad man who looked like him that did all the bad things?" Renee asked.

"Yes!" I jumped to my feet and walked swiftly around the room. Renee sat quietly in her chair, waiting for my panic to subside some. "My daddy wouldn't hurt me like that. He loved me. He must have gone away, but someday he'll come back. You'll see. Then he'll beat up the bad man and chase him away. Don't you see?" I wiped angrily at my tears with my shirt sleeve.

"I see, Kate," Renee said.

"Yah, you see all right. You see me being four and denying like crazy. Even I see that." (Where did this switch come from? Who am I now? God, what am I doing!) "Renee," I wailed, "help me!"

"I'm here, Kate, I'm here," she said as she moved toward me. Somehow she got me to the couch where I collapsed into a fetal position. As I sobbed, she knelt on the floor and held me.

When the tears had subsided some, she handed me several pieces of Kleenex. "You should make me bring in a case of these, Renee," I tried to joke.

"Shush now, it's okay."

"Renee, I'm sorry that I had to act that way. I hope you know that my anger wasn't at you." I was feeling guilty for having yelled at her. "I don't know where it came from. I walked in here planning to tell you about after my mother died, but suddenly I was about four again and a little crazy. I'm sorry."

"There's nothing to be sorry about," she said. "You're still dealing with that flashback of a couple weeks ago. It's not crazy, believe me."

"I wish I could. Why does this keep happening?"

"My guess," she answered, choosing her words very carefully, "is that you have been in shock since the day that your father first threw you. All these years, nearly thirty, you've been in a state of shock, I think. That explains a lot about you, Kate."

"Not to me, it doesn't. How could I persist in denying so completely? That's crazy!"

"No, it's not. You do know what shock is, don't you?"

"I think so, but maybe you had better tell me."

"When something very, very bad happens, our minds refuse to acknowledge it at first. It's a way of protecting ourselves until it's safe to deal with emotionally. Until we are sure that the knowledge won't destroy us, we won't let it in."

"But it took me 29 years!" I exclaimed in self-disgust.

"Which is," Renee responded, "a measure of how traumatic it was initially and how unsafe you've felt since then."

With her words, I began crying again, but this time, very softly. "What is it, Kate?"

"That poor child, Renee. I think she's still inside me, absolutely terrified. She's still waiting for her father to return."

Chapter 17

After my mother died, I returned to Atlanta and buried myself in my family and my Ph.D. program. I had fallen in love with chromosomes many years ago and now I finally had the opportunity to study them at my leisure. Although I was very much in mourning for months, there was a quiet humming inside as I peered through the microscope at my beloved chromosomes for hours at a time. Here, right before my eyes, were what produced laughs in children and tail-wagging in dogs. I longed to know absolutely everything about them.

Once a week or so, I tried to call Spens until his phone was disconnected. Mike and I talked infrequently. Bill and I wrote and called each other often. He went through a bout of heavy drinking for about two years after Mom died, and he frequently called me at midnight or later to talk about his loneliness. I lost some sleep, of course, but it seemed a small price to pay in exchange for giving him the easing effects of sorrow shared.

In May of 1972, however, he hung up in the middle of a conversation about a friend of his. The friend had lost his wife nearly two years ago but was about to remarry. "That's great, Bill!"

"No, it's disgusting. His wife just died, for Christ's sake!"

"It's been nearly two years, do you expect him to live alone forever, just mourning her?" When I said that I was glad for his friend, Bill hung up. I called him back, he hung up. I wrote him, he returned the letters unopened. I was only partially confused

117

by his behavior because Bill had, in fact, never ceased to mourn my mother.

Mike divorced Michelle, married another woman, had a child, then divorced her. Each of his children he left behind, just as he had vowed he would never do. The last time that I talked with him was in the fall of 1974. I told him about my fear of his disappearing, the way Spens had, and he assured me that he would always keep in touch. Then he disappeared.

My girls grew quickly and well. As each year passed, I silently celebrated the fact that I was doing ever so much better as a parent than my mother had. Never did we have any violence in our home.

After I received my Ph.D., I taught college for a year, then Joe, I, and the girls moved to Connecticut in 1975. Both of us went to Yale where he was on sabbatical and I was a postdoctoral student in biochemistry. Now I was going to study DNA, the essence of chromosomes.

The girls were eleven and nine at the time, and both were furious about the move. They wanted to stay in Atlanta, with their friends. What they didn't realize was that the move was a last desperate attempt by Joe and me to save our marriage.

The year went badly. In Atlanta I had had many friends who had acted as a buffer, provided me with the emotional support that Joe didn't give. In Connecticut, deprived of the web of friendships dating back nine years, I had to depend solely on Joe, and I gradually came to realize that he could not give me what I needed. We tried marriage counseling, which served to clarify the difficulties between us but did little to alleviate them. At the end of the summer he went back to our house in Atlanta, and the girls and I stayed in Connecticut. We had not decided on divorce, or even separation. We tried to continue working on our difficulties by phone and by mail.

The girls were outraged at having to stay in Connecticut another year and demanded to be allowed to return to Atlanta with Joe. I took the brunt of their anger, since they were with me, and began to fear that they would leave me, too. The battle went on between us, day after day after day. It seemed that the whole world was deserting me: Spens had been gone since Mom died in 1969, Bill closed me out in 1972, Mike disappeared in 1974, Joe left in 1976. I had no friends near me. I had no family. I felt desperately alone, out of contact with everyone. I felt as if I had been plunked down onto the earth, with no connections to anyone. Everything I touch falls apart on me. Obviously there is something wrong with me if all those closest to me eventually leave. It began with my father, and it is still going on. Maybe I am crazy after all, and I am driving everyone away from me just as my father did. I stopped eating, had terrible dreams of Germans trying to kill me.

. . .

"That's it, Renee. I've brought you from childhood to the present. I called you for an appointment the first time when I got that letter from my father. I still haven't answered it, and he's written several more times, complaining that I haven't. What am I going to do about him?"

"Why don't you tell him that you're in therapy and need not to hear from him for a while? Say that you'll write him when you can. Can you do that?"

"Yes, no problem. . . . Look, where do we go from here? I've told you just about everything that I know about my extended family. What more is there for us to do? I feel kind of lost without a historical structure to guide me."

Renee laughed as she said, "There's plenty for us to talk about, don't worry. Where do you want to start?"

Silence. She was going to leave it up to me, but I didn't know where to begin. After all, I'd never been in therapy before, how was I supposed to know what to do? Very tentatively, I said, "Joe?"

"Okay, Joe. What about him?"

"I don't know. But he is the most pressing problem and I have got to come to a decision about him. When he was here at Christmas it was terrible. Since going back to Atlanta he has been angrily spewing out letters. Here I am in New Haven, faced with a major career decision, with two angry girls and what has become an almost total dependence on you. What in the hell am I going to do?"

"What are your options?" she asked.

"Divorce, move back to Atlanta and try to work things out, stay here and float as I've been doing."

"Could you get a job in Atlanta?"

"Not in my field, and my future is too shaky to abandon it for the sake of trying with Joe. If it didn't work out, I'd be in a terrible mess. I've been thinking, though, about trying to get another postdoc at Oak Ridge. That's in weekend distance of Atlanta. We need to be closer if we are to have any chance. If I could get it, then somehow I would learn to do without you."

Chapter 18

I applied for the position and didn't get it. The letter arrived on the same February day that Joe did. I didn't know how to tell him. We were tense, awkward, nervous with each other. I had never felt loved by him and didn't now. He had badly run roughshod over my feelings, desires and needs for so long that I didn't believe him when he said he would change. The only changes he had made recently were for the worse. Still, maybe he could. Maybe, together, we could find a better way to live with each other. If it meant giving up on my research to return to Atlanta, maybe I could do even that.

We went out for dinner to a small Mexican restaurant in New Haven that had always been my favorite. We had a drink, then supper. Finally, over coffee, I broke the news to Joe about Oak Ridge. I hated telling him because we both knew that it was about our only chance unless I returned to Atlanta without a job. I expected sorrow and sadness from him; I didn't expect his huge burst of anger. It came ripping out of him in fury. He began to catalog all my failings once again, and I felt overwhelmed by so much of the past. And then, beyond his words, I heard John Denver singing "My Sweet Lady" in the background music. John was singing so sweetly, so tenderly, with so much care and concern for the woman he loved; Joe was pouring out venom. I listened to each, alternatingly; one was fantasy, the other was reality. I needed Joe to speak, just occasionally, like John; but he never had and he never would. And then I said the words that wound so deeply that they can never be retracted: "I want a divorce."

Joe leaned back and smiled a little, as if he had finally gotten what he had been wanting all along. When he spoke it was without either anger or sorrow. "Okay, it's yours. You can have the kids, I'll take the house." This was no time to be bargaining over the girls. What was going on?

"Joe, none of that now. There'll be plenty of time for discussing that later. If you want a divorce too, we should tell the girls soon, preferably while you're still here. They need to hear from you that you will still be part of their lives."

"Okay, but I want to be the one to tell them."

He did the next day. Becky sat and cried; Carole screamed around the house, kicking furniture and slamming doors. Both demanded to be allowed to return to Atlanta and howled at my firm no. Never, never had I felt worse about what I was doing than I did at that moment. I saw our lives as a complex and beautiful web that I was ripping apart strand by strand. I was the destroyer, causing hurt to everyone closest to me. I could still hear my mother's words far too clearly.

Joe left the next day, and I set about trying to order my life. I needed a job for the next year, preferably in New Haven so that we wouldn't have to undergo further dislocation. We had to get out of the house that I was renting because I could not afford it. I needed a lawyer. Most of all, I needed to find some way to reach the girls. They were miserable and blaming me for everything wrong in their lives.

I applied for, and received, a research faculty position at Yale. After weeks of hunting I found a house that we could rent beginning in September. The girls were to spend the summer with Joe, so I rented a room in an eighteen-person co-operative for the summer to keep down expenses. I found a lawyer in Atlanta who would represent me. But I didn't find a way to reach the girls.

Now the time with Renee focused on my feelings of guilt for what I was doing to the four of us. Again I stopped sleeping or, when I did, awoke panicked from nightmares that I couldn't remember. I was bad again, dangerous to everyone again, afraid to cry again lest I not be able to stop. Whatever progress I had made was destroyed by my decision. And yet, it was the right decision; I never doubted it once from the moment that I reached it. Ultimately, despite the pain we were all suffering now, divorce was better for us than yet another attempt to fix something beyond repair. The marriage was over, dead.

Once I had reached a new balance point, therapy turned back to my family again. All the self-destructive feelings I had in response to divorce had their origins in what had gone before. Somehow, I had to exorcise the ghosts that had been haunting me for so long. It became a time of new-seeing for me.

Part II: A Time of New-Seeing

Chapter 19

"Renee, I think that I might have learned something yesterday, something very important."

"What, Kate?" she asked.

"Well, I went with two friends of mine to hear a talk on battered women and how they are handled in the medical system. It's really bad, by the way, but I don't want to talk about that. I went for two reasons. First, there was a free lunch. Second, I've always wondered if Mom was battered, and I was curious about what the speaker would say. Whether she was battered or not, you know?"

Renee nodded her head in response, and I continued. "So I was sitting there, listening, and by the speaker's definition Mom was a battered woman. My back started hurting then. It got progressively worse over the next few minutes. It was so bad that I considered leaving, but I couldn't without disrupting the speaker. I stood up in the back of the room, kept shifting my posture, trying to find a position that would relieve the pain. It got worse and worse, to the point that I couldn't focus on what the speaker was saying.

"Just when I thought that I couldn't stand it any longer, an idea occurred to me, and the pain totally disappeared. I thought, 'I was beaten in the same way that Mom was.' Does that make me a battered child, Renee?"

She smiled gently as she said, "Yes, Kate."

"I thought so," I said, feeling relief. "It had never occurred to me before that I had been battered. I've known all about child abuse for years, but I never connected it with me before. It sounds kind of dumb, I guess, but I just never realized."

It was quiet for a while in the room while I thought about the implications of that label. Then Renee asked, "What do you think was blocking you, Kate?"

"Pain, I, I guess. If I was an abused child, then my parents abused me. But they are the ones who are supposed to have loved me. Either something was wrong with them, both of them, which is a horrible thought, or something was wrong with me. You know that I've always feared that something was wrong with me. Either choice is kind of hard to take.

"I feel really dumb that I didn't see it before, that I, I was abused. For m-m-months we've been talking about my childhood, how I was hit and thrown against the wall and stuff, and I never once attached the label 'abused' to me. At the same time, I'm very glad that I finally know."

Renee smiled as she said, "You sound relieved."

"Yes, I am," I agreed eagerly. "It gives me a way to understand what happened. I had all these memories that I was trying not to believe. You must remember how I felt so distant from myself that I sometimes talked about me in the third person." Renee nodded yes and smiled again. "If I believed my memories, if they were real, then something was very off in my family and it had to be either them or me. If my memories weren't real, th-th-then the fact that I had them meant I was crazy, just like my father. I'd rather have it be something was wrong with me, I was bad or something, than th-that I was crazy. You know, I was bad so my totally normal parents had to punish me."

"Maybe something was wrong with your parents, Kate," suggested Renee.

"All the literature on child abuse, and a book that I got from the library last night, s-s-say it was my parents, not me."

"Do you believe what you read?" asked Renee.

"Sort of," I said slowly. "Part of me would like to be able to. At the same time, I know that I had a role in what happened. If my parents had had a different child, somebody not like me, that child wouldn't have been abused."

Looking puzzled, Renee asked, "How do you know that?"

"Nothing happens in a vacuum," I said, beginning to feel angry. "I was interacting with them, which was why I was abused. Somebody else interacting with them wouldn't have been abused. So it has to be something in me that led to the abuse. The problem is, I don't know what was wrong with me that made them so angry with me. I'm really afraid of finding that out, Renee, but I keep trying to figure out what it is. If I could figure it out, then I could change whatever it is in me."

"What could it possibly have been, Kate?" Renee asked.

"I don't know," I replied. "Didn't you hear me just say it? Maybe I was crazy. Maybe I didn't obey as much as I thought I did. I was always doing things w-w-wrong or making a m-m-mess like spilling my milk. And I didn't eat like I should have. Maybe there's just something really b-b-bad about me, deep down, you know?"

"I haven't seen anything bad in you, Katie, and you're not crazy." Renee said that gently, and I longed to be able to believe her.

"Yah, but you don't know me," I answered angrily.

"What do you mean, I don't know you?"

"You just don't," I insisted. "If you did, you wouldn't talk to me anymore."

"How many hours have we talked together, Kate?"

"It's probably close to 200 now," I answered, puzzled by where she was going.

With her next words, I knew exactly where she was headed. "Do you think that I don't know you after nearly 200 hours of talking with you? Do you really think that?"

"You know parts of me, yes. But not all parts of me," I insisted.

"I don't know the bad parts, is that what you are saying?"

"Yep."

"Okay, so tell me about the bad parts. Prove to me that you have them," she said with a slight smile.

"I can't, Renee! The problem is that I don't know what those bad parts are. If I did, I could c-c-change them, maybe. All I know is that my parents were reacting to them. If the parts hadn't been there, my dad wouldn't have beaten me and Mom wouldn't have let it happen." I was feeling terribly frustrated by our conversation. Why wouldn't she believe me?

"Okay, Kate, what would it mean to you if you have no bad parts and you're not crazy?"

"Simple logic: it would mean that there was something wrong with both of my parents," I answered, feeling very scared.

"How do you feel about that?"

"I can't accept it. I just can't."

"Because then it would mean that they didn't love you the way they should have?" persisted Renee.

"Yah. . . . Look, I'm getting bored with this. We're going in circles. Can we change the topic?"

"No. Why didn't they love you as they should have?" she persisted.

"Because there was something bad in me, dammit! Are you satisfied now?"

"Kate, Katie. Don't you think that it's time to let yourself off the hook? We've been going in circles because you're caught in circular reasoning. Even when you temporarily assume that there's nothing bad in you, you conclude that there's something bad in you. . . . Come here, let me hold you. . . . Good. You are not crazy, Katie. There's no hidden badness in you deep down inside. You've shown me pictures of yourself as a child, and that child that you were was beautiful. You've told me what you did and how you felt as a child. That child that you were was a delightful person. You tried so very hard to do what was asked of you. You were bright, eager, curious, imaginative - all the things that I adore in my Dawn. There is nothing bad in you, Katie."

When I could talk I asked, "Then why did my parents treat me that way? Why did Mike and Spens disappear from my life? Why does Bill have nothing to do with me? Why are Joe and the girls rejecting me? In each case, it can't always be them, not me. It just can't be! If I thought that, I'd be thinking in a paranoid fashion, just like my father."

"You are ignoring so much that you know, Kate," said Renee as she gave me an extra hug. "Shall we go through the list again? You don't know why Bill hung up on you. Mike and Spens weren't angry at you the last time that you spoke to them. You are rejecting Joe, he's not rejecting you. Your girls are having a normal reaction to divorce. You father wants to hear from you."

"Renee, you just do not know me! I'm bad, you're just too dumb to see it."

"Anyone who would like you either doesn't know you or is too dumb to recognize what they see in you?"

"Yes," I said firmly, drawing away from her.

"That reminds me of an old joke: 'I wouldn't join that club; they accepted me for a member.'"

"Laugh at me if you want, I don't care," I said, turning my back to her.

"Okay, Katie," Renee said as she forced me to face her again. "Can you accept this, then? You are bad inside, but it doesn't bother me at all. I like you anyway, and so do most people who meet you."

"Do you know what's bad about me?" I asked fearfully.

"Yes. You refuse to believe that anyone could like or love you. That's very bad. You turn people away because of your refusal to believe it. If you could change that, you would be getting rid of the badness inside you. Do you think that you could change that about yourself?"

"I, I don't know," I said slowly, thinking about what she had said. "Do you r-r-really think that that's why my parents treated me as they did?"

"No, I don't," Renee answered firmly.

"Then why did they?"

"I think that they did not learn how to love in a healthy way."

"You mean that they loved me but just didn't know how to go about being parents?"

"Yes. They loved you, but they didn't know how to give you the nurturing you needed," she answered.

"Was there something wrong in me for needing all that nurturing?" I asked, feeling a rush of anxiety.

"No, Katie. You needed exactly what every child needs, what you've given to your girls, but your parents didn't know how to give it to you. Can you accept that?"

"I'll try, Renee. I'll try because it's the way I want it to be, given what happened. . . . Do you know how stupid I feel about what I've been saying? I see the illogical statements, but I had to make them if I were going to tell you how I feel, which is about five."

She smiled as she said, "I know that. It's okay. You were doing exactly what I wanted you to do. You were talking from your child, and I needed to hear how your child feels. That part of you isn't logical in anyone. I needed to speak directly to your child, and you let me. Thank you very much for letting me in, Kate."

Chapter 20

"There's nothing that I want to talk about today, Renee."

"Fine. Do you want to take a nap? I could get caught up on my paper work," she responded.

"Jesus! You can be such a shit at times."

Smugly she said, "Yep." We both started laughing then.

"Okay, I can be, too. Will you answer a question?" When Renee nodded yes, I continued. "Last week you said that I was speaking from my child. Could you explain what you meant?"

"Sure. I was using Transactional Analysis language. Each person, no matter what their age, has three parts to them: a child, a parent and an adult. The child is the feeling part. Hopefully, the child is spontaneous and playful. The parent is also a feeling part, but in a different way. The parent is close to the Freudian super-ego. It has a lot of shoulds in it: you should brush your teeth, you should do your work, that kind of stuff. The parent also nurtures the child. The adult is the rational part. It makes reality-based decisions, processes information, is all business."

"Thanks. Then when we were talking last week about my hidden badness, was it my child or my parent speaking?"

"Basically it was your child," she said. "But your child is heavily contaminated by a very punitive parent."

"You've lost me, I don't understand at all."

"When you were a child, Kate, you were given many bad messages about yourself from your real parents, so you split your own parent part in response. One part of it became rather punitive, the other part remained nurturing. The part that is punitive won't let your child feel good about herself."

Feeling scared by the way she was describing me, I said, "You're talking as if I have multiple personalities."

"We all do," reassured Renee. "When you're in the lab you certainly behave differently than when you're playing softball, don't you?" When I nodded yes, Renee continued. "Sometimes we're all child, sometimes we're all parent, sometimes we're all adult. Mostly, we're a mixture. You seldom are all child because, every time you begin to be a child, to be playful or happy or loving or sad, your parent gets scared for you. That's because, when you were actually a child, you weren't allowed simply to be a child; it was too dangerous. You had to watch, always, for the next blow. So now your parent gets scared when you act from your child and then, in a confused sort of way, your parent protects you by being punitive."

After I had digested that, I asked, "Sort of like the way my parents treated me when I was a kid?"

"Yes. You learned how to treat your child from your parents, after all. If we can get your parent to feel less scared and your child to feel better about herself, therapy will be over."

A bit confused still, I asked, "Do you mean that now, when I want to feel happy, my parent still thinks it's dangerous? And because it's dangerous, my parent makes me feel badly about myself so that I won't be happy and, therefore, won't be in danger?"

"That's how it is," said Renee. "It's being a protective parent, ultimately, but it's also being a parent who isn't very good at nurturing your child."

"But if that's real, then my real parents were trying to protect me when they were being so mean?"

"You could look at it that way," answered Renee.

"Renee, if I'm not a child very much, what am I?"

"Mostly you're an adult. You're so very serious, you know. Always very logical, always all business, always very controlled."

When she said that, I felt as if I had been hit in the stomach. "Oh, god, I remember when it started! I remember exactly when I decided that I was going to be totally rational! It's horrible, Renee."

"When, Kate?" Renee asked quickly.

"Mom was talking to Con, after my dad had been committed. She was telling her that Daddy had paranoid schizophrenia. She said it was too early to know if Spens or I had it. I got really scared. Mom had said so many times that I was just like him. That meant that I was going to become crazy like him. I decided then that I would be totally logical all my life so that I wouldn't become like him. Even if I were crazy, if I could behave logically, then I wouldn't be acting like him. If I weren't totally logical, I would hurt those who were closest to me, just like he had done. I had to be logical to protect them from me."

I was crying then, quietly, softly. Renee said nothing. She looked at me, watched me, waited for me to speak again. When I didn't, after a while she said, "Katie. You made that decision so very early to protect everyone whom you loved or would ever love. Is that the choice someone would make who is intrinsically bad?"

When I shook my head no, she continued. "You've limited yourself all your life out of love. If you could love yourself the way you've loved everyone else, then you could begin to protect and nurture your child in a better way. You were the one who chose to be all adult out of love. You could now choose to allow your child to exist out of love. It's the child in you that other people love. Can you give more of that gift to other people? More of your child?"

I nodded yes slowly, still crying quietly. "If you don't want to be like your parents, Katie, then you are going to have to start taking care of the child inside yourself in the same loving way that you have nurtured everyone else. You're going to have to tell that child that you love her, that she's beautiful, that her very existence delights you. You're going to have to be very gentle with her because she's been severely traumatized. When she gets scared, you're going to have to protect her in a new way, a nurturing way. You're going to have to be patient with her fears, to reassure her constantly. You already know how to treat her because you have been a nurturing parent to Carole and Becky. Can you assume that same loving responsibility for your child inside, even if she doesn't respond for a very long time?"

It was time to go. There was nothing else to say. Slowly we each unwound from our chairs, stood up. I could feel the lack of an ending to the session acutely. Renee stood waiting silently, unmoving, watching me intently. I wanted to hug her, I could feel the need pounding at me, barricading me in the room. Fear swept over me, anxiety poured in on me. I wanted to hold and be held. That was the only proper end to our conversation, but I was afraid to try it. I walked slowly toward the door, my head down in shame at my defeat.

As I stretched out my hand toward the knob, Renee spoke quietly. "Kate, what does your child want?"

"To hold you," I mumbled.

"Are you going to make sure that she gets what she needs, or are you going to be an abusing parent?"

I turned slowly toward Renee. "It's not that simple," I pleaded.

"It is," she said firmly. "You've read the emotional content of our conversation correctly. You're wanting to respond normally, but you're afraid to ask for a hug because you might get rejected. Either you will do your best to ensure that your child gets what she needs or you will abandon her in her need. What you do will tell her if you are going to be a protecting or an abusing parent."

For the first time I looked up at Renee. She was looking at me intently, eyes pleading with me to make the right choice. I wanted to tear out of the room and down the stairs. I wanted to run to the arms that I knew would welcome me. Immobilized by my internal struggle, I began to hate Renee for not making the decision for me. All she had to do was to walk across the room and hold me, but she refused to do that simple act for me. "You don't really care! Whatever happens, whether I hug you or not, you'll still get your money for this hour. Therapy is the female equivalent of going to a prostitute. I pay you, and you talk to me and hug me if I want it. I'd rather play it honestly and pick up some guy on a street!"

What I'd said filled me with a sense of horror. I didn't mean any of it. Oh, god, how could Renee stand working with me! I was a vicious shit. No wonder all my family had rejected me.

"Kate, your parent just talked to me. Could your child talk to me now?"

I nodded my head slowly, ashamed to look at her. "I'm so scared, Renee, so all alone. I don't really feel that way about you. My parent was trying to reject you before you rejected me. She does her best, but she doesn't know yet how to protect right. Please forgive me, I'm so sorry if I hurt you, my parent is just so scared that I'll get hurt again.

I'm terrified that you will be mad and not want to see me any more. Please don't do that, Renee. I need you right now."

"Let me talk to your parent now, okay?" I nodded yes slowly, fearfully. "Do you understand what your child just said?"

"Yes. I understand. She's a lot more healthy than I am. Maybe I can learn from her, follow her lead."

"You can, Kate. Your child has all the right instincts. Together, all parts of you together, will do just fine. Where was your adult in all of this?"

"Paralyzed by the conflict."

"It's time to bring her in now to make the decision between the needing child and the scared, protecting adult. Your adult knows which way is best for all of you."

As I switched into the adult mode, the decision was obvious and easy. "Renee, please, I would like to hold you and be held by you. I need it badly. Is it okay with you?" She nodded yes and, as I moved across the room toward her, what had gone on seemed to be so terribly silly. Loving was so easy once the fear was gone. As she held me, she asked me softly if I could remember how the holding felt. I answered that I would try.

Chapter 21

One day I learned with Renee that a person could fight with someone without destroying their relationship. She said something, I don't remember what, and I started arguing with her. I continued for most of the hour before I apologized and said that she must be angry with me.

"No, I'm not, Kate."

"You must be. I've been ridiculous for the entire hour. It's been a waste of time."

She smiled as she said, "I'm not angry, Kate."

"You have to be," I insisted. "If someone had behaved with me the way I've been with you, I would be terribly angry."

"I'm not."

"Well, that's because you don't care what happens in here. You get paid no matter what. But it still was a waste of time."

Renee sighed when I said that. "Yes, it was a waste of time, but I'm not angry."

"I don't believe you," I continued to insist. "You're just saying that to shut me up. You've got to be angry with me."

"Okay, Kate," Renee said, "I am angry with you."

"About what?"

"Everything that has happened here today," she answered grimly.

"How much can I believe you?"

"Completely. I'm mad about everything." When Renee said that, finally, after all my begging her to say it, I went a little crazy. There seemed to be a tremendous amount of movement and noise in the room. It confused me. All I could see was a bright glaring nothing in front of me. I sat immobilized by fear. She said something to me, but I couldn't hear her through the fog and confusion. It was as if Renee were very far away.

She quickly ran over to me and pulled me out of my chair. She yelled my name several times, then hugged me very hard. I could see her looking at me, concern and almost fear written on her face, but she seemed so very far away that there was no point in answering her. Then she pushed me across the room and into her chair. Next she sat down in my chair.

"Listen to me, Kate. Raise your head and look at me. Come on, look at me. Good. Now listen carefully. You are me, sitting in my chair. I am you. Do you understand? Nod your head if you do. Good. Now, watch me be you."

Then Renee-me looked very sad. Her head was down, looking at the floor in an unseeing way. She told me how angry I must be at her for being ridiculous and wasting the hour in bickering with me continuously. As I sat and watched her, gradually I became Renee and could feel a rising affection for poor Kate across the room. She had no idea that I loved her very much. No one could get angry with her for being so scared by what I had said that she used the only tools available to her to keep from hearing me. The buzzer rang several times, indicating that the next client was here and the hour over, but I couldn't leave Kate feeling the way she did. I'd have to find some way to reach her quickly.

And then I snapped out of it. Renee was Renee, and I was me. She wasn't mad at me for being who I was. I jumped up with a big smile on my face. I was laughing as I interrupted her act, pulled her up and gave her a quick hug. Then telling her that I would explain during my next appointment, I ran out of the room and down the stairs feeling exultant.

I tried figuring out what had happened during the next several days but couldn't. When I saw Renee again, I told her about the confusion, noise, sense of motion and white fog. She asked me if I had ever experienced anything like it before.

"It seemed very familiar, like a nightmare I have had many times. It also seems like I'll have it again."

"Do you know why?" pursued Renee.

"No, but it's a part of me. I know that."

She thought a minute, then asked, "When you were a child and your father was coming at you, do you remember how you felt?"

"Nice, Renee," I said with real admiration. "That's how I felt. Your being angry with me was as terrifying as his being angry with me. A fight with you could destroy me because I'm so dependent on you right now."

"Don't forget that you survived, Kate. What was that laughter about?"

"You weren't like him. You wouldn't hit me or leave me just because you were irritated with me. You could both be angry and love me at the same time. You weren't really that angry with me, anyway. You understood that I was being stupid only because I was scared."

She smiled as she said, "That's right, Kate. It's safe to be angry. You can be angry and love at the same time. You wouldn't leave someone you love because you were angry at them, and no one will leave you just because they are angry at you."

"That's not true, Renee," I said, shaking my head. "My father did. Bill did. Mike and Spens did. When my mother used to get very angry with us after our dad left, she would walk out of the house and be gone for hours. She used to threaten leaving us for good if we didn't behave better."

"Your father was off the wall, remember? Besides, he didn't really leave because he was angry," Renee patiently explained again. "Remember his last letter to you? He's still trying to reach you. As for Bill, what he did was totally irrational. You don't know why he hung up on you. Mike and Spens weren't angry the last time you talked with them. You don't know why they disappeared, remember?

"I don't know what to say about your mother. Maybe she would leave so that she wouldn't hurt you. Maybe she was trying very hard to be a good mother, and that was the best that she could do at the moment. She never left permanently, did she?"

"No," I answered. "But when she used to walk out the door it felt like she was leaving permanently. I remember crying, begging her not to go, promising to be better."

"What did you do that would result in her leaving?"

I didn't want to answer Renee, but I had long since learned that she would not let me duck a question. "I don't remember every time, just twice. Once it was that Mike and I had been fighting a lot. I guess she got tired of listening to it. The other time was worse.

"She used to spank us with a paddle that came from a game I had. Do you remember those paddles that had a red ball attached to it with a rubber string?" When Renee nodded yes, I continued. "It was one of those, minus the ball and string. Anyway, that paddle hurt. Mike wasn't getting spanked any more, but I was. He said that he had broken her of the habit by laughing each time she hit him. 'The more it hurts, the more you have to laugh,' he said. 'She'll hit you harder and more times than she would otherwise,' he said, 'but then she'll scare herself and she won't ever hit you again. Just laugh as hard as you can and don't let one tear out.'

"One night when she came home from work, I had not started supper as I was supposed to. I had been playing softball at the park and didn't want to stop. So she started spanking me, and I laughed. She kept hitting me harder and harder, and I held on to what Mike had told me and laughed and laughed and laughed and . . . god, it's sick, now in retrospect. My stomach is heaving just from thinking about it after so many years." I sighed deeply, then continued. "Finally, she threw the paddle at the couch, shoved me off her knee and walked out the door. I lay on the floor for a while, then got up and started supper. When she got home, it was ready."

Renee was quiet for a while as she held me and stroked my forehead. When she started talking, her question was asked very softly. "How old were you, Katie?"

"About nine, I think. It's hard to remember exactly."

"I think that she walked out because she didn't see any way to stop what she knew was bad for you except to leave. What do you think?"

"It's possible, I guess."

"In a strange way," said Renee, "I think that she was trying to protect you. Your mother loved you, Kate, I'm sure of it. But like I said last week, she had not learned to love in a healthy way."

"Renee, would you hit a kid with a paddle for not getting supper started?" I asked.

"No."

"Neither would I. I wouldn't even ask a child that age to be responsible for cooking dinner," I said sadly.

"Well . . ." Renee was quiet for a while. Her hand moved gently over my forehead, and I greedily absorbed her comfort. "Look, we started almost an hour ago talking about what you discovered last week. I don't want that to get lost. It's safe to be angry, Kate. You and I can fight, and the fighting will allow each of us to learn more about the other. Fighting of the type that we did last week doesn't kill love. It doesn't drive people away. In the long run, it helps two people to become closer. I know it scares you now, but you'll eventually get used to it. You need to be able to fight, to let the anger out in small doses so that it doesn't build and build to an explosion. When explosions occur, real damage can be done. Trust me on this, will you?"

Chapter 22

Gradually a rhythm to my life began to develop. I went to work, where I worked very hard in the laboratory, then I went home and tried to reach the girls. Twice a week I saw Renee. Therapy bounced back and forth, between past and present. More and more Joe became a non-topic as I repaired the hurt and began to move into my new life as a single person.

Suddenly it was June, time to move and to take the girls back to Atlanta for the summer. The time had crept up on me unawares, because during the last month I had met a man whom I liked very much. He was Coe, soft-spoken, gentle and loving Coe. He was the first man I had dated since my first year in college, and he was extraordinarily patient with me. I had met him while I was house-hunting and had responded to him with an intensity that frightened me.

Coe helped me put most of our possessions in storage, move what I needed for the summer into the co-operative where I was to live, and pack the car. When I got back from Atlanta we were going camping on the Cape. I would badly miss his support while I was gone.

The drive to Atlanta was an agony. The VW was jammed with three people and two dogs, and it was hot and humid. The girls would not speak to me unless it became absolutely necessary, and when they did it was with a snarl. The only laughter during the entire trip was at toll booths, when the frenzied barking of the dogs and their wild leaping about caused the tiny car to sway back and forth. For the rest of the time it was silent. I felt completely closed out by the girls and was convinced that they would leave me as soon as it was legally possible. I looked at them and saw all the years of loving care wasted. Somehow Joe's and my failure had become totally my fault. Didn't they remember anything? I was not as bad as they thought, I just wasn't.

When I drove up to the house, Joe was waiting for us on the porch. The girls and dogs piled out of the car while Joe came up and asked me to have a beer with him at the picnic table in the back yard. Once there, I sat and looked at what used to be our house, the gardens in which I had worked so hard, the lovely old trees that rose gracefully to the sky. Over there were the hydrangeas that kept their big purple-blue balls of flowers for over a month. The dogwoods had grown at least a foot since I had planted them. The fig trees needed care badly; honey suckle was beginning to choke them. The yard needed work, and I longed to get down on my knees and begin weeding. But this wasn't my house anymore.

Joe looked at me solemnly and asked me to reconsider. We had had a good life together and it could be that way again. I knew that it couldn't be, and I sadly shook my head and said no. He had tears in his eyes, the first time that I had ever seen them, as he said, "Kate, I gave you the best years of my life."

I answered, "Hey, that's supposed to be my line!" and instead of a laugh, his anger burst forth once again. He never did have much of a sense of humor. I quickly left, driving to a friend's house where I was going to stay.

During the week that I was in Atlanta, the girls refused to see me, go out with me, or talk with me. At first I saw a few friends, but it was so painful trying to talk with them that I soon stopped. I felt that everyone must think me to be a horrible person since Joe and the girls were furious at me. My shame and sense of guilt were so huge that they became a barrier between me and the entire world. When I left I tried to kiss the girls good-bye, but they ran from me.

I drove the thousand miles to Connecticut stopping only for gas. I needed Renee and Coe so badly that I could feel their absence as a physical ache. By the time I arrived, gray and shaking from fatigue, the pain over the girls had turned to a bitterness. I hated the thoughts that I had as I watched young couples tending their children: "Just you wait, someday all the love you lavish on them will be returned with rejection," or "Enjoy them now, while they are still nice." I remembered the walk with Becky on the beach at the Cape when she said to me: "Mom, do you know how Carole gets embarrassed by things that you do? Well, I'm getting to the age when you're going to start embarrassing me, too. It's okay for you to say 'hi' to seagulls or kiss me, but please don't do it in front of my friends." What had happened to all the trust and openness between us? How could it have disappeared so rapidly?

Coe and I had as good a camping trip as anyone can have when one of the people keeps bursting into tears without warning. His sympathy and understanding seemed to encourage the flow of tears instead of making me feel happier. I was sure, now, that I was close to a nervous breakdown, but Renee told me that I was mourning properly for the first time in my life instead of repressing my sadness and slipping into depression. My reaction was appropriate but, oh, how it hurt.

By mid-July, however, my life seemed to be a lot better. I was enjoying my new work, and enjoying the novel experience of living with seventeen other people. Coe and I were spending every evening together and, one magical night, the girls actually talked to me when I called them.

With Renee I had gone back to my family again, and hour after hour I spoke of my longing for a sense of belonging to someone, to be part of a group again. When she suggested that I contact some of my mother's family, however, I refused. None of them had cared enough to intervene or to try to stop the violence in our house. I wasn't about to go back to them. They had abandoned me when I was a child. I had had no interaction with any of them since I was twelve, and I wanted to keep it that way. The only ones I cared about were my brothers, and they were gone. "Well, then, why not try to find your brothers?" she asked.

It had been two or three years since last I called the San Francisco operator to see if Spens had moved back to town. What was the point? He had been missing for eight years, so how could I expect to find him now, with 2,500 miles separating us? He probably wasn't in San Francisco, but it cost nothing to call. Try. I can't. She pushed,

I resisted. Who needs him anyway? Who needs anyone? I had been alone all my life, I could continue that way very happily. Who's happy? All right! I'll do it tonight, now let's talk about something else for a change.

I called the operator, and she gave me Spens's phone number. Now I had to face my anger at Spens for disappearing so long ago, and my fear that he, too, would reject me again. I had a choice: I could be honest with myself and acknowledge that I needed him, or I could continue to be alone. It took me three days to find the strength to place the call.

As the phone began to ring, my anxiety was so high that I was not sure that I could talk if he answered. I stuttered out his name, almost crying in fear.

"Yes?"

"This is Kate. The operator gave me your number."

"Oh. Hello."

"How have you been?"

"Okay, but I'm sure that you didn't call just to ask how I am. What do you want?"

"I've missed you so much, Spens. I tried to find you for years after Mom died."

"I took off." (Spens, talk to me!)

"Yes, I gathered as much. Where did you go?"

"Up in the Sierras, down to L.A., lots of places."

"Spens, Joe and I are getting a divorce. The girls are staying with him for the summer. I'm miserable."

"I've been through that, too. Kathy and I split when John was two." (Did he really name his son after our father?)

"I'm sorry to hear that, Spens. I had hoped that things went better for you. How is John?"

"Okay, I guess. We put him out for adoption. Neither one of us could give him what he needed."

"I'm sorry, Spens, so sorry. Do you ever see him?"

"No, that was part of the agreement. He's better off having no contact with me. . . . I've missed you too, Kate. You're the only family that I have." (Oh, Spens, finally!)

"I have no one else besides you, Spens. I was heart-broken when you disappeared. . . . So, you don't see Dad?"

"No, the last time I did was in 1974. He told me that I was no longer his child. I took him at his word."

"Beat you on that! He told me the same thing in 1956. Congrats on joining a select group." Spens laughed, finally, and we continued talking. Before hanging up we exchanged addresses and promised to write. Both of us kept our promises, and near the end of the summer Spens's letter said he would come for a visit in September.

Meanwhile, my success with Spens gave me the courage to acknowledge that I would like to rejoin Mom's family. Nana was dead but her sister Nettie and I had always remained in contact and her letters for years had kept me current on all the people. I knew who had married, who had divorced, the names of new children, all the details of their lives. I just didn't know them, the people. One day late that summer Renee asked me whom I liked best, besides Nettie, in my mother's family. Chuck, there was no question about it. Okay, where did he live? In New Jersey, just a couple of hours away. Good, how about visiting him? No! Again she pushed and I resisted. And again, I finally yielded.

Chuck was delighted that I called, delighted that I wanted to come see him. He had an apartment with plenty of room for me to spend the night and would eagerly await my arrival on Saturday. Going to see him was almost easy.

When Chuck came out to greet me, I saw the uncle who had been so nice to me so many years ago. He was older, of course, and quite sick now, but his smile was unchanged and his hug felt even better than it used to. We went out for dinner and caught up on over twenty years of living.

Back at his apartment later, we continued talking over a drink. He played the organ for me, the song "K-K-K-Katie." He said that he had gotten the music after I called him, and I thanked him through my tears.

Later he started talking about my mother, how much he had loved her and how he missed her now. I didn't respond very well to that. For months I had been furious at her for what I had lived through as a child. I said something about her not being able to be strong enough to protect her children, and Chuck looked puzzled.

"Wait a second. Do you mean that you don't know?"

"Know what, Kate?"

"That my dad beat all of us and Mom never did anything to end it?"

"What are you talking about?"

"You don't know! My god, I've made a terrible mistake for years! I thought that you knew and just didn't care enough to help. That's why I've stayed away. I was sure that you knew and didn't care. All the years I've spent, rejecting everyone because they didn't help; maybe they didn't know either. What a complete, total waste! Damn her for keeping it a secret!"

"Wait, Kate. I don't know what you're talking about. Slow down. What happened?"

And so I told Chuck, and he cried as he learned the secrets from so long ago. "Do you really think that I wouldn't have helped her? She was my sister, I loved her. I would have killed John if it were necessary to stop him. What was wrong with her? Even animals will die to save their young. What was missing in her?"

Chuck and I talked late into the night, first about my family, then about his. He, too, had been beaten by his father, Bert, the man I loved so much as a child, and he shook with rage as he spoke about it.

While trying to get to sleep later that night, I suddenly wondered if I had made it all up. No one had ever talked directly about it, not even Mike and I. Chuck had not known about it, and probably no one else did. Maybe none of it happened. Was I so crazy that I had made up all the details just because I was angry at my father? His letters, after all, had expressed puzzlement for years at my continuing anger at him. Did I really make up everything? Who knew besides me? Mike, but he was gone. Maybe Spens, but he had been a baby. Mom and Nana were dead. Con? She would remember, she had to remember. I had to find out finally if my memories were real.

I left Chuck the next day, with promises to keep in touch, and hurried back to New Haven to call Con, my neighbor from so long ago. I hadn't seen her for two years, but I could always count on Con. She had become like a second mother to me and called herself

"Grandma Ass," grandmother by association. Con would tell me if I were living in a terrible fantasy land.

When I finally reached her, she was in Massachusetts on vacation. She drove down immediately and confirmed my worst memories. She added details that I had forgotten. Yes, it had been as bad as I had remembered, I hadn't made up anything out of anger.

Over the next couple of weeks I relaxed considerably. My crazy memories were real, Spens would soon be visiting me, my anger at all of my mother's family was slipping off of me like an old coat that was no longer necessary, and the girls would be back soon. It was nearly time to move again, to make a home for my girls. I was stronger, more able, than when they had left. Surely I could reach them in some way. I had to find a way.

Coe and I had had a turbulent summer. It could not have been any other way, given what I had experienced, yet he had stuck with me. He had taught me how to fight without overwhelming fear and how to say what I felt instead of what I thought he might want to hear. We had had fun and love. But now, as my mind became more and more filled with the girls, as he realized that most of my time would be taken up by them again, he began to withdraw. It had to happen, our relationship had to change now. Both of us were filled with a bittersweet sadness as he helped me move and organize the new house.

Chapter 23

The girls came back angry, of course. Becky seemed to be tiring of her stance, but Carole was even worse than she had been the previous year. She began to be defiant in a reckless, self-destructive way. Spens's month-long visit, which I thoroughly enjoyed and which reassured me on some deeply basic level, acted as a buffer for a while, however. Chuck came to visit that fall while Spens was there, and it seemed that my family from childhood was pulling together while the family I had established was falling apart.

One night early in November, I received a call from my eleventh grade chemistry teacher. He and his wife had become good friends with Mom and Bill many years ago, and through him I had kept track of Bill since he had hung up on me in 1972. Bill had had a major stroke and was completely paralyzed on his left side.

After we talked I sat in the kitchen, on the floor where I had slumped down during the call, in the dark, and went through all my memories of Bill. ("How's the water, daughter?" "Ten feet high and rising!" Oh, Bill! Do you remember still how that really meant 'I love you?' It must be so hard for you to be sick, to have to depend on someone else for everything. I ache for you. I wish that there were some way I could wave a magic wand and make it all better for you.) I still loved that gruff, stubborn old man very much. If he would see me, I would fly to San Francisco immediately. But when I called, he refused to speak to me. (I wish that you would let me back in. I love you so! I accept, I don't understand, but I accept). I wrote him and he did not return my letter. He didn't answer, but at least he read what

I had to say. Thereafter, I wrote him frequently, hoping someday for an answer.

It was Renee who solved the puzzle of Bill for me. The abrupt change in his behavior toward me five years earlier could easily have been caused by a minor stroke. Even if it hadn't been, it would be easier on me to think that it had than to assume he had rejected me for some as yet undiscovered badness.

. . .

All that fall my lawyer called, angry at Joe. He had demanded the right to sue for divorce, but was refusing to file. The property settlement was getting nowhere. She fought with his lawyer, also, who was recently divorced and was being as unreasonable as Joe was. Then one day just before Thanksgiving, my lawyer called with ominous news.

The next day I felt terribly ashamed as I told Renee what my lawyer had said. "Renee, Joe is going to fight for Carole in court starting next February when she's fourteen. He's not going to fight for Becky. I can't let that happen."

Renee looked startled before she said, "Surely the court would award her to you!"

"No, it's not that way. It's not that simple. In Georgia, a child of fourteen has the right to choose in a custody suit. The only way that I could get custody - because I know she would choose Atlanta over New Haven - is for me to prove that Joe is an unfit parent. Then the court would take away her choice. But I'd lose if I did that because I would be proving that the girls' father is unfit. I'd lose both of them emotionally, even if I won the suit. Their anger would be enormous."

"Have you talked with Joe? I thought that he had agreed to your having custody."

"He did, last spring. But right now he feels as if he is losing everything. He doesn't really want Carole, he just wants to salvage something from our years together. She's like a piece of furniture to him, something tangible, a possession.

"The worst part is that that's how he'll treat her. When the girls were little, I used to beg him to spend more time with them. He always refused, saying that it was natural for mothers to be the primary parent with daughters. He said that if he had a son it would be different, then he'd help more. But, once he has possession of her, he won't know what to do with her, so he'll bury himself in his books as he's always done and ignore her. He's horrible at the day-to-day parenting that she requires. He doesn't even begin to understand that a parent must lead a child and listen to a child, not dictate behavior from some idealistic pattern that exists only in his head."

"Then what are your options," she asked, her face a study in concern.

"I've been thinking about it since my lawyer called last night. All I've done is think and cry. Carole will say in court that she wants to return to Atlanta, there's no doubt about that. If I let her say that formally, in court, the breech will be too large for us to recover. My hurt will be too strong, her guilt will be too great. Becky will be terribly hurt when she finds out that her father isn't willing to fight for her. She'll see Carole's leaving as an abandonment, too. Carole will cut Becky off emotionally because it will be too painful for her to acknowledge that she chose to leave her behind. The only way that I can see to avoid the horrible consequences is to give her a free choice now. But that leaves Carole at the mercy of Joe!"

"Sometimes, Kate, you are powerless to block all of the consequences. Maybe the best that you can do is to minimize the damage."

"The minimum is so horrible, Renee. What will it do to Carole to be raised by Joe? He's so rigid, so harmful emotionally. He loves her, I don't doubt that. But he has no idea of her emotional needs, needs of any kind scare him. He'll destroy her."

"He won't," Renee responded. "Carole is tough, you've told me that repeatedly. Her behavior for the last year and a half is proof of her toughness. She's bright enough and healthy enough that she'll come back to you if it gets too bad. She won't let herself be destroyed."

"Yah, you're right. But I hate to think of her growing up without the care she needs."

"When her need gets to be too much, she'll find a way to get what she needs," she reassured.

"But what will it do to her to live until then with her needs unmet?"

"My guess is that she will learn some important lessons. She'll learn that what is really important is not the place where you live but who you live with. She's always had your loving concern, so she doesn't know what it's like to be without it. She'll learn that love and care feel better than being ignored. She's never lived with just Joe, so she doesn't know his emotional limitations. She'll learn that there are consequences to acts. She'll also probably begin to see the two of you more as individuals; that usually happens with a divorce. And the more that she sees each of you clearly, instead of dimly through a cloud of anger, the less will be her anger over the divorce. Remember that she is now about to find out why you decided to leave Joe. He's not going to be any more caring of her than he was with you. It won't take her long to figure out why you left him. Until now, you've had the full brunt of her anger over the divorce because you are the one in her mind who is supposed to protect her from all upset. She sees you as the one who failed because she never expected anything from Joe. But living with him, having to depend on him, she's going to put expectations on him that he won't be able to meet. She'll learn from that. All in all, she's going to learn many very important lessons."

"If she survives."

"She will. She's your daughter."

"Yah, she will. I don't know if I will though," I said in despair.

"You will, too," she reassured.

For a while I sat quietly, acknowledging that somewhere inside myself I could find the strength to live through even this, the worst that I could possibly imagine. "Renee, maybe the worst thing about this is that my family is about to repeat the mistake that my mother made. I see it, but I'm powerless to stop it. Like Spens and I, Becky and Carole are going to grow up apart, separated by many miles. Eventually, they'll be as angry at me as I am at my mother for letting it happen. Carole is going to feel guilty, just as I felt guilty for complaining about Spens." My God! Tears are running down her face. Renee is crying! I'm not, why is she? Is she crying instead of me? I guess that someone has to cry at these words, but I can't. I'm too far past crying to shed tears now.

"Becky is going to feel rejected, as I'm sure that Spens must have. It's not right, but I can't stop it! We're going full circle, as if there's a curse on this family that makes it fragment into pieces just like mine did. I am so frustrated that I want to scream 'No!' I want to throw things, break things. Doesn't anyone but me see the disaster that looms over us? I feel so horribly guilty for not being able to block this, even though I clearly see that there is nothing I can do about it. Who I am has led to this!"

Wiping the tears from her face she asked, "What do you mean, Kate?"

In anger, I began to explain the obvious. "I was so determined to provide my girls with the proper parenting that I never let them suffer because of Joe's lacks. I kept stepping in, taking over, buffering them from him. I did it because of what I experienced as a child, of course. But now, I'm about to lose Carole because of it. Had I been less of a mother, they would know that Joe can't care for anyone, and I wouldn't be losing Carole. God! That's so terribly ironic. It truly meets the definition of tragedy. Because of who I am, what I have feared most for nearly fourteen years is now happening even though I was aware of the possibility and did everything I could to protect against it. By protecting against it, I made it happen. I . . ."

"Whoa, Kate," interrupted Renee. "You did not make this happen even if you feel that you did. Joe is choosing to fight for Carole. It will be Carole who chooses to go to Atlanta. You could choose to fight this in court, and you could probably win, but it would make matters much worse. You said that yourself. Instead, you are choosing to minimize the damage to everyone. What you are doing now is continuing with the same parenting, loving and concerned and self-sacrificing parenting, that you have given the girls all along. Do you really wish that, long ago, when the girls were small, you had been less of a parent so that now Carole would choose you over Joe?"

"No."

"Then stop blaming yourself about this," she said gently. "It's happening because of who all of you are, not just you alone. Joe is trying to salvage what he can from your marriage. Carole is trying to get back to the city where everything was good in her life, not realizing that you were who insured the good for her. You are trying to minimize the damage. Each of you is doing what you feel you must. Joe will never grow up, that's why you left him, but Carole now has her first chance. She's your child much more than Joe's. You've taught her what's important in life. Trust her to have learned from you. It won't take her too long to realize her mistake."

Then I began the searing work of letting my daughter go.

Two nights later I told Carole that she had finally convinced me. I believed her when she said that she would remain miserable until she went back to Atlanta. So now she had a free choice. The only restrictions were that she could not tell me her final decision until the end of January and, if she decided to leave, she must wait until the beginning of a new school quarter in March. And, I wanted to see a complete end to all her nonsense from now on, she had to be co-operative.

Carole was shocked and serious, Becky stomped off to her room in fury. That she, too, could choose when she was fourteen was no consolation at that moment.

Carole had promised to behave, and she kept her promise. Within a week she was full of laughter again, something that had disappeared for over two years. Becky's mood lightened in response to the change and, once again, we had a family to which it was fun to belong. As Christmas approached, though, Carole began begging me to move back to Atlanta. Each time I assured her that I wanted her to live with me but that I had no job in Atlanta and had to stay in Connecticut. The girls went off to spend Christmas with their father, and I sank into gloom.

· · ·

Coe and I had planned a quiet Christmas by ourselves. The day before, we went shopping together for ingredients for our supper. On Christmas we exchanged gifts, then began the elaborate preparations that filled most of the day. Both of us were sad, he was missing his son who lived in New Jersey and wouldn't arrive until the next day, but we were determined not to spend the day in depression. We could acknowledge our unhappiness and then go on to enjoy each other.

After getting everything into the oven, we both showered then shared some pot. Coe had been completely surprised that I, a child of the sixties, had never used pot or any other drug and had brought some along with him for me to try. Somewhat reluctantly, somewhat apprehensively, I took three puffs on the cigarette he made and decided that I didn't like the burning sensation in my lungs. I was drifting off to sleep on the couch when the nightmare began. Like so many times recently I jerked awake, but this time the nightmare did not go away. It was the old one, from childhood, and I was terrified to be having it while awake. I told Coe to say something, anything, and not to stop talking until I said that he could. He talked, I focused on his words and gradually the nightmare receded. It started again as soon as he stopped talking. Finally now I knew what it was like to be crazy, and I also knew at the same time that I had never been crazy before.

For the next three hours, until the pot wore off, I had to struggle to remain in contact with reality. I began to be able to control it some. I could go into the dream a little and then come out at will when I grew too frightened. Finally, though, I decided that it would be dangerous to explore the dream without Renee. We ate our delicious supper, took a walk in the snowy woods, and I held the nightmare at bay.

The next day I saw Renee. I let myself go into the nightmare, and it came back with intensity undiminished. I was a Jewish child, pursued by German soldiers. When they caught me, they would kill me. I ran in the dark with them getting closer and closer. And then Renee asked me who the soldiers were. They were my father. He was going to kill me.

"What are you feeling, Kate?"

"Stark terror," I panted. "I'm very dizzy. I keep getting very hot, then very cold. I can't move. I'm going to be sick. There's a bright glaring nothingness surrounding me. I can't hear. And I'm feeling so very alone! Please hold me." Renee held me while I cried and cried for the many times that my father had pursued me and I had endured alone.

Later, she asked me why I had been Jewish in the nightmare, but I couldn't answer her because I didn't know.

The next day, anxiety set in. Never before had it been so intense. Within a couple of days I was exhausted from lack of sleep, had sharp cramps in my stomach whenever I tried to eat, began to suspect that everything in the refrigerator had spoiled, even the frozen food, and was afraid to go out of the house. Renee had the flu and couldn't see me. When she suggested that I needed Valium, I refused a prescription because I was afraid that I'd become addicted to it. I called her repeatedly, begging her to do something to help me. Finally, she made a deal with me: if I went and got the prescription, I could come over to her house the next night if her fever were down.

I went and got the pills at the pharmacy and took one right there, and I barely made it home before I fell into an exhausted sleep for four hours. I took another and another, every four hours, and caught up on five days worth of sleep. The next night a sick and weary Renee explained that I was having an anxiety attack that would probably continue until I discovered what scared me so much. No, it wasn't the dream; I'd probably never have it again. It wasn't my childhood, we had explored it in detail without such a severe reaction. It was something from now, my current life, that I was trying to avoid recognizing.

The anxiety attack continued into January after the girls came home, after the divorce, without settlement yet, went through the court. It continued until Carole and Coe both told me within an hour of each other that they were leaving. Each was gentle with me. Carole said that if only I lived in Atlanta, she would continue to live with me. Coe said that he had to get back to New Jersey to his son. The anxiety left, the waiting was over.

Carole left on a snowy night in February, my birthday. She had turned fourteen years old three days earlier. Fourteen years ago, I had taken her home from the hospital on my birthday. She came, and she left, on the same day. The ride to the airport was one of strained silence. Becky had chosen to stay home with Coe. There was just the two of us, my heart feeling as if it would break with sorrow. I had prepared for this day for over three months, but no amount of preparation could have prepared me for it. We kissed good-bye and I numbly watched her walk away, her guinea pig hidden in her coat pocket. I drove home, and Coe held me through the night while I cried. Then he left, too.

Chapter 24

So now my family was down to one, Becky. She brightened up within ten days, recovering from the weeks and months of constant strain. Both of us spoke to Carole four and five times a week, and I handled by long distance the minor problems that Joe should have been able to help her with. I even tutored her in algebra on the phone, though Joe had been a math major for a while in college.

I also wrote her at least one letter a week. Sometimes the letters were signed by her dog, supposedly. Sometimes a TV commercial character, Big Fig, was the writer. Both her dog and Big Fig could broach topics that I couldn't. But most of the letters were directly from me to her. I was determined that she remain my child. Making the best of a bad situation, I felt that we had an unique opportunity, the two of us. She could get to know me through the letters long before most kids learned who their parents were, without the necessity of an immediate reaction on her part. All she would have to do was read. I could become real to her, instead of Mommy-who-is-always-taken-for-granted. I wrote and wrote to keep our relationship alive.

And with Renee the subject was once again, still, my family. Spens and Chuck were back in my life, I hadn't been able to locate Mike, and my father was still waiting to hear from me.

"Maybe it is time to do something more?"

"No, I am too afraid. Nothing good can come from it."

"You said the same thing before contacting Chuck."

"Chuck is different, I had good memories of him."

"Maybe your father's brothers are nice."

"They couldn't be."

"You don't know, Kate."

All my life, until I had begun talking with Renee, I had tried to put the past behind me, but my fear of my father had contaminated every aspect of the life I was trying to lead. With all our work together, I had not been able to change my reactions in any substantial way. My normal anxiety level was incredibly high, the nightmares continued with little modification, and I suffered from terrifying flashbacks. The formal name for my problems was post-traumatic stress syndrome which, according to the literature, was strongly resistant to treatment.

Renee, however, was convinced that if I could see my father with adult eyes instead of childhood memories, I would lose my fear. I was convinced that I needed to see him once in order to prove to myself that I would not be destroyed by contact with him. I favored immediately flying to see him in order to get the horrible task over with but Renee insisted that I go very gradually, in order to ensure that I had a sense of control over the process and to avoid being overwhelmed by anxiety and fear. We argued for weeks as we worked out our plan of moving backward in time for a while so that I could move forward in my life.

His brothers were to be my first step toward my father. Because they were my father's brothers, they would be similar to him, and I would be able to get a sense of my father by getting to know them. The more that I was able to learn about my father's past from them, the more real my father would become to me. The more real he would become, the less scared I would become. Eventually I would be able to meet my father without terror. That was the plan at least.

In March of 1978, I wrote my father's brother, Art, a letter of introduction, and my response to mailing it proved that Renee was right about going slowly. During the day I was filled with an anxiety that made it almost impossible to work. I dropped things in the lab, going through expensive glassware at an appalling rate. I made errors in calculations that ruined experiments. I left out critical steps in experiments. I locked myself out of the lab and car continuously, to the point that I had to set up multiple safe guards by leaving keys with friends. I went places and forgot why I had gone there. One day I went into a grocery store and, after wandering up and down the aisles for nearly a half hour without taking one object off a shelf, fled in panic. Later that day I went back with a list of five objects and forced myself to move methodically through the store gathering them. I was irritable and ready to explode at the most minor of difficulties. At night I kept awakening again, ten to twelve times a night, screaming from nightmares of men trying to shoot me. That went on for nearly two weeks while I waited for Art's answer.

Towards the end of that two-week period, I started going home during my lunch break, a round trip of twenty-two miles, to see if an answer from Art had come. When it finally did, I sat and cried as I read his gentle, welcoming letter. I had wanted so badly to hear from him, but I had been afraid that he would tell me that he wanted nothing to do with me simply because I was my father's child. Instead of my worst fears coming true, he had written an extremely warm letter, and the relief was tremendous.

When it came to answering him, however, I found myself incapable of doing it. His response had stirred up so many memories and feelings that I could not force myself to write a social, chatty letter to him. Each time that I tried to write Art, I was overwhelmed by anger. The anger, of course, was supported by the previous total lack of communication from him. He had known where I was as a kid; he could have written to me then and let me know that he cared. Why did it take over thirty years and my initiative to activate him? Also, in addition to the anger, fear of my father was blocking me from answering Art. At that point, to me he was my father's brother instead of Art, a separate individual who might be very different from his brother.

After six weeks of not writing, during which time I struggled with my anger and fear, Art wrote a brief note expressing his hurt that I had not answered him. That was enough of a push, and I started writing. I told him about the anger and the fear, then asked that he be patient with me as I worked through my confusion.

Art's next letter triggered even stronger responses in me. He completely ignored what I had said about being abused. He made no mention of my anger and fear. The closest that he came to acknowledging what I had said was that the past was too painful to remember and that he refused to discuss it. I overreacted to that, and I could not figure out why.

"What is going on, Kate?"

"I don't know, Renee. She is so furious at Art that I never want anything to do with him again. I feel like he has totally rejected her. I know that he hasn't, but that's how I feel. He ignored every single emotionally laden topic in my letter. How can you read that your brother beat his child and not show some sort of response to it?"

"He responded," she said. "His response is to ignore."

"But that's a totally crazy response!"

"If he could deal with it, Kate, he would."

"What in the hell are you saying?"

"What I'm saying," Renee went on patiently, "is that I suspect Art is teaching you about your father. What you said must have been threatening enough to him that his only choice was simply to block it out. Remember how your father has always denied that he hurt you in any way? Denial is just a more active ignoring. I think that getting to know Art is going to be identical to getting to know this aspect of your father. What concerns me right now, however, is your reaction to his letter. Talk to me about it."

Feeling disgusted with the world, I slumped into the chair and began. "I feel rejected by Art, but the truth is that I want to reject him. He's being like everyone else in my family, ignoring what I said. To hell with them all!"

"Why are you so angry?"

"I'm not only angry, I'm totally and completely disgusted. I feel invisible and I'm angry at the people who make me feel as if I don't exist." I stopped talking then and stared out the window. I could feel my jaw muscles so tight that my teeth hurt.

After a while, Renee's soft voice brought me back to the room. "When you were a child, Kate, were you invisible then?"

"Yah," I answered, anger welling up in me at the memories. "I was invisible in all sorts of ways. I tried to be invisible. That way, I could avoid being hurt. I stayed outside as much as possible. When I was home, I was super-careful to blend into the wallpaper whenever possible. I never left my things in any part of the house except my room. The one time that I did, I came home to find that my mother had thrown my stamp album on the front lawn. She said that if I didn't care enough about it to put it away, it didn't deserve any space in the house. God, I was angry about that! She had tossed it from the porch and most of the pages were bent." I stopped talking, feeling again the rage that I had felt as a child at the violation of my property.

"What did you do about it?" asked Renee.

"Became better at being invisible," I answered bitterly.

"Okay," said Renee, "you tried to remain invisible. What you've said so far doesn't relate to the anger you're feeling about Art's letter, though. What is it in it that is making you so angry?"

With Renee's question, my anger faded rapidly to sorrow. "It feels," I slowly began, "no…" I couldn't find the words to explain. In exasperation with myself, I said that I didn't know.

"You know," Renee encouraged.

Sighing deeply, I started again. "I want just one single person in my family, I don't care who, to say 'Gee, Kate, that happened when you were a child and it was terrible.' I want validation or recognition or something. I'm angry at Art because he totally ignored what I said. It's like I didn't say it and it never happened."

"Do you feel like it didn't happen?"

"Right now, yes. I know it did because my neighbor Con said it did, but I feel so remote from the kid that it happened to. She's another person, Renee, and I don't want her to be. I want her to be me!"

Renee handed me a piece of Kleenex before she began talking. "I wonder, Kate, if what you're feeling now is the same way you felt when, as a child, you tried to talk with your mother about what your father did to you."

"I don't remember ever trying to talk about it." (*you dumb stupid kid no one not anyone i know has an elephant's trunk in their pants*) "What was the point? She wouldn't have done anything."

"What are you overreacting to in that letter, Kate?"

"Dammit! I am not overreacting to anything!" *(the elephant's trunk walks up my stomach leaving sticky patches in a random pattern)* "Why is it that I'm overreacting every time I get angry about something? Don't I have a right to get angry if what I say is totally ignored by someone?"

"Yes, you do, Kate. But the anger you're feeling now comes from more than Art's response to you. Think."

"My father has told me for years that he never hurt me, Renee." (*the elephant's trunk waves in front of my face*) "His letters are so convincing that I wonder if I made up everything each time I read his denial. But I didn't, I didn't." (*it hits me on the nose moves up toward my eye*) "I didn't make up anything." (*it slides down my cheek leaving a trail of wetness.*) "You believe me, don't you?" When Renee nodded yes, I could continue. "When he denies my reality, it feels like he denies me, my existence. When he says that he doesn't understand why I am angry, it's a denial of my memories, the entire history that lies between us, what I am today." (*it caresses my neck*) "It makes me into a non-person. I am who I am because, in part, of what went on between us." (*i hold my breath hoping that it will go away instead of eating me*) "If he denies that, he denies the parts of me that stem from what happened." (*i try to move my head from side to side both ways are blocked by his legs*) "I feel so damn fragmented right now. I feel like there are parts of me that I don't know. Huge parts." (*it pushes hard under my chin and now I can't breathe*) "There's no continuity between what I was and what I am, or there's no continuity between all the parts of me that exist right now." (*i gasp for air*) "I can't explain any better than that right now, Renee. I can't, I'm sorry. All I know is that I will no longer tolerate anyone denying what happened. It's too tempting to begin denying it myself again." (*as my mouth opens the elephant's trunk dives into it*)

"Is that what's really going on? You feel tempted to go back to denial yourself?"

"Yes," I reluctantly admitted.

"I have no doubt that what you say happened truly did happen, Katie. No one could invent the terror that I've seen in you at times. All of it, unfortunately, was very real." When Renee said that, I began crying in relief. Then I went home and began to write a letter to Art that left out what he couldn't acknowledge.

Each time that I wrote Art for the next four months my reaction decreased as I became desensitized to the indirect contact with my father. By the beginning of summer I was able to look forward to meeting Art without overwhelming fear. If things worked out very well, someday I could also meet my father that way.

Chapter 25

In June Becky and I drove to Atlanta. She was going to spend the entire summer with her father. Although both girls were supposed to be with me for half of the summer, Carole had strongly protested going back to Connecticut after living only four months in Atlanta. She had a strong need to remake a home for herself again in Atlanta which I thoroughly understood. While I could have insisted that she spend six weeks with me, I decided that two good weeks together in Atlanta would be much better than six in Connecticut with Carole angry and hostile the entire time. Because I also thought that it was very important for the girls to have as much time together as possible, I yielded to Becky's plea that she be allowed to spend the entire summer with her father and sister.

I stayed with friends in Atlanta, and during that time sorted through my possessions that were still in Joe's house. Although we already had a no-fault divorce, we had yet to reach a property settlement. He was taking the position that I had abandoned him and was, therefore, entitled to nothing that I had not had on the date of our marriage fifteen years ago. While such a position was a legal impossibility, it was blocking the settlement at that point because he refused to discuss anything. It was incredibly hard to sort through my school papers, books and clothes in a beautifully furnished four bedroom house and not compare it to the unfurnished two bedroom house into which Becky and I had just moved. We had two mattresses on the floor, a table and chairs loaned to us by a friend, a popcorn popper and a yogurt maker. Friends had also loaned us dishes, one lamp and a rocking chair. We had nothing else. Many hours were spent with my lawyer during that period but nothing was resolved.

The time with the girls in Atlanta was very painful. Becky was understandably eager to be with her old friends after the long separation, and so she spent very little time with me. Carole and I did not know how to be with each other. Even though our last three months together in Connecticut had been quite good, both of us were haunted by the prior year and a half when she had been so terribly angry about the move and divorce and had blamed me for everything wrong in her life. I had tried hard to understand her, but I still felt her leaving as rejection. At the same time, I tried hard not to make her feel guilty about leaving because I did not want guilt as yet another barrier between us. I did not want her to grow up feeling guilty the way I had. Gradually, tentatively, we worked toward each other over the two weeks. It was awkward and painful and only slightly reassuring.

As soon as I arrived back in Connecticut I got the flu. For two weeks I lay in that deathly quiet house with a temperature ranging from 100-102 degrees. I went back to work too early, had a relapse and spent another two weeks alone with even higher temperatures. During the relapse I suffered nerve damage and permanently lost some hearing in one ear. That may have been the low point in my life. In the course of two years I had lost a husband and house, moved away from all of my friends, neither of my children was with me, even the animals were gone, and I was lying in an unfurnished house at times literally unable to get to the kitchen. I kept a jug of water, a jar of peanut butter, a loaf of bread and a jar of aspirin on the floor next to the mattress. When I had to go to the bathroom, I crawled.

By late July I was becoming very worried about my upcoming trip to visit Art. The flu had lasted so long that I was sure it would go on forever. Even if I were well in time, I was worried about the stress of the drive to Buffalo, which was five hundred miles away. But, if I did not go at the planned time, I would have to wait until Thanksgiving to make the trip, and I was unwilling to do that.

I finally left for Buffalo on a Saturday morning in early August, still shaky and down ten pounds from my normal weight. I drove slowly, stopping often to rest, and covered a little over 300 miles that day. I was very worried about what the next day would bring. Peggy, Art's wife, had written that she was planning to have both of her daughters' families for supper. Also, my father's older brother Nat, and his wife Ivy would be there. Meeting any one of those people would have been difficult for me; all of them together seemed close to being overwhelming. What kept going through my mind was something my mother said once: one of my father's brothers was just like him and one was very nice. I could not remember, however, which was which. Art seemed very nice from his letters, I had accepted the fact that he refused to talk about the past, but something bothered me about him. I had had no communication with Nat at all, but I did remember that he had turned up at my house when I was eight. After my father had been committed, he had come to offer help. Finally, I decided that I would have to think of both as nice until such time that I had reason to conclude the opposite. That made the next day seem easier to face.

By two o'clock the next day I had located Art's house. Then I went to a nearby park and sat under a tree until I felt ready to handle the unknown.

As I parked the car in front of Art's house, my father walked out the door and limped toward me. Although prepared by a picture he had sent, Art's resemblance to the image of my father I had carried with me since I was twelve was so strong that I froze for a few seconds and stared at him.

Art was about six feet tall, with a long narrow face. He was going gray at the temples only and had a thick head of very dark brown hair. As he limped closer, I could see a warm gentleness in his eyes and knew that he was okay, safe, non-violent. At that, I quickly got out of the car and hurried up to him. He reached for me and held me tightly for a long while, and both of us had tears in our eyes as we separated.

Peggy came out onto the porch and looked questioningly at Art and me. Then, all three of us started talking at once. Art would have recognized me anywhere because I looked just like their younger daughter, Peggy had been worried that I had gotten too scared and changed my mind about coming, I had driven on back roads and had not realized how much longer it would take. After our burst of conversation, there was a long silence as each of us stared at the other and tried to figure out these strangers to whom we were closely related.

Peggy broke the gathering tension by offering me a cup of coffee and then leading us anxiously into the house. As Peggy bustled in the kitchen, Art sat down on the couch, motioned me to a chair opposite him, and started talking in a very formal manner. "Kate, I've thought a lot about your visit and want you to know that we have a rule in our house. No one has to talk about anything if they don't want to. I don't want to discuss the past and ask that you respect that." It was said gently, but something in his voice told me that he was capable of asking me to leave the first time that I broke his rule.

"Art," I said carefully, "what I'm interested in is getting to know you and your family as you are now. If I ask a question that you don't want to answer, please just tell me so. I, too, have painful events in my past that I find difficult to discuss."

The business concluded, we went into the dining room and began to try to know each other as we munched cookies and drank too much coffee to cover uncomfortable silences. They told me about their daughters, who would be coming soon, and I told them about mine. I found out that Art limped because he had been hit by a car at work. The conversation kept lagging and then going off in spurts as someone thought of a new topic. It was uncomfortable, but it was not as bad as I had feared.

Once their daughters and their families arrived I withdrew some and became more of an observer. When Nat and Ivy arrived, the tone of the gathering changed considerably. There was a wariness in the air that had been lacking before.

Nat did not look like my father and did not sound like him. He lacked Art's gentleness but, at the same time, seemed more vulnerable than Art simply because he honestly and directly showed his feelings. Whereas Art seemed to contain everything deep inside, Nat was much more open. As he spoke about his daughter, Autumn, the hurt and bitterness were readily apparent.

Nat and I stood on the front lawn, separated from everyone else as we talked. The more he said, the harder he chewed on the remnant of his cigar until he had reduced it to such a pulp that he took it from his mouth and threw it as hard as he could toward the street. It flew apart in the air. The previous summer he had declared Autumn dead to him. Art, under similar circumstances, would have declared the topic out of bounds, but Nat said very clearly and very sadly that Autumn was no longer his child since she had gone with her husband instead of staying in Buffalo and helping him with Ivy. I liked Nat but his words had a chilling effect on me. Here was yet another father declaring his child dead to him simply because she did not meet his expectations.

And, his expectations were clearly off. Ivy had been depressed for years, going in and out of mental institutions with appalling regularity. Autumn had also had been hospitalized several times for severe depression, and her fourth husband had moved back to Buffalo at her father's insistence. Nat had bought them a house directly across the street from his house, arranged for employment for Autumn's husband, Jack, and then expected Autumn to help him care for his wife. After several months, Jack had returned to their original home and Autumn, several weeks later, had followed him. Clearly, Nat had expected her to abandon Jack and to stay with him and Ivy.

Ivy was a vague, nebulous person, completely ignoring what was going on around her. Whenever she roused herself enough to speak, her topic was Autumn, of whom she was highly and indiscriminately critical. Before Ivy had arrived earlier that afternoon, Peggy had told me that Ivy had long ago stopped cleaning and cooking. As a result, she and Nat ate all their meals in restaurants and never entertained. Although they lived only one block from Art and Peggy, they had not invited Art's family into their house since before 1960, over 18 years ago. When they were invited, they were invited into the yard only.

The evening together was long and exhausting. More and more as it progressed, I withdrew and tried to look for patterns of interaction. I pulled out my family album and watched closely as the brothers reacted to pictures of my father. Peggy brought out her album, and I tried to note who said what, and who remained silent, as I asked casual questions that occurred to me as I looked at the pictures. By the time everyone left, I had gained far more information about them than they would have guessed.

. . .

Peggy and I talked continuously the next day while Art was at work, and it was a very difficult conversation for both of us. Art's prohibition on the past obviously extended to her, yet it was also clear that she wanted to tell me more than she was allowed to say. I wanted to learn as much as I could, but I had to do it in such a way that I did not directly violate Art's prohibition. I was glad that I had conveniently left out of my life description the fact that I also had a masters in marriage and family therapy, because the training was extremely helpful as I talked with Peggy. Because I had to restrain my curiosity, I seldom asked specific questions and had to be very patient as I drew her out. I spent the entire day on two levels. I was Kate the real person, focused on Peggy, reacting to what she said and revealing myself. I was also Kate the observer, deciding which of my reactions I would allow to show, probing, forming hypotheses, testing, subtly directing the conversation, monitoring my response to what she said, tying separate images together. It was exhausting work.

Gradually over the course of the day I developed pictures of how her family worked, how Nat's functioned and how the two interacted. I also became increasingly puzzled by the numerous areas of discussion that were included in Art's prohibition. Peggy lied frequently to me, as judged by a jump in her anxiety level as she answered some of the few direct questions I risked. I came away from the day with hundreds of questions and a suspicion that the family was Jewish.

That night - my last night with them - was also very uncomfortable. Peggy was exceedingly tense, and I could only guess that she was worried about some of the things she had told me. Perhaps she feared that I would ask Art all my unanswered questions. I felt frustrated by Art's rule of silence, I did not understand it, but I also felt that he had the right to impose it. Unlike the previous evening, Art acted as if he felt no obligation to participate in conversation. He was silent all evening, inhibiting further the flow of talk between Peggy and me. I pleaded fatigue and a long drive the next day in order to remove myself from the situation.

On the long drive back to New Haven, I tried to draw pictures in my mind of what I knew about all the people I had met in Buffalo. If I could define what I knew, then I could perhaps begin to erase some of the confusion I felt. Also, my real reason for going there had been to re-experience with adult eyes the interactions that had shaped me as a child. As I sorted through the facts and looked for patterns, I realized that the confusion, puzzlement, frustration and anger were coming from my interactions with those people and were identical to what I had felt in every interaction with my father. By the time I arrived home, I had a fairly clear idea of what I had experienced as a child.

So what was it that Peggy told me during our day together? Well, my grandfather's name was Sam, which I vaguely remembered. Sam had been born in Odessa, Russia, not France as my father had told me. At the age of thirteen, in 1906, Sam had left his family. He had worked his way across Europe on foot and sailed from Antwerp to Montreal. He had then gone on to Chicago where he worked to bring all the rest over. Rest? How many were there? Where are they now? Who are they, my family? There were twelve others, but she didn't know where they were now. And she lied as she said that.

Okay, so Sam brought them over. What did he do next? Well, he opened a car repair shop that did very well. Then, when your grandmother died, he and the boys moved to Buffalo. No, John and Art moved with him, Nat remained in Chicago. Hold it a minute, my grandmother: what was her name? Where was she born? Why did she die? When? I don't know, Kate, and she lied as she said it.

So they moved to Buffalo, but Nat didn't. He was sixteen at the time, in about 1933. My father ran away. Sam raised Art in a succession of boarding homes. Art was only six when they moved. My dad came back, met my mother, married her, and then went off to fight in the war. Nat moved his family to Buffalo in 1952 and joined Sam and Art in the family car repair business. Sam got stomach cancer and died in 1966.

So what kind of man was Sam? He was a good man, a gentle man. He lived with us for a while and was a loving grandfather. And my grandmother, what was she like? I don't know, Kate, and she lied as she said it.

Why did Nat declare Autumn dead? The real reason, underneath everything, was that Autumn refused to take care of her mother. Her mother is crazy, and Autumn's not in such good shape herself.

You know, you should write Autumn, she lives in Atlanta with her fourth husband. Do you mean that my cousin and I lived in the same city for four years without knowing it? We could have been friends, helped each other. That was it, the entire family story except for all the holes in it.

When I got back Renee and I went over the few facts I had gathered, but she didn't think the family was Jewish. "Nat, Art and John weren't Jewish names, you know."

"But Sam is."

"Not exclusively. And the picture Art sent of himself included a Christmas tree."

"Yah, but that's what you would do if you were hiding it."

"No one is hiding anything, Kate."

"They are, I know it. Peggy lied too much."

"Maybe she simply forgot."

"No, she was hiding something."

"And did they welcome you well?"

"Yes, it felt good to be surrounded by family."

I wrote Autumn, my cousin, and asked her all my questions that Peggy had left unanswered. I wrote my father, too, and told him that I had no sense of him as a person, that I needed to know him better. Then I leaned back and waited. Soon now, I would begin to understand.

And then Autumn's letter arrived and shattered my world.

Chapter 26

This is what Autumn's letter said and my reactions to it.

Anna, my grandmother's name was Anna. She was a Jew from Odessa, not a Methodist from France. Sam was a Jew, too. Anna had not died in the early 1930s in Chicago; she was still alive, not dead. I could see her, talk with her, touch her if I went to Canton, Ohio, where she was in a nursing home. As a child, Autumn had gone there several times with her father Nat.

I had guessed correctly about my family! My middle name, Ann, probably came from my grandmother's name. I was named after her. My grandmother was alive and she could tell me what had happened, to her and her family! She, like me, had been excluded by them. She would feel a kinship with me, and she would tell me what she knew. She just had to, she was my grandmother. Grandmothers take care of kids even if parents don't. They're a refuge for the youngest generation. They understand more than parents because their perspective is larger.

I would go to her, she would welcome me with surprise and delight, we would sit for hours and talk. She would tell me about her life in Russia. I would hear about her travel to Chicago as a young girl, not more than fourteen. She would tell me how she met Sam her husband and how they struggled in the ghetto of Chicago. She would teach me to light the *Shabbes* candles and tell me stories that could have been straight from Issac Bashevis Singer or Shalom Aleichem. I would tell her that my father had been like a Cossack or a Nazi to me and she would understand what I meant. Together we would face the world and laugh.

She wasn't crazy, she couldn't be, not my grandmother. There must be some other explanation than that. Sure, she had been in a mental hospital since the thirties, but that didn't necessarily mean she was crazy. She had just been depressed and none of the doctors spoke Yiddish. Running naked through the streets of Chicago sounds like an apocryphal tale, not to be believed. If Sam had been having the affairs of which she had accused him, it would make sense to refuse to cook, to scream obscenities, to threaten to poison him. Even attacking him with a knife, if it weren't an exaggeration, would be within the realm of the semi-normal. No, my grandmother wasn't crazy, there had to be another explanation.

After Anna was hospitalized, they all moved from Chicago to Buffalo. Ariel became Art. Nachum became Nat. Shmul became Sam. Their last name, Bozeman, became Duboze and then DuBose. Was John, my father, once called Jacob? When did those Orthodox Jews become Methodists? When did they begin saying that they came from France, not Russia?

And what about Sam? He left Odessa in 1906, the year after a massive pogrom in that city that killed over 800 Jews. At the age of thirteen he left by himself. He left as an Orthodox Jew, he raised three sons as Orthodox Jews, including my father, and he gave his granddaughter, Autumn, Easter baskets every year. Easter was the trigger for pogroms in Russia, yet he ended up celebrating the holiday. How could any man travel so far from what he was?

Maybe the plan to hide existed before Anna's commitment and it was her refusal to go along with it that led to her commitment. Maybe because she spoke only Yiddish they had to get rid of her if they were to change who they were. With husband and sons preparing to give up land, language, name and religion, it's no wonder that she screamed and threatened. She became depressed, and then she couldn't tell the doctor what was wrong because of the language barrier. No wonder she screamed. It must have been a scream of absolute terror at the thought of what her husband and sons had decided to do.

Maybe, though, maybe all the lies developed to cover their shame of her real craziness. Her son, my father, was crazy. That I know beyond doubt. Her diagnosis was the same as his; maybe hers was accurate. Maybe she was the reason that my father hated and feared females. No, no, not my grandmother! She couldn't have been the source of what happened to me.

Okay, they couldn't bear the stigma of a crazy wife and mother. But, they shouldn't have abandoned her. She would have gotten better with their help. How could they have done that to her? How could they have left her totally alone for nearly fifty years, locked away from people whom she loved and who spoke her language? If she could have moved in with Nat in the early fifties, that meant that she no longer needed to be hospitalized, whatever the original situation had been. She had been locked up for at least thirty years for no reason except convenience. How could they have done that to my grandmother? Damn them for what they did!

Only Nat stuck with her at all. He even took Autumn to visit her when she was a child. Nat stuck with her, he stuck with her until she could have come live with him. But then he transferred her to a nursing home and moved to Buffalo.

Not once did her husband Sam visit her. Only once did Art visit her. My father? My father never visited her, not once, and not once was he man enough to say, "This is who I am." Even his brothers were capable of more than that. Their daughters, all of them, knew about Anna. But I didn't.

They lied to me, all of them. My father lied to me all my life, from the very beginning. Art and Nat and Peggy knew that I was confused, seeking information, trying to understand my terrible childhood and how it led directly to a disastrous end to my marriage. They knew I needed to have the truth in order to make sense out of my life. How could they have done that to me? Did they laugh to themselves as they told me their lies? What kind of people are they? Damn them for what they did!

As I read Autumn's letter, years of puzzling memories dropped away. Now I knew why I had hated Christmas as a child and was never allowed to have an Easter basket. I knew why Saturday mornings were always so tense in my house, with my mother resenting the expensive and lavish breakfasts that my father demanded. I knew why my father drove us to church but never went inside. These things, and so much more, became understandable with the missing piece: my father was not what he said he was. He was not comfortable with the image he had chosen for himself, and I had noticed without knowing. My memories finally made sense, and I was delighted by that, at least.

All those years when I kept wanting to convert to Judaism, identifying with Jews, and not understanding why. What a waste. I had called myself neurotic to feel that identification. I had told myself that I had no right to intrude on the sorrow of a grieving people. I was morbidly attracted to them for the wrong reasons. No. Stay away, you have no right, I said. And all along I was already what I had wanted to be. I had lost my past because of my family. No wonder I had felt disconnected, not linked with the world. They had destroyed all of my links. And now it was too late to be what I was. I couldn't erase thirty-four years of life as a non-Jew and substitute life as a Jew. I had raised my girls in the Christian traditions, I had thousands of memories centering on those traditions. How could I possibly be a Jew now? Damn them for what they had taken from me!

. . .

"I read the copy of Autumn's letter that you put in my mailbox, Kate. What do you think of it?" Renee began.

"I believe her. No one could make up that kind of story, it's too crazy. I was right. Peggy and Art were hiding something. My father's family is Jewish."

She smiled as she said, "Yes, you were. I should have remembered that you have a built-in lie detector."

I smiled weakly. "But I don't understand anything at all, Renee," I said plaintively. "Suddenly I'm Russian, not French. Suddenly I'm Jewish, not vaguely Christian. My grandmother's alive, not dead. I have an aunt, or a cousin or something, named Belle, and she's an Orthodox Jew. Someplace in this country are the descendants of ten or twelve family members. The name I grew up with turns out to be a fabrication. I don't even know my father's first name. Who am I?"

"You're the same Kate whom I've known for two years," she tried to reassure.

"No, I'm not anymore," I said, shaking my head in negation. "That Kate thought that she had one set of forces acting upon her. It turns out that she knew nothing about what was affecting her. Look, I have memories of my dad surrounding the yard with string. He made a string fence every year. I thought that it was because he wanted to keep kids off the grass. I was all wrong! He was doing it so that he could carry things in the yard on Saturdays. The string was an *eruv*, or artificial boundary that made the yard into part of the house. In Orthodox Judaism, one can carry inside a house but not outside on *Shabbes*. Or what about my memories of Easter? I thought that he was mean not to let me have an Easter basket but it turns out that he was reacting to pogrom season in Russia! Don't you understand? There's my Christmas memories, all interpreted incorrectly. What about the horror that was Saturday mornings and his demands for elaborate breakfasts that caused so much trouble? I was living with a Marrano, a Converso, a hidden Jew, and I didn't understand what was going on. I am so fucking angry that I could scream!"

"Go ahead."

Angrily I turned away from her. "You know what I mean, come off it."

"I think that I do, Kate. What are you overreacting to?" she calmly asked.

"I am not overreacting! How would you like it if you found out that everyone in your entire family had been lying to you for your entire life? Even you might overreact to that!"

"I would be furious," she answered.

"Well, I am! Oh, Renee," I said, my anger disappearing, "I am so confused that I don't even know my name now. Last night I had to introduce myself to someone, and I almost couldn't because I suddenly didn't know my last name. There was about a five second silence after I said 'Kate.' I couldn't remember what came next."

"What name did you use?" she asked.

"Slaboda, but it didn't feel right," I replied, remembering the sense of distance I had felt from my name.

"What did it feel like?"

"A lie. I'm no longer Kate Slaboda either."

"Who are you? Do you know?"

I sat looking at the floor, shaking my head. "No, I don't know, and I'm scared. Whose blood is running through my veins? Whose eyes look out at me when I gaze in a mirror? When I was a kid, I used to stare into a mirror, trying to figure out who I was. I was looking for indications that I was French, but I couldn't see them. No wonder I couldn't!" I said, feeling the anger rise in me momentarily before slipping away again. "I was confused, Renee, horribly confused. I was told that I was something, French, but I didn't match what I was supposed to be. Do you know how confusing that can be?"

"I can only imagine, Kate," she answered with real sympathy in her voice.

"Well, it's shitty. It's like walking through an earthquake maybe. There's no solid ground to stand on. That's how I feel right now, as if the ground has suddenly shifted on me. Name one fact about my past that you are sure is right. I can't. How can I trust my memories if I wasn't seeing what was really going on?"

"Kate," Renee said with a touch of urgency, "your memories are very accurate. They stuck with you and you told me about them because there was something wrong in the scenes that you remembered. If there hadn't been, they would have slipped away from you. The wrongness in them bothered you, and so you remembered them. You are excellent at detecting lies."

"Yah, sure."

"I'll prove it to you," she continued. "I'm willing to bet that you know if your mother knew that your father was Jewish. Think a moment. Did she ever talk to you about Judaism?"

"Yes, she did," I said with some surprise.

"Try to remember your response," she urged.

"I was puzzled. Out of nowhere, several times she praised Judaism. Said it was an extremely healthy religion and the only one to which she would convert. I couldn't figure out why she was telling me that. She was giving me an important message, but I didn't know what it was."

"She knew. See?" Renee said proudly. "You remembered those times because something was emotionally off in them. That's why they puzzled you. You can trust your memories, Kate. All of them."

"But that means she lied to me too! How could everyone have done that to me? What is wrong with me that everyone in my family lies to me?" I asked in renewed despair.

"Kate, Kate, it's not you; it's them. You didn't make them lie to you. When did it start, what's your earliest memory?"

"When I was three or three-and-a-half years old. My dad told me that his father was from France. He taught me several French words, but I don't remember what they were."

"What could you have possibly done at that age that would make him lie to you?"

"I don't know. It must have been something," I stubbornly insisted.

"No. It was nothing, believe me. They lied to you for the same reason that they lied to everyone: they were afraid of the truth."

"But why?"

"I don't know, Kate. I do know that they were afraid of the truth."

"If the truth were that I were a Jew," I slowly said, "I would be proud of it."

"Why?"

"I just would be. I've identified with Jews since I was a little kid. Several times I thought seriously about converting. Shit. In one sense I already was what I wanted to be; I just didn't know it."

"In what way did you identify with Jews? By becoming a scientist?"

"God, that's a dumb question! Being a geneticist has nothing to do with being a Jew. I don't even know why I'm talking to you today." I had had it with therapy, with Renee, with every goddamned person in my life. To hell with them all!

"What scared you about my question, Kate," Renee persisted.

"Nothing, nothing! I'm not scared all the time, you know."

"But every time you've been hostile to me, you've been scared."

"Who's being hostile? It was a dumb question, and I can't cope with dumb questions right now."

"Why can't you cope right now?"

"Aw, Renee. I feel so confused. I feel fragile. A light tap on the head would send me flying into a thousand fragments. My whole world has been rearranged on me. I've heard of identity crises, but this is absurd."

"It is, but you've been having one since you were born. You can handle this," she reassured.

"I guess so," I said without any conviction.

"I know so. . . . Try to step back for a moment. Can you?" I nodded yes. "Good. You went to Buffalo because you wanted to get a sense of your father from his brothers. Learning about them would be learning about him. Well, now you know. Your father and his brothers lie; their entire lives are lies. For some reason that we don't know, their lives are lies. You have found out the central secret that eventually will explain what happened to you. You've accomplished a tremendous amount."

"But why couldn't Art have told me?" I persisted. "I wrote him and said that I needed to understand the family's past in order to make sense of what happened to me. Why didn't he respond?"

"He couldn't, Kate. Autumn wrote that his own girls were in their twenties before he could tell them. He couldn't do what you were asking him to do."

"Was I asking too much?" I asked, suddenly feeling guilty.

"Of him, yes."

"But I needed to know, he knew that."

"Yes, but he can't give you what you need. I doubt if anyone in your family can."

"Are my needs so great that no one could possibly satisfy them?" I fearfully asked.

"Normal people could and would. Your family is not normal, Kate."

"Renee! Do you know how it makes me feel to hear you say that? I feel terribly alone, cut off from everyone. How can I make it in life, with no family to help?"

"Small children need family help to survive. Adults can find the support they need from friends. You can do that, Kate."

"I haven't been so good at it so far. If I had been, I wouldn't be in therapy," I said, feeling totally defeated.

"If you hadn't been good at it, even as a child, you wouldn't have survived. You're very good at it."

"If you say so." I was beyond arguing.

"I say so. . . . Kate, we've got to end now. Don't do anything until I see you again. Don't write anyone in your family, don't call anyone. I'd even be careful about talking to friends about this right now. You and I have a lot more work to do on what you've learned. Okay? Come here, I want to give you a hug."

Chapter 27

"So what's been happening, Kate?"

"It's such a mess, Renee," I said, wanting to dump it all simultaneously. "Last Friday when I got Autumn's letter, I was so excited. Really excited, really happy. My grandmother was still alive. I could see her. My father was a Jew; that meant I was a Jew, even if not by Jewish law. I was delighted to be a Jew. I had guessed right and caught the bastards in their lies. I was almost euphoric. By Monday, when I saw you, I was furious. My family had stolen my heritage from me. Their act of theft had resulted in the confusion that I've suffered for years. Maybe if my father had remained who he was, instead of living a lie, maybe he wouldn't have gone crazy and I wouldn't have been battered. Maybe the only reason he beat me was that he had gone crazy from the stress of living a lie."

"Maybe," she responded slowly. "But maybe only someone crazy would try to deny everything that they were."

"Okay. Your point's well taken. Anyway, I'm still angry and I'm still confused and I still don't understand. How could they have done that? My father was an Orthodox Jew; then he became a Methodist and completely hid his past. That's crazy."

"Yep," Renee said smiling. "They don't come much crazier than that."

"Maybe my grandmother wasn't crazy at all. Maybe she was just appalled at what her husband and sons were doing, so they had her committed. Maybe she flatly refused to go along with their scheme, so they had to get rid of her."

"Or," Renee cautioned, "maybe they were so ashamed of her craziness that they went into hiding. It goes both ways, Kate."

"Yah, but Autumn said that she could have lived with them in the early fifties, but Nat put her into a nursing home. She couldn't have been crazy then; maybe she never was crazy."

"Maybe," Renee said non-noncommittally.

I looked at her closely. "Why are you defending them, Renee?"

"We don't have enough information, Kate. We don't know what happened. You're trying to make them into bad guys who victimized your poor sweet grandmother. What comes next is that you can rescue her from their evil clutches. You're repeating the family pattern with a vengeance."

"You're right," I laughed. "I've gotten caught by that. I've had all sorts of fantasies surrounding my grandmother. I was going to be a comfort to her in her old age, make up for all the pain she's suffered at their hands. She was going to rescue me by telling me the truth. She was going to teach me how to be a Jew."

"So you're their victim, too."

"Yep. But look, that pattern exists in my family because people do hurt each other. To stop the hurt is a normal tendency."

"It is," she said with a nod, "but you can't stop it."

"What am I supposed to do with the information, then," I asked in exasperation.

"Instead of having expectations that she can rescue you or you can rescue her," Renee said, "you could decide that you simply want to get to know her. She might not be very nice, you know. Remember that you weren't too fond of Nana. Let's say you rescued her. You stole into the nursing home in the dead of night and helped her climb out the window. You escaped back to your house. Now suppose she turns out to be a horribly nasty old lady. They do exist, you know. Aren't you going to be angry about all you did for her? Wouldn't it be better if you simply got to know her first, before you go to all that effort?"

By that time we were both laughing at the ridiculous picture she had painted. "I gotcha! First I get to know her, then I rescue her if I like her."

"When? How?"

"Writing is no good, I have to see her. I can't drive to Ohio until next summer because of the kids and work. I'm going to try to find someone in town who will teach me Yiddish so I can speak to her."

Renee looked surprised at that. "Do you think you can learn enough Yiddish to make it worth the effort?"

"Sure. I'm pretty good at learning languages rapidly."

"Now what about everyone else? How are you going to deal with them?" she continued.

"I'm not sure. I could write them, I guess, and tell them what I've learned. I could ask them to help me understand."

"Your father too?"

"No, not him. I can't deal with him right now. You know, before I got Autumn's letter I sent him that letter full of questions. I didn't know what I was asking. He's going to think that I knew all the answers when I wrote it. He's going to be very mad at me, Renee."

"Are you scared?" she asked.

"Yes. My nightmares have been horrible. They're filled with men trying to shoot me. I've been sleeping in ninety-minute segments, then I'm awake for a couple of hours."

"How much sleep in total?" she asked with concern.

"The maximum is about four-and-a-half hours. When I awake at night, I'm terrified. The dreams are really bad, Renee."

"Do you want to go into them?"

"No. I'm too afraid right now. If I can get some more information, understand why they did what they did, I think that the dreams will stop. I'd rather spend my time trying to end the dreams than to spend it exploring them. I know what they mean now."

"Okay," she said, "but I'm here if they get to be too much. . . . Who do you want to write first?"

"I already wrote Autumn. I thanked her for telling me and asked her for help in understanding."

"Kate, I told you not to do anything until we had talked about it!" Renee was looking very exasperated at me.

"Well I did it."

"But why?"

"Autumn and I are okay. I'm not going to mess up anything with her. Besides, I'm not a baby. I don't need your approval on everything I do."

"You're not a baby, but the way you're sitting right now suggests a rebellious teenager." Her eyes were twinkling. I looked down at myself and saw what she did: slouched, feet sticking out and crossed, arms crossed on my chest. I could feel almost a pout on my face.

Laughing, I said, "I'm progressing, at least. I used to act like a baby in here. In a couple more years, maybe I'll make it to my twenties." Then we both laughed at the way I was behaving. "I shouldn't have written Autumn, you're right. *Mea culpa*, and all that. But I've done it, and I'll live with the consequences. I may complain about them, though."

"I'm sure you will, but it's okay. Kate, I'm not sure that you really fully know what you're dealing with in your family."

"I don't. I'm confused."

"I am too, but not in the same way," said Renee. "We've got to go very slowly and very carefully. You've been having a toxic reaction to some of the things that have happened. I'm not trying to protect your family, I'm trying to protect you. If you hadn't said no to writing your father, I would have. I don't want you to endure unnecessary nightmares and extra anxiety. I think that you can handle anything that happens, but there's no sense in moving too rapidly so that you get extra pain out of this. For a while, would you please turn over responsibility for the pace to me? Right now I'm a better judge of your fear level than you are."

Renee had never before asked me to give up responsibility for the pace. Always, it had been me who set the pace of therapy. I had been the one who decided on each new step. I didn't understand 'toxic;' I did understand that she was worried. I was afraid, horribly afraid. So I agreed to let her determine the 'when' of each new step for a while. "What' was my responsibility, though. The 'what' I wanted was to write Art, and she agreed that I could try over the weekend.

Into the midst of this emotional turmoil dropped three letters from my father. His lies were continuing and I felt as if I would burst if I didn't do something, anything, with the anger that was overwhelming me.

DUBOSE MORTGAGE COMPANY
Our Investments Will Earn You More Than Will
The Sweat Of Your Brow
August 1, 1978

Dear Daughter Kate:

Your welcome note of 7/17/78 received via the Pony Express, but as is not unusual in my business, have not had a moment to get to this reply of mine until today.

The news about you and husband Joe being divorced is not pleasant to contemplate especially when two lovely children such as you have are also effected, but I trust that you and Joe decided as best will in time prove to be beneficial to all concerned.

Having finished your postdoctorate does that make you a Ph.D. and in what?

Glad to hear that you and Spenser had a month's visit together giving you a greater insight into each other's merits (?) etc. You did not state just what he is presently involved in as a goal, permanent or otherwise. When I read that you needed to know me, that you have no sense of me as a real person, I questioned whether that could be accomplished by me if I prepared that which is commonly called a resume. Outside of that which would be prepared for a prospective employer quoting dates, incomes, ambitions, etc., an uninteresting compote of statistics, to really tell you all that has occurred since my birth in Chicago about one hundred years ago would require many hours to relate. Incidentally, after graduating from high school (four years completed in three) I wound up in phase one of my peregrinations at the age of fifteen and one-half as a assistant strawboss on the Sugar Loaf Dam and Tunnel in 1927. When I quit that job I came into New Haven, had a haircut and shave, bought myself new clothes to replace my working ones, then took off, winding up in the Hawaiian Islands for three years. Left there for San Francisco with a motorcycle, later caught my first ocean liner as an able bodied seaman, traveled the world considerably including the Far East, then wound up in Brazil where I stayed about three years, then anticipating getting married to my employer's daughter number three, I returned to Chicago and my parents for a final visit there. That trip to Chicago and circumstances there prevented my return to Brazil. (But Peggy said that you bummed around the United States for several years. Mom said that, too.) Sold out in Chicago, so with my Dad and younger brother Art moved to Buffalo leaving my other brother Nathan in Chicago where he preferred to stay. Next I worked as a criminal investigator for the New York Banking Commission, then later for a group of attorneys plus in my spare time as a detective. Entered the Army in March of 1942 as a private, worked up to a Staff Sergeant in five months, passed the IQ test with a mark of 145, entered Officers' School at Fort Knox, graduated from there with a score higher than 13,000 previous officers (so I was told by the General who pinned my bars on that morning) making me a second Lieutenant. In Holland or Belgium won a battlefield promotion to first Lieutenant during combat; also won medals. Had my name picked out of a hat entitling me to a vacation to Paris where several others and myself spent five days and five nights. A day or so after our return from Paris I was wounded, taken somehow to Liege, Belgium, then on to a big hospital in Wales. Prior to my being wounded our battalion colonel had made me an acting Captain, promised he'd promote me to a Captain, but after being wounded my papers for same never came through. In 1956 where I flew to eventually meet my present wife May, I also by chance met said Colonel, a big oil man. We wound up at his private club, he, Spenser and I, and during our quite long stay with him at his club, he stated that he had really goofed back in Germany where I'd been wounded, ordering us all to button up our tanks. I disobeyed his order during the tank attack at night, did not button up my hatch, and thereby was blown out of the turret, to live. But when I wrote him and his superiors after being hospitalized, due to my brain damage, did not know what really happened, how or where I had been wounded. Said Colonel having investigated knew just how, told me I had been blown out of my tank turret, the other four men dying in the same tank. (But Mom said that you drove a stolen jeep into a tree while drunk. They were going to court martial you.) He also said that he had put in for a Silver Star for me but that I got only a Bronze Star because I got injured.

By the way, I never knew wife May until 1956, long after divorcing your mother. In August of 1957 Spenser and I after bidding goodbye to your mother and you started our drive to California and after several days we arrived in Menlo Park. The day we arrived I got myself my new job and a place for us to live; we ate all our meals outside except for breakfast which I prepared each morning before Spenser left for school and I for work. I worked at this job for several months, left and took work with a company in Sacramento, and the second company transferred me to Sacramento. Early in 1958 May and I re-united, started going fairly steady then in July she agreed to marry me, which we did in Carmel. Spenser and I moved to Sacramento, followed by May a couple of months later after she completed a job in San Francisco. Then we moved into a leased house as large as two railroad cars until we would become acclimated and satisfied that we were going to stay in Sacramento. Eventually we chose a lot, bought it, had our large beautiful home constructed in which we still abide. May practically designed its construction and every morning I inspected the work being done according to plans and specifications, after an architect drew the plans.

As stated above, shortly after my return from Paris I went into a night attack with my company of tanks in Germany, was blown out of my tank turret, then much later I inadvertently learned that my back from brain stem to and including my coccyx were broken and otherwise severely damaged, plus my right kidney ruptured then necessarily removed. Then after all those years of pain and incompetency to do any hard work (even though when we all lived together in Royal Oaks I was compelled to take out large garbage cans full of ashes from the basement weekly with neither your mother or your half-brother Mike ever offering to help; later I even scraped and painted the exterior of our two-story home with again NO help being offered or given; even had to come down the ladder in order to get a drink of water or fruit juice for myself), in 1974 my left side and shoulder started becoming paralyzed. After a myelogram in San Francisco my doctor told May and I that I required two operations. In December of 1974 instead of May and I going on a several weeks' vacation as we usually do in December,

I submitted to an operation from my brain stem downward twelve inches. It was predicted that by the following February I'd be free of pain (and to this date I am still NOT free), so when I last met with the doctor in February, he denied being able to relieve the pain and I refused to go through the second operation which would have been on the small of my back. May stayed with me at the hospital every minute of my stay there, from the initial wait of nine hours following my operation (the time in operating room and recovery room). They even supplied her with a bed in my room and she had it decorated in more beautiful and expensive fashion than any room ever was for anyone. Since then as I promised May in the hospital, I work shorter hours than before; from 10 A.M. to 3:45 P.M., five days per week, taking pills galore three times each day. I would have been dead long ago were it not for May and for how constantly she looks out for me. Used to love working hard in our gardens front and back which contain about 250 various plants which she and I have installed, but now she will not even permit me to pull a weed. May, a housekeeper and gardener do all the work, the latter two being barely effectual as help usually is.

May and I have always loved animals. She would just love to have a donkey. We've had as many as seven golden-mantle ground squirrels and one large, gray squirrel in our living room (of all places) at one time. Also purchased a baby, white rabbit for May one Easter and she raised it. Before Peter passed on he was about 13 pounds in weight, followed her around as would a dog, barked like a dog while mimicking our lovely Siberian husky dog which May originally bought for Spenser. We always feed the raccoons in Yosemite Park with food May saves up for them and the bears, in our freezer. I would NOT shoot a bird or animal except if my life depended upon it. (Would you kick a dog to death?)

This has taken me about a week to write in my spare moments and though I originally planned on re-typing it in order to look better I do NOT have the time to do so. Now you have a fairly comprehensive resume of my life. Much detail has been left out, but the highlights should give you a much better indication of what I have experienced. Drop me a line or two periodically so that I can follow your progress.

All my very best to you.
Your father, John

...

DUBOSE MORTGAGE COMPANY
Our Investments Will Earn You More Than Will
The Sweat Of Your Brow
8-30-78

Dear Daughter Kate:

Your's of August 19th. received. Warm and friendly though it is, I am puzzled by the seemingly text-book-list of questions asked. I have no qualms about answering them, as I have nothing to boast over or hide, after I have heard from you again in answer to this note. That which I take into account is Spenser's last visit in 1974, his most critical unfriendly manner. Then his complete lack of concern and also interest following my telling him I was going to have a myelogram taken then afterward be operated upon. Since then, no word from him to either ask about my welfare or to ask if I even recovered.

Were I to answer all your questions as I intend doing as stated above, after hearing from you again following your receipt of this from me, I am fairly certain that my information will differ from what you were told by another, now gone (Mom?), or from that which you may have concocted somehow, by yourself(?). Whatever the differential or how it could affect you bothers me, as I do not wish to brand anyone as this or that, or hurt you in ANY way. And there is this thought as well: how, what and why did your therapist bring you to this point in time. I have no idea what he accomplished.

Many years prior to my father marrying my mother, my mother's father deserted her mother and a total of five daughters (my mother one of them). There was no welfare forthcoming in those days and years, no child support, nothing but the absolute need for my mother's mother to go out to work at menial tasks, having no talents developed for anything else. Throughout all the years I spent at home, not one word of anger or other emotion was ever spoken by my mother; no mention of her father was made at all by her. My father once, long ago, briefly mentioned it to me without rancor. You, though never deserted, built up an anger against me because of information, what not; probably a lot of misinformation, even though I regularly sent you gifts (still unacknowledged), regular monthly support payments, and letters while you were still at home with your mother, and they were not answered by you. Really a puzzle that ever defies solution considering your unbridled and unwarranted anger towards me. Until now, when I hope and pray it may have finally abated. Do not wish to bring up anymore of the past, as that can do you hurt and possibly worse.

Would appreciate some clarification from you, Kate.

You mentioned remembering a period in our family's life during which money was in short supply. During my sojourn in the Army as an officer, I sent (allotted) two-thirds of my pay home to your mother after having left several thousands of dollars before I went overseas. She did not go out to seek employment as most servicemen's wives did, possibly because her only talents when I met her were as an insurance typist for her father Bert's business friend. (But she had two babies to care for!) During my incarceration following our move from Flint to Detroit, she obtained a job (?) with the Army because of being an officer's wife. Upon my return from overseas to a stateside hospital, she had saved but $50.00 out of all I had left her, then later sent her. That is why there was a period of short money supply. Let me hear from you soon, Kate, then we will take it from there. Okay? Your Dad,

John

. . .

DUBOSE MORTGAGE COMPANY
Our Investments Will Earn You More Than Will The Sweat Of Your Brow
9-22-78

Dear Kate,

It is almost a month since last I wrote, and no word from you yet. I am I believe much busier than you; still I find time for you. Your check list, so I said, is about the kind of list I too would make, and so I understand you.

Just do not be angry, answer me, for I have never stopped or even hesitated loving you. I can and do remember much about you, dating back to your first return home after delivery, my washing your diapers in the bathroom on my knees in Flint, my bathing you in Royal Oaks. *(The warm water slaps against my chest as I lean forward to push the blue and yellow tug just a little. I laugh at its bobbing motion, then smile up at him. He is sitting on the closed toilet lid. He smiles back at me, then kneels next to the tub. His khaki-colored shirt sleeves are rolled above his elbows, his man's arms covered in black, curly hair. He leans forward and fishes out the wash cloth and the white, gooey cake of soap as it floats on the tiny waves.*

He takes my hand and helps me to my feet. Then he soaps the cloth. Gently, he washes my neck, my shoulders, and under my raised arms. I shiver once with a slight chill. The cloth flows soothingly across my chest and belly. It strokes my back. It begins to caress my pee-place, and I freeze. "It" is going to happen again. No, not "it!" I can't let that happen again. Never, it is too horrible. And then I start screaming. Hands clenched, arms stiffly at my side, head thrown back, I scream in terror.

He rocks back on his heels, hands holding cloth and soap extending over the tub, a look of puzzlement on his face. My shrill screams echo in the tiled room as he shrugs, then begins rapidly to rinse me off. Quickly, then, he lifts me and stands me on the shaggy pink rug next to the tub. As he wraps a towel around me, my screams stop abruptly. I look at him, silently wondering what the word is for "it.") Love you, Kate. Please, no anger and answer me.

Dad, John

Chapter 29

During those days I would have been lost without Renee. She kept me from acting blindly out of uncontrolled anger. She reminded me again and again that people do only that which they are able to do. Had my uncles been able to talk to me about their history, they would have. What Art had not done for me he had barely been able to do for his own daughters. Renee helped me to define my goals and begin to move toward them in such a way that I would not block myself from what I wanted.

I had two primary goals: I wanted to see my grandmother and I wanted more information so that I could begin to understand what had happened. I began studying Yiddish with an Chassidic rabbi so that I could speak with Anna. Information could only be gained slowly, through gently teaching my family that they need not fear telling me the truth. There were five potential sources of information: Autumn, Art, Nat, my father, and a second cousin named Belle, also in Buffalo, of whom Autumn told me. I wrote them all, except my father. Renee helped me write some of the harder letters to make sure that my anger was kept out of them. She checked all of them before they were sent to make sure that I had not said anything that would scare or offend.

I wrote Art of what I had learned and from whom. He wrote me back about the weather. He said that he and Peggy had had some good hot dogs, with all the trimmings, and seen a friend's boat. He made not one reference to my letter.

I wrote Nat, and he didn't answer.

I wrote Belle, and she didn't answer.

I wrote Autumn a letter of thanks for revealing the family secrets to me, and she wrote back a letter filled with anger at me that had me completely confused. I wrote her again, and she didn't answer.

I called Spens and told him what I had learned, and he got angry at me for disrupting everyone's life.

I called my old neighbor Con and told her about the astounding facts that I had learned, but she wasn't surprised by them. She had known since 1952, when my mother had told her. She had always assumed that I had known them. I hung up even more angry at my mother than I had been before. She had had the key to my confusion and never given it to me, not even when I had wanted to go to Israel. Months later, though, another interpretation of my mother's silence occurred to me. Bill had been haunted by the concentration camps. Before Mom began dating Bill, she had spoken several times to me about Judaism. Never once after she married Bill did she talk to me about Judaism, however. Perhaps, together, they had decided that it was dangerous still to be a Jew. Perhaps they did not want me to be emotionally linked in any way to the camps. Maybe they decided to protect me from what I was. I had had two fathers, not one, who couldn't talk about Jews.

Since Nat, Art, Belle and Autumn would not tell me anything, my father was the only possible source of information. It took Renee and I over a month to write the letter to him. We were sure that he would answer it.

He did not answer.

Chapter 30

"What is it, Kate? You look terrified."

"Another flashback," I managed to get out. "No . . . it's not a flashback. It's . . . it's a picture. I see a little child, Renee." Right then I could go no further. I looked at Renee and knew that I had pleading in my eyes. Maybe she could find a way for me to tell her what I was seeing so clearly.

"Okay. Take it easy, Kate," she said. "You'll be able to tell me. Let's get your breathing calmed down first. Take a deep breath and let it out slowly. . . . Good. . . . Do it again. . . . Good. Now, once more. . . . Can you sit down?" As she gave me instructions, I could feel myself beginning to gain some control. "All right, now. You are seeing a picture of a child. What are you seeing?"

"She's about four. She's standing with her head thrown back, screaming silently, arms rigid at her side. There's a white glaring nothingness surrounding her."

"Do you know who she is?"

"No, no I don't," I answered with growing panic.

"Slow down, Kate," Renee coached. "Close your eyes and look at her. Have you ever seen her before?"

"No, Renee. I don't know who she is. She's so scared!" I could feel myself right on the edge of panic. I stopped then and took several slow breaths before continuing. "I-I would like to h-h-help her, Renee. I want to. Help me to help her. Please."

Renee picked up an empty chair and moved it right in front of me, then she sat back down next to me on the couch. "Okay, Kate, the child is sitting in the chair in front of you. Try to tell her how you feel."

I tried but there were no words. I looked up at Renee pleadingly again. She gave me an encouraging look and then looked back at the chair. I, too, looked back at the child. I wanted to reach her, comfort her in some way, but I didn't know how to do it. Feeling like a total failure, I burst into long racking sobs.

When I became aware of Renee speaking in an hypnotic fashion, I began to focus on her words. "Someday you will be able to help her, I promise. Someday you will know who she is and what she needs. Someday, she will be able to stop screaming and relax and smile at you. You will be able to help her someday, I promise. Until then I will take care of her for you. Can you trust me to do that for her?"

Of course I would. I would trust Renee to take care of any child who needed help. That's why I had brought this one to her.

. . .

"What is it, Kate? You look terrified again."

"It's another picture, Renee," I wailed. God, when would they stop? For two weeks now I had been haunted by them, one right after another. What did they mean? Where were they coming from? Becky would be back from her summer in Atlanta in less than two weeks and I was in no shape to give her what she needed. I had to get myself under control very soon.

Renee actually smiled at the news that yet another picture was filling my vision. "I bet it's another child," she said, her eyes twinkling.

"How did you know?"

"A lucky guess. All right, Kate, let's hear about child number two. Can you tell me?"

Caught in her casual mood, I actually smiled back at her as I let my eyes unfocus and gazed at the inner picture. If Renee wasn't worried by what my mind was doing to me, there was no reason for me to worry.

"I see a child of eight standing with her back to me. Her head is bent and her shoulders are slumped." (Hey! This is getting almost easy!) "In front of her is a huge dark judge's bench. At the bench there are one and two, alternatingly, adult forms with no detail. They flicker in and out so fast that I can't see them." Finished with the description, I looked back at Renee and smiled.

"Good, very good, Kate. You're getting to be a pro at this. Let's make it a little harder this time. Can you tell me the feelings in the child?"

That *was* harder. I narrowed my concentration to the picture again and, very surprisingly, I felt what she was feeling. "Shame, sorrow, isolation, desolation, abandonment . . ." I looked at Renee, amazed at what I was doing. "There's something else, Renee. It's strange. There's a sense of about to go into exile."

Renee looked thoughtful for a moment before asking, "How can you help her best?"

"I-I think . . . I think that she needs someone beside her so that she knows she's not a-a-alone, Renee. I think I c-c-can do that for her. No matter what she has done, she sh-shouldn't be alone in front of the judges." I turned my attention back to the child. Then I walked up to her. I tried to take her by the hand and walk out of the room, but I couldn't budge her. It was as if she were rooted there. So, I joined her. I turned her around and held her for a long time. Then we both faced the judges, side by side, my arm around her, our heads up.

With Renee's next question, the picture and my mood shattered. "Who are the judges, Katie?" The child was alone again, her head and shoulders bent again.

Shaking my head in sorrow at what had just happened, I softly answered, "I don't know."

"Why is she standing in front of them?"

"I don't know."

"When she goes into exile, what will that mean?"

"She will be kept from all people," I said slowly. "No one can get near her. That way, she won't be able to hurt anyone again."

"How long are you going to remain in exile, Katie?"

"It's not me!" I screamed at Renee. "Don't say it's me. How could you? I'm not in exile, she is!" This was it, it was finally it. I quit. No more therapy, no more stupid questions, no more getting upset about dumb pictures that didn't exist anyway. "I quit! I have had it with these games. Mail me your bill. Good-bye, thanks, so long, have a good life!" With that I got up and ran out the door.

I ran for nearly three blocks before my panic was exhausted. Then I sat on a stone wall, gazing into the distance, seeing nothing. Then I slowly dragged myself to my feet and back along the route I had just come. Then I walked into Renee's office again and she put out her arms to me.

. . .

"You're as white as a ghost, Kate. What happened?"

"Nothing, Renee, nothing. It's what's going to happen," I said in despair. "I've been holding a flashback at bay for almost two hours. I don't think that I can hold on much longer, Renee. Can you help me, please?"

Renee took my hand and led me to the couch. I pulled my thighs to my chest and rocked back and forth while I waited for her to settle next to me. "Shush, you'll be all right, Katie. Take it easy, Little One. Tell me what happened."

"I was seven. Our family was eating. I was sitting at one end of the table, my father at the other. Mike was to my left. Mom and Spens, in his highchair, were to my right." Having set the scene, I shook my head, trying to force myself to go on even as the static picture changed into one of motion. Now the task was to keep up with what was happening. "Suddenly, my father is standing. He's going to attack me again, Renee! Hold me tight, please!" I could feel her arm go around me, but she was so far away that she almost wasn't there.

"Mike is quietly pushing his chair backward. He's trying to put a barrier in my father's way without him seeing. Mom's hand tightens on the rolling pin that she has in front of her on the table. Spens is crying now. His eyes, Renee, they're so huge. I feel as if I can't move, he's paralyzed me with them. He's coming, coming, oh, god, why doesn't he move fast and get it over! He's coming so slowly, Renee! He slowly pushes past Mike. Mike falls forward onto the table slowly from the blow. My mother just sits there, watching. She isn't doing anything but watching, Renee! Why won't she help me?" And then I was screaming without words. Somewhere, I knew, Renee was holding me, keeping me unalone. Without her, I couldn't have continued to exist. I was close to fainting. I put my head between my knees and tried to block out the horror in my mind.

Later, as Renee gently rocked me, she asked if I could remember what had happened when my father reached me. I couldn't.

"Are you feeling strong enough to try something new, Kate?" I nodded yes. Anything was worth trying once. The film was on an endless loop, showing again and again with no pause. I had to cut it.

"Okay, then," she said. "I want you to bring Big You into the picture." I looked up at her as if she were the crazy one this time. She smiled. "Go ahead, do as I say. Have Big You step into the dining room."

Almost laughing, I closed my eyes and visualized myself stepping into the room. Immediately as I did, I could feel the seven-year-old's eyes swing to me. Beneath her terror, a flash of hope passed over her face. I flexed my muscles in a clowning manner, and she smiled, she actually smiled! When I nodded to Renee to indicate that I had done as she had asked, she said, "Now, I want Big You to stop your father. Stop him, Kate, any way that you have to."

I looked at Renee, totally confused. "No one can stop him. He's too big. My mother didn't even try."

"You, Big You, can stop him, Kate. Do you have a gun? You could shoot him."

"No! No! I won't kill him! Don't make me do that," I begged.

"Then find another way, Kate. You must not let him hurt you again." Renee's voice was like iron. "What about a knife?"

"No! Not that way either!"

"Then find your own way, Kate, but stop him."

"There is no way, Renee," I pleaded.

"Find a way, Kate. You are an adult, your child is about to be hurt. Stop him."

"I would have to kill him. I can't do that. He's too strong just to stop, but I can't kill him. Don't tell me to do that, Renee, please don't. I can't kill my father. I already did once. Don't make me do it again. Please, Renee, don't make me do that again. He can kill me, it's okay. I don't mind. Let him do it. Really, it's okay. Don't make me kill him again, please!"

"Find a way to stop him, Kate."

"I can do it without killing him maybe. Please don't make me do that. There must be something I can do." Frantically trying to avoid killing, I flew at him, knocking him down. He got up. I knocked him down. Over and over, he got up and I knocked him down. Then I picked him up by his feet and swung him so that his head smashed against the wall. I smashed him and smashed him against the wall, without hurting him, until my child was convinced that I would never let him hurt her again. Then I carried him to the front door and threw him outside, gently.

When I had rested from the fight, Renee asked me why I had refused to kill my father. Still exhausted, I dragged the words out of me. "I couldn't kill him because I love him." Renee gasped and, when I looked up at her, I saw tears running down her face. I didn't understand, but I accepted her extra hug with no questions. In fact, I almost burrowed into her as I sought to get closer.

Still later, she asked me if I could summon up the picture of my four-year-old. I did. She was still standing with her head thrown back in a silent scream.

Then she asked me why I had said that I had already killed my father once, but I couldn't answer that question because I didn't know why.

. . .

Later that night, I checked the picture of my child and it had finally changed. The soundless screaming had stopped, the white glaring nothing was gone. She was sitting on the floor, with her knees drawn up to her chin and her back to me. I couldn't get her to turn around, I didn't know how to reach her, I couldn't even begin to guess at her emotional state. Before it had been stark terror; now, I didn't know where she was. A change had occurred, but what?

A few days later the picture changed again, this time without me doing anything to make it change. She was facing me, about five feet away. I couldn't see her face because her head was hanging down. She was just standing there, looking alone and sad.

That night I awoke from a dream and found that the picture had changed yet again. For the first time she was definitely a little girl. Until then she had been almost sexless. There were details in the picture now. She was wearing long heavy braids as I had when a child. I asked her if she wanted a haircut, since I had longed to get rid of the weight of my hair as a child, and she answered with a weak smile. She was about four and had fat cheeks. She was wearing a white shirt with ruffles at the neck and dark green corduroy pants. I finally recognized her: not surprisingly, except to me, she looked just as I had. The image of her was so clear that it superimposed on my real vision for several days.

For nearly two months the picture stayed unchanged. My child was five feet away. Sometimes she would smile, mostly she looked very sad. I tried everything I could think of to bridge the gap between us, but nothing worked. Then one night in late October, I was thinking about the imaginary fight I had had with my father. I remembered that Renee had gasped and cried a little when I had said that I loved my father. As I remembered her crying, I felt the love again and started crying myself. It came and it went very quickly but it caused a drastic change in my child. She smiled at me, her eyes twinkled, and then she ran to me. I held her for a very long time, and then we started playing together. Four-year-old me has been with me since that night. Sometimes she gets angry at me still, but she hasn't gone away again. Mostly we play together; when she needs it, I comfort her.

. . .

My eight-year-old child, the one who stood in front of the judges' bench, was nearly as difficult to reach as the four-year-old was. She stood, with Big Me beside her, in front of the bench for nearly two months also.

"Renee, I can't get her to move, to pay any attention, to listen, nothing. She stands there, feeling terrible about herself."

Renee nodded, indicating that she knew that the child was still there. "Do you have any idea what she has done?"

"Don't ask, Renee, please. I can't say it."

"Does your other child know?" I nodded yes. "Do you think that she could tell me?" When I shrugged, Renee continued. "Let me talk to your child, Kate." I looked at her. That child would tell, I knew it. The question was, was I ready to deal with what would happen then? Taking a big breath, I nodded yes again. It was going to have to come out sometime.

Speaking as if to a young child, Renee asked what it was the older child had done. Even while I could feel the resistance building in me, I began talking. "She planned to kill my father. She had it all worked out." When she said that, I burst into tears.

Taking the Kleenex from Renee, I continued. "I-I knew th-that I couldn't . . . kill him with a knife in self-defense, when he was angry and could over-power me. I had to be able to g-get v-v-very close to him before revealing what I was going to do if I were t-to succeed. That m-m-meant I would have to pre-pretend affection and . . . then, then stab him as he h-held me. I was eight b-b-but the plan would have w-w-worked because I knew enough to predict that a non-angry father would open his a-a-arms to me." That was as far as I could go without taking a crying break. I could feel deep shudders of self-revulsion ripping through me.

Then, from somewhere I could hear Renee's voice. I focused as much as I could. "Kate, I asked you if you ever tried your plan. Did you?" I shook my head no. "You never actually tried?" Again I shook my head in negation. "Then you aren't guilty, Katie. No court in the land would find you guilty."

A rush of hope went through me, until I remembered. "You don't understand. I didn't try because Mike came up with a better plan." Despair washed over me. "Mike and I met in the coal bin in the basement. He was the one who first mentioned killing. Honest. But I remember that I felt relieved to learn that he had come to the same conclusion as I had. I told him my plan, and then he told me his. His was safer so I agreed to it," I said in total shame.

"What was the plan?"

"Every June Joe Bruster, the policeman who lived across the street, went on vacation. I always took care of his dog. If we could hold out four more weeks, then Mike could look for his gun. Mike was sure that he wouldn't take it on his vacation."

"And?"

"My father was picked up by the police before Joe Bruster went on vacation," I said in anti-climax. "His doctor was convinced that he had planned to kill us all that night with the stolen gun. Murder must have been floating through our house."

In sadness beyond tears, I stared at the floor. "You did not do it, Katie," Renee repeated.

"Yah, but I would have. I was just lucky. For all intents and purposes, I killed my father. I know that I am capable of murder, I've known it since I've been eight."

"Kate, listen carefully. I have to ask you some very important questions, and I want you to hear me." I nodded okay. "Kate, how long is the average murderer kept in jail?"

Puzzled some, I answered, "I don't know, maybe five years."

"And then his debt to society is fulfilled?"

"Yah, but I wouldn't want to live next to him."

"Why?"

"Because someone who has killed once can never be trusted again."

"Kate, is that why you have kept yourself in isolation for over 24 years?" Her question was like a blow in the stomach. My god, that's exactly what I've done to myself! When I could nod yes in reply, Renee continued. "If you had killed him and been convicted, you would have been in jail five years. Because you didn't try to kill him, only thought about it, you have kept yourself in jail for 24. It's time to come out, Kate. You've more than paid your debt."

. . .

After that hour with Renee, I began two months or more of reading everything that I could find on the concentration camps. I didn't know why I felt the need to do it, especially since immersion in that literature was one of the most depressing things that I could have chosen to do, but it felt necessary. Had Renee known, she probably could have gotten to the reasons very quickly, but I kept that from her. Whatever it was that was driving me, I had to deal with it myself.

Finally, one day in January I understood what I had been reading and why. Everything I had read had emphasized the passivity of the Jews in the face of extermination. At the same time, there had been long descriptions of smuggling operations in the camps, organizations that sprang up in every camp in order to help people, attempts at Treblinka to ensure one survivor who could tell the world what was happening. People refused to die, which was one way of fighting back. The Jews had tried to help each other, had tried to warn the world of what could happen when hate became too strong, they had not been passive at all. They had fought in the only way possible given their situation. Even the parents who had walked with their children quietly to the chambers had fought in their own way. They had calmed their children, knowing full well what lay ahead of them, and in so doing had prevented their children from dying in terror. They couldn't stop the killing, but they did remain protective parents to the end.

When I realized that passive Jews were a myth, when I realized that my identification with Jews came out of a fierce longing for protection from the death that had swirled around me as a child, a great weight lifted off of me. Self-protection had been part of the Holocaust, I just had not consciously recognized the form it had taken, and it somehow legitimized my own attempts at self-protection when I had been eight. This time, Big Me and my four-year-old walked up to the child who stood before the bench. Both of us held her, then all three of us turned our backs on the judges and walked out of the room.

Chapter 31

11-17-78

Dear John,

Now it's my turn to write it: it's been six weeks since I wrote you and still no response; aren't you going to answer my letter? You don't have to answer my questions. Please, just write. I want to hear from you in a way that I've never wanted before. Please write.

Kate

. . .

DUBOSE MORTGAGE COMPANY
*Our Investments Will Earn You More Than Will
The Sweat Of Your Brow*
11-27-78

Dear Kate,

Trust and hope you and your two darlings are well, shall enjoy the Christmas holidays to the fullest. Am preparing this card and many more during the third week of November as I have to each year to keep pace. Since your note of 9-25-78 asking me to be patient, I have NOT received a word from you. (You haven't received two letters from me? How dumb do you think I am?) I feel that after having waited over a year recently, much longer before that, I can continue to wait. Whatever, I hope it shall NOT be upsetting to

205

me, as my health is not worth talking or writing home about in any respect; that very bad.

Your Dad, John

. . .

12-8-78

Dear John,

From your Christmas card it's clear that you did not receive a letter I wrote you during the first week of October. In it I explained why I had asked you all those questions. I also told you that I had been in contact with your family and why. Since I have a copy of that letter, I could send it to you again. Should I? You say that you're sick and don't want to be upset. My letter will probably upset you some, but it will also make clear that I want to establish a new and better relationship with you. Please let me know your answer.

With love, Kate

. . .

DUBOSE MORTGAGE COMPANY
Our Investments Will Earn You More Than Will The Sweat Of Your Brow
December 12th, 1978

Dear Kate:

This morning I received your's of the 8th. Had intended initially to write this longhand but changed my mind. I change my mind more frequently than most women are accused of doing. Why not? Just now I was interrupted by a phone call from a friend wanting to advise me that he is no longer with a large mortgage company doing mortgage-banking; also wanted to wish me all the best for the holiday season, and to get together afterward to talk business.

To get back to you - no, to date I've not received your letter written as you say, the first week in October. That is not strange at all with our pony-express-post-office's-services. I have received checks from here in Sacramento ten to 14 days late (I service monthly, most of the loans I make) and it has been necessary to charge the trustors late charges. My terms in the promissory notes that I prepare stipulate that payments must ARRIVE in our offices by certain dates; that postmarks or dates on checks are not honored by us. At times payments are also lost.

As to sending a copy of the above-mentioned letter - forget it. I have a feeling that I do not want to read it's contents, and that feeling is quite strong. I have often thought that if I had followed my hunches most of my life I could have retired very wealthy before I became 50 years of age. This is such a hunch.

Pleased all to h--- and back that you express your desire to establish a new and better relationship with me. Also over the fact that it has been more than twenty (20) years that you have signed yourself, "With love". Were you before me, I'd say that you still need a spanking; a little one, anyway. (You bastard! You goddamned bastard!)

John

Chapter 32

"I understand, Renee, and I've remembered so much more. Do you want to hear?" I asked anxiously.

She smiled at me. Of course she wanted to hear.

"I remember everything now. It came back last night. I remember my grandmother's call and the horror in my mother when she learned that my grandfather was planning to shoot my father. I remember the drive to Mom's parents' house, my mother talking all the way about it. She and my grandmother sat and talked. He was a foolish old man to think murder solved problems, he was crazy, out of his head, had lost his mind. Besides, he was dying in his back bedroom, didn't he recognize that? It was a horrible thing that he planned to do. And then my mother went into his room and forced him to give her the gun. They buried it in the back yard. They buried the bullets in the front yard. And all the while, it never occurred to either of them that I was there, hearing and seeing everything.

"After they took the gun away from my grandfather and buried it, they had tried to talk me into going to see him. I refused to do it, and then he died three days later. So I never saw him again. I remember being afraid to see him. I knew that he would be dead soon. He hadn't been able to kill my father because he had made the mistake of talking about it. He had also waited too long, until he had nothing to lose by doing it. Anger? Mom and my grandmother had been horrified by what he was going to do. Fear? Yes to them both.

"I remember riding in the car with those same two. They were discussing Chuck, my mother's brother, and how he must not know what my father was doing to us. Chuck would have tried to kill my father, which couldn't happen. It would be horrible. It would destroy Chuck's life. It would destroy all of us. No one could know because they might tell Chuck.

"And then the police came because my mother wanted them, but she sent them away as soon as they came. So, I had to do something because there was no one left to help. Do you understand? I didn't want to do it, I had to. It was the end, there was no one who would help save us, no one at all in the entire world. He was going to kill us and there was no one to help. Please, do you understand?" Renee nodded yes.

"I think that I was invisible during those three weeks between the time my mother took the gun from my grandfather, my grandfather dying two days later, my father killing my dog, and when he was hospitalized after stealing that gun. I heard everything and no one remembered that I was a child. An hour after I was told that Bert died, I was in school. The next day I was sent to Chuck's house for three days while everyone else went to Hamilton for the funeral. When I got back, my dog was dead.

"I think that's when I decided that something would have to happen. When the police were sent away, I decided to make it happen. He had killed my dog. He would kill us. My grandfather had been more right than either of those two women. I would just have to live with what they would think about me, because I wasn't going to let my father kill all of us. While I was thinking those things I was staying with my grandmother. Mom said that I had to comfort her, but I couldn't. For the first time I see that Mom was trying to protect me, maybe, from what she thought would happen at home. Except, she brought me back home again.

"It was maybe two days after Mike and I met in the coal bin that my father was picked up by the police. He was going to kill us all! I had been right, Mike had been right, but what we had planned to do . . ." for the first time in my recital the tears were flowing. But I was determined to get it all out, for once and forever. "Then I overheard Mom and Con talking about what the psychiatrist had said about schizophrenia: it was hereditary. Because I had planned to kill, I had inherited it. I had to watch myself from that point on. If I failed to do so, I'd become like him. I couldn't forgive myself for my plans, because then I might stop watching myself. I had to be careful, so very careful, for the sake of everyone around me. I had to protect them from me."

Chapter 33

By mid-November I had been ready to try again with my father's family, just as I had tried with him. I wrote Art a chatty letter, saying nothing, and he responded in kind. We kept that up until March, when I casually mentioned that I was studying Yiddish. He didn't answer any of my letters after that.

I felt cut off, excluded from my family. I gave up on everyone for a while and concentrated on trying to learn Yiddish, trying to make sense out of what I had learned and trying to calm down.

All that fall I read only about Jews and Judaism. I was trying to reach some understanding of what my family had given up and why. If I could understand how they must have felt, then maybe I could shrug off the sense that they had made their lives a lie in order to do well financially and socially. If the pressures on them had been intolerable, then I could forgive them for the hurt their decision had caused me. Unfortunately, the more that I read, the more I saw their acts as cowardliness.

One of the things that surprised me was the way other people reacted to what I had found out about my family. Some were fascinated; others could not understand why I wanted to learn more and see my grandmother or why I felt angry. The message from the latter was definitely that I was overreacting to basically unimportant things. Perhaps I was overreacting, but what happened was not unimportant to me.

Another, even more surprising, reaction was specifically related to Judaism. While most people interacted with me in the same way as before, some immediately changed their response to me. A few people with whom I had been fairly close, within the limitations of a work relationship, withdrew noticeably over a short period of time. For instance, I had been car pooling with a woman in my lab for over two years. She was divorced also and had children about the ages of mine. For two years, our families had celebrated Thanksgiving and other holidays together. Within a week of my telling her about my family hiding their Jewishness, we stopped sharing the ride to and from work. Each day she came up with a different excuse for not riding together the next day until it was clear to me that she never wanted to ride with me again. And, in the lab, she grew increasingly distant until I gave up trying to be anything but polite with her.

Others, Jews, seemed more warm towards me. Avi, for instance, was an Israeli postdoc in the lab who responded to my story with deep sympathy. He offered help, at any time, in such a tactful manner that he forever endeared himself to me. "Judaism is like a big lake," he said. "You can walk around it, dip into it a little or fully. Much of what it really is, is hidden. To know it fully, you must submerge yourself in it. I'd advise just getting your feet wet at first; save submersion until you are very sure that that's the way you want to go because it will change you forever." His wife, whom I had not met up until that point, called and invited me to supper, and Becky and I soon became part of their extended family. We were invited often, and Becky quite frequently babysat for their two boys.

Overall the response to my having a Jewish father was rather subtle, but it was there. I had thought that antisemitism was a thing of the past; I learned that antisemitism and anti-goyism exist.

For my part, I must admit that I gradually changed the way that I saw people, also. As I integrated what I had learned and learned more about Judaism and Jewish history, I shifted more and more to feeling Jewish. With that shift, for the first time in my life I began to see the world in terms of us and them. By late spring, I realized that I no longer found non-Jewish men attractive and that it had been several months since I had dated a non-Jew.

Part of my shift in viewing the world undoubtedly came from my intensive study. Certainly, as I read everything I could find about the Jews of Odessa and learned that the Nazis had gathered them together in one place and poured gasoline on them, I wondered how many of my family had burned to death that day. However, I think that most of my shift was due to the many years when I had felt unconnected to the world; at last I had a place.

It is ironic that, for most of recorded history, being Jewish meant to have no place and not to belong and that the place I was beginning to find in the world was with those who have no place. It is only recently that I have recognized this additional link with Jews that I had had since I was a child. I, too, had had no place in a dangerous world. As a young teenager I had wandered the streets at night, looking at families through the lighted windows of the houses I passed, longing to belong. When I returned home it was out of tiredness or in retreat from the cold; it was not to return to my family. By moving toward Judaism I was joining the Jews, finally. I was also joining all those unknown people from whom I came who also had wandered through the world with no place of their own. I felt strongly linked to them, whoever they were. Someday, I would find them.

As I read about Judaism, I had to begin considering the concept of God. When I was seven or eight I had concluded that all of religion was a bunch of nonsense. Religion was the way people avoided confronting their unimportance and aloneness. Not for me were those false comforts; I was alone in the world and had better keep that in mind if I wanted to survive.

With Renee I realized that such dogmatic independence was my response to my father's abusiveness and my mother's lack of protection. I had learned that I could not count on those whose job it was to protect me. In fact they were the source of my danger, and I feared trusting in anyone except myself. If I trusted no one, no one could hurt me.

The problem was that those attitudes almost resulted in my emotional destruction. The isolation in which I had lived had been nearly as extreme as had been my isolation from my father's family. As I began to give up isolation as a self-destructive protection, I became more open to everything. It's not that I began to accept everything that I had previously rejected; rather, I became better able to reconsider previously rejected concepts and ideas without fear as a barrier to understanding.

. . .

In New Haven the only place I could find to study Yiddish was at the Chabad House, which is an Chassidic study house established by the Lubavitcher Rebbe. It was located in a flat above a popular men's clothing store just off the Yale campus. I talked Avi into joining me in studying Yiddish.

"This is aleph, the beginning. It was the first sound that God, blessed be His Name, made as He was about to create our world. The sound is like an English short 'a'. Aah. Say it, now. . . . Good. That is aleph, with which everything began. Now, look at it closely. See how the lines flow? Aleph is especially beautiful. It stands on two points, like feet, all by itself. It comes from nowhere, it points to nowhere. By itself it stands, complete, needing no other letter to make a beginning.

"This, now, is bet. The sound is like an English 'b'. Bet flows from aleph, it has its back to it, and is open to all the other letters of the alphabet. It is a very sturdy letter, it rests firmly on its broad base. Meaning could hide inside of it and be safe. Can you see what I mean? Say it now, slowly. Good. With aleph, the beginning, you have not really entered into the alphabet. It stands alone. But once you begin with bet, you have truly begun. The only way is forward now, through to the end."

With a charming intensity, Shmul led me through the Yiddish alphabet, carefully characterizing each letter for me. It was clear that he knew each intimately, had pondered its shape and size, tried to tease from it the significance of what it was. They were holy letters to Shmul.

To me, they were the pathway to Anna, along which I wanted to run just as fast as I could. Barely controlling my impatience, I nodded and smiled as Shmul slowly taught me the shapes and sounds. Somewhere along the way, though, much to my surprise I found that I had favorite letters, just as Shmul did. Lamed, 'L', was one; shin, 'S', was another. Their lines, their sounds, they fit together beautifully. They were a pleasure to draw. Soon, I too was lost in the letters, my sense of urgency forgotten.

Avi stared at me in amazement as I got caught up in the letters. He knew them all, of course, since Yiddish and Hebrew use the same script. His amazement came, I think, from watching the developing rapport between Shmul and me. Avi and I had worked together for two years at that point. We were close friends. He had seen me depressed, ecstatic, exhausted, joyful, overwhelmed, triumphant, but he had never seen me caught up in mysticism. Neither had I, and it was only afterwards, as I walked to my car after the first lesson, that I began to chuckle to myself about what had happened.

Shmul, our teacher, began to intrigue me. He was highly educated. He was filled with curiosity about the work Avi and I did, asking many questions and going one night after class back to the lab with us, just to see it. "And what does this do?" he asked, pointing at the gigantic model E centrifuge used to characterize DNA. He probably did not follow the explanation, but he was fascinated. He was amazed to see cells growing in culture, he hadn't realized that they, like his holy letters, had different sizes and shapes. The cells, just like his letters, could be combined in different ways to create new meanings. He marveled at all that he saw, asking question after question.

At the same time that Shmul was entranced by modern science, he was garbed in the clothes of an Chassidic sect that denied evolution. His broad-brimmed black hat, his beard and ear locks, his buttoned white shirt with no tie under his long-coated black suit, all that he wore said instantly to an observer that nothing fundamental had changed since eighteenth century Poland.

Shmul was more open to the world than I would have guessed before I came to know him, and I was more open to him than I would ever have believed possible before I came to know him. I watched Shmul closely, at first intrigued by what I saw as contradictions in him, later amazed by his ability to compartmentalize what did not fit with the Chassidic world view. Whenever those views were threatened, his highly trained mind turned itself off and clung to magic and mysticism. How he was able to exercise such self-discipline I never understood.

Avi and I made slow progress with Yiddish at first. Avi had no trouble with the letters, obviously, but the language itself, with its medieval German syntax, gave him a great deal of trouble. The learning was from English, of course, which he did not speak that well. I had no trouble with the language because at one time I had been close to fluent in German, but the letters seemed impossible at first, as did learning to read from right to left. Eventually, though, I mastered letters and direction. From that point I took off, far out-pacing Avi because I could lean so heavily on the German I retained.

To my delight, I found that Yiddish was like German set free of its rigidities. To my despair, I found that Yiddish destroyed forever the German I still knew when I began. I could speak and read one, or I could speak and read the other; they were too close to each other, though, for me to retain both without constant confusion. So, for Anna, I gave up German.

As time went on, I found myself more and more able to enter Shmul's world for the duration of a lesson. I grew accustomed to the fact that he always glanced obliquely at me, never did our eyes meet. Automatically, eventually, I kept the proper minimum distance between us. I learned not to offer my hand to him. Still, what happened one night told me that I actually knew very little about his world.

It was a cold February night, with sleet in the process of changing to snow. The wind from the Sound moaned about the building as I climbed the dark stairs to the second floor, waved to Shmul sitting in his office and walked into the darkened classroom. Finding the light switch, I proceeded to shed my layers of clothes, stomp my feet to get my circulation going again and blow on my numbed fingers to warm them. Then I sat at a table reviewing the lesson, determined to read aloud without error for the first time. I had studied the passages for hours during the week and was anxious to show off how much I had improved.

It was a long while before I became aware that Avi was very late and class should have started at least fifteen minutes earlier. In fact, it was not until Shmul came to the doorway that I emerged from the lesson.

"Is Avi coming, Kate?"

"I saw him just before I went home for supper, and he said he'd be here. He hasn't missed a lesson yet."

"Okay, I'll do some work while we wait."

Again I buried myself in my book. Having thoroughly studied the assigned work, I moved on to what we would cover in class that night. A little advanced exposure never hurt. Some time later, Shmul again brought me to awareness.

"He's not here yet," he said, stating the obvious.

"Nope. Shall we start without him or wait some more?"

"We'll wait. I have some phone calls to make."

Once more I lost track of time in my book, once more Shmul eventually interrupted me. "He's not here yet."

"No, Shmul."

"He said he would come?"

"Yes."

"We'll wait. It's time for my prayers."

This time I did not return to studying. It was about four hours past the time for Shmul's evening prayers, even I knew that. I looked at my watch and was amazed to see that class should have ended twenty minutes earlier. Shmul obviously didn't want to teach tonight.

Closing my book with a sense of uncertainty, I dressed for the mini-blizzard outside and walked to Shmul's office, where he sat reading. A bit puzzled, I said that I'd see him next week. I was almost at the bottom of the stairs when it hit me, and I barely contained my laughter until I was out the door and a few steps from the Chabad entrance. Shmul couldn't sit alone in the same room with me, a woman, and he was too embarrassed to tell me that.

Again and again, Shmul and I experienced culture clash. Since I was in the only flexible system, I learned to adapt to him and to be more sensitive to his rules. That was as it should be, for I was the one who was drawn to his world, not he, despite his curiosity, to mine.

Chapter 34

"I've been thinking about all I've learned, Renee. I've been trying to put it all together in one coherent picture. Do you realize how well my mother fit with my father? It's horrifying almost."

Renee shifted in her chair and gave me an encouraging smile. We were into the third year of working together. After so many hundreds of hours of talking, there was much that no longer needed to be said between us. By the tone of my voice she could tell that I had entered one of my periodic reflective states again.

"My mother, my mother, she was such a child. Once she said to me that she didn't begin to grow up until her father had died, and she was so very right about that." Poor Mom. During the last year of her life she still felt guilty about my father's commitment. She had told me, had I loved him more and put him before you children he would not have behaved as he did. She never realized that the situation had been hopeless from the start.

"Come back, Kate," Renee said. When I looked up at her I gave her a quick smile before continuing.

"It's okay. I was just thinking that I'm glad Mom died before she understood what she had done."

"Why?"

"She never realized that she always put my father first, that she had never considered us. She thought that Mike and I, and even Spens, had come through without any scars. I'm glad that she didn't know the truth because I don't think that she could have survived the knowledge of what she did to us."

"You're no longer angry at her," Renee said, stating the obvious.

"That's right," I said with a self-deprecating smile. "I have every reason to be, of course. Her role in what happened to me was huge, but she didn't know and she didn't understand and she didn't intend for it to be that way. She thought that she was being a good mother. And, when you get right down to it, she had been so damaged by her own childhood that she had no chance."

Renee looked thoughtfully at the floor. Then she raised her head and looked directly at me. "Once you said that understanding saps your anger. Is that what is happening?"

Sighing, I responded. "I guess so. She's guilty as hell, if you want to be legalistic. I don't want to be. I'm glad that she's dead because if she were alive, I would be continually newly angry at her for things she would do and say. She's dead, though, and it's time to stop being angry." (Mom, I love you despite what you were and did. I can't forgive you, but I can put it all to one side. That, I do because I love you.)

Renee handed me a Kleenex. "Anyway," I said through my tears, determined to convey to Renee what conclusions I had come to over the weekend, "she fit perfectly with my father. They were made for each other. No marriage could have been better."

"What in the world are you saying?" Renee had a surprised, almost startled look on her face.

I laughed. "Don't worry, I haven't flipped out. Look, Chuck told me all about his family, remember?" Renee nodded. "Here's what I see in that information now. My mother was adored by her father and hated by her mother. Right?" Renee nodded again. "They played a game, those three. Her mother, Nana, verbally attacked my mother. Then her father, Bert, jumped in to rescue my mother. Then Nana attacked Bert verbally, and Mom jumped in to rescue Bert. Sometimes Chuck got to play Mom's position. Then, Chuck was adored by Nana and Bert hated him. They simply reversed the direction of their circle. Unfortunately, when Chuck played there was physical, instead of simply verbal, abuse."

"And?" Renee encouraged me, a look of almost fascination on her face.

"Around and around they went, and my mother arrived at adulthood dizzy from eighteen years of the family game. Don't you see? My mother had learned three roles, all of them sick. She was her mother's victim, and so she felt badly about herself much as I had concluded that I was bad because my father beat me. As her father's rescuer she had failed and felt guilty, just as I did when I failed to stop my father from beating her. Her third role you could call 'the bad guy' because, having failed to rescue and having concluded that she was bad, she deserved everything that happened to her. She had learned three roles, she had learned that parents involve their kids in their fights and she had learned that child abuse is something to be tolerated."

Renee continued to look very interested in what I was saying. "Where does this take you, Kate?"

"My mother came to my father with three interchangeable roles, a son, a history of two failed marriages and, I suspect, a horrible fear of failing yet again. She had to make it work this time, don't you see? My father beat her during the first year of their marriage, before he went off to fight in Europe, she said that herself. Any normal person would have used his absence to break away psychologically, then get a divorce. But my mother couldn't." I stopped talking for a moment. My poor mother, I felt so sorry for her then. "While he was gone," I continued with a sigh, "she set me up as the victim she would eventually rescue."

"How do you know that?" Renee interrupted.

I smiled. Reaching down to the floor I picked up my purse and withdrew an ancient envelope containing photos. "These are pictures of me at six months. The handwriting is my mother's and they are addressed to my father. Don't bother with the pictures, read what she wrote on the back."

Renee took the envelope from me and extracted the photos from nearly thirty-five years ago. With a tone of discovery she read my mother's words. "Kate refused to behave for this one." "Kate raised hell in this one. My posture is horrible due to her struggles -- sorry, sweet." "Kate was so devilish she wouldn't stand still -- her perpetual state of being -- devilish and not standing still." Renee looked up at me with amazement in her voice. "Where did you get these?"

"My Dad, actually. He sent them to me when I was twelve, when he declared me not to be his child. I don't know why I kept the envelope, too."

"Why didn't you show these to me when we were looking at your family pictures months ago?"

I could feel a half-smile on my face. "I was too ashamed. I didn't want you to know that I was bad at that age, even. Please don't be mad at me."

Renee gave me a smile to indicate that she understood, then turned the photos over, looked at the pictures, turned them back over and re-read my mother's words. I knew what she was thinking because I had gone through the same process myself. "You look like a normal, active baby to me in all these. It's strange that she labeled your behavior so negatively. Not one of them says anything nice about you." She looked up at me and I nodded in response. "You're right, Kate, she was setting you up as bad."

"Yah," I said, feeling a wave of bitterness for a moment. "When my father got home from the war, my parents began to play the family game. This time, however, the roles were more rigid and very much more dangerous. My father became the consistent bad guy. Mom and I took turns being victim and rescuer. Mike got to fill in for me some, but not Spens. He was left out of the game in the same way that my mother's youngest brother, Tom, was. Child abuse was unpleasant but tolerated, just as it had been when Mom was a child. My father was insane, but my mother showed him how to act while insane."

I could go no farther right then. Unsuspected tears flowed once again. This time I was so deeply mourning that I no longer knew exactly which loss was racking me.

Renee gave me the time I needed before responding to what I had said. "How far back do you think this game went?"

"Do you mean generations?" Renee nodded yes. I shrugged, then tried to find a verbal answer. "It's funny isn't it. I'm a geneticist and I'm discovering that roles are also part of the inheritance of each child. Who would have thought that? I could draw a pedigree for the inheritance of violent behavior. It's an autosomal dominant, with high penetrance and variable expressivity." Feeling the irony, I was quiet for a few moments.

"I don't know for sure, though. On my mother's side, I think it came from my great-grandfather. On my father's side, who knows? If my mother chose my father because she could set up the same dangerous game with him, the game that was so familiar and felt right to her, then he must have chosen her for the same reasons. I don't know what my father learned from his family but I suspect that he knew the game already."

Renee looked thoughtful before asking me to continue. When I said the key was that his family was Jewish, she smiled to herself in an indication that she had guessed correctly. "Antisemitism is the reason why I think my father knew the game. I think that my father knew how to play the game because his family had internalized society's view of the Jew. Jews were evil, dangerous, non-human - bad guys, if you will. They seemed to threaten majority society everywhere. So they were victimized. Ultimately, what I experienced as a child was due, in part, to the interaction of Jews and non-Jews for the last twenty centuries."

Then Renee asked, "What happened to the rescuer? You've left that role out."

"I'm surprised at you, Renee. Didn't you ever study any Jewish history? No one ever rescued Jews."

Chapter 35

DUBOSE MORTGAGE COMPANY
Our Investments Will Earn You More Than Will
The Sweat Of Your Brow
February Eight, 1979
RE: In answer to your's of August Sixteenth, 1978

Dear Kate:

To begin with, in your's of Dec. 8th you say you have been in contact with my family. Whatever you have been told I do not know or care. This much I do know, that being the first and oldest son I was 'privy' to much information that the two younger sons may not have been, as you are now being my oldest child. So now I shall answer your's of 8-16-78 as written by you.

I noted while growing up that my parents spoke with an accent, so when I reached the questioning age I asked my father what he and mother spoke other than American. He replied, "Russian." Later on, a month or year, whatever, I asked if they were both Russian born. He told me he had lived and grown up in what later I identified as Chaumont, France, and Antwerp. He also said that mother had been born in Odessa, Russia. That he, Dad, had an uncle who became a doctor (physician) in the then Czar's court (a thoroughly Russian Orthodox Catholic court which did not countenance 'anyone' other than a member of that church), another brother living in Turkey, another in Constantinople, another who lived in South America, two uncles in Paris running a ballet school.

Dad was one of thirteen children. Bilingual? - I know a smattering of five or six languages; spoke Portuguese fluently once. Methodist? - According to a Reverend James Story I know here in Sacramento, who was in my office about ten days ago renewing friendship and wanting to know if I could arrange financing for a 2nd Methodist church for him, both France and Belgium have many Methodists. College? - Yes, I wanted to be a physician all the time I was growing up. Had four years of Latin, two years of German, two years of Greek, and in High School which I started at twelve, physics, chemistry, even Calculus. My mother's over-protectiveness caused me to leave home. How long a sailor? - Long enough to between Oct. 1930 and Dec. 1933 see Northern Africa's Cairo, several, other cities there, then return towards South America, jump ship then wind up in Belem, aka: Bahia, Brazil. There I remained for almost three years working as a labor boss on a tobacco ranch. Met your mother at Crystal Beach, Ontario on a dance floor accompanied by her parents and Mike your half-brother. After I became an Army Officer we married in Yuma, Arizona. She and Mike lived in Palm Springs, with me training on the desert with General Patton's Army.

Yes, I was changing jobs when we moved from Detroit to Flint, then to Royal Oak, for then I became the business manager for U.S. Gypsum-Steel in Detroit. Moved all the way to California to get away from so much UN-happiness. May my wife whom I met almost seven years after divorcing your mother, the most lovely woman a man could ever hope to meet, has worked all her life, through choice and not through necessity. For many years as even now, works in Intensive Care and Coronary units. She's extremely competent, works only part-time and will probably retire this year, I believe. My brothers and infrequent contact? - True, for we have never been close, as we are so vastly different from each other. I have always felt I am their superior intellectually and worldwise. I say this without conceit! Recently read that many doctors feel that first children inherit that virtue genetically. Name change? - My Dad told me long ago that his name originally was -- DuBosee, that he "-cut off his tail" the final -e- and used a small -b- when he left Europe, landed in Montreal, then to Chicago, in order to

Americanize his name. When I entered the Army I used the single -e-, then had my name changed using a capitol -B- on the advice of my boss.

There, I have answered all of your questions as written by you. Briefly, because of time pressure, but as stated above, 'privy' only to you on the above and the following. In ALL my life I have never considered myself a Jew, never attended a Jewish temple, never married a Jewish woman, as did neither of my two brothers. (Oops, Dad. You forgot that you never received the only letter in which I mentioned being a Jew and Judaism.) May and I feel that Jewish people for the most part are extremely intelligent, industrious and successful; plus we have many fine Jewish friends in the medical profession.

Brother Nat is married to I believe a Hungarian and Art is married to a French-Canadian. As a child I was known as Jack by parents and all others. When young my Dad told me that my middle name of Stephen was Etienne in French. I accepted that which he told me, most of the time. When we all lived together in Royal Oak, one Sunday a.m. I stayed until Noon in bed. Came down to find all of you at dining-room table. Your mother asked me why I was so late and I answered "Because my back was so painful". To which she replied, "God damn - your back, you S. O. B. -goddam Jew." The only time I ever raised a hand to her was that Noon-time when I walked into the kitchen to where she had retreated, sitting in her chair. I took off her eye glasses, set them down, then slapped her across the face.

You have nothing over which to be concerned or ashamed. Though I have never presented to the world or its peoples, a forbidding facade, even though I have been in the past in places where life was rigorous and very demanding. Right now I am very tired from all this talking and explaining which I have never done before. Do you follow?"

Sincerely,
John

. . .

DUBOSE MORTGAGE COMPANY
Our Investments Will Earn You More Than Will
The Sweat Of Your Brow
March Twelfth, 1979

Dear Kate:

Very much appreciate your taking the time & effort to describe the facets of your life, with a bit thrown in about your two daughters, Becky with you, & Carole evidently staying with her father in Atlanta. Though fairly certain that you & Spenser undoubtedly posses some traits &/or characteristics of mine, you both appear somewhat enigmatic to me. Growing up, whenever I saw or knew something needed doing, I would deliberate briefly then do what I thought best, but right NOW. You two seem less deliberate in thought & action, preferring the leisurely approach to life. Time will, I imagine, prove who or which is right. I have long felt that life is too short - do it NOW! May & I both feel that I could live to be 100 had I not been so severely injured physically & emotionally

Several months ago when I began having severe back-muscle-spasms (not spasmodic but like giant cramps) we visited with the neurosurgeon in San Francisco who operated in December of 1974. Do you ever hear from Mike, your half-brother? I never have. In July of 1969 when I had the floral arrangement sent to Oakland for her funeral by the most outstanding & expensive florist in San Francisco, I did not know that Mike was in California. Though the phrases, Thank You or Thank you very much, are considered by me as the most obnoxious in the American language, I am still in doubt if either you or Spenser even saw it with both your names thereon, as neither of you acknowledged it to me.

You studying Yiddish - I can't understand why. Steve Allen the comedian, married to a dopey woman in my opinion (but HE loves her), is a fluent speaker of Chinese. Had I the choice & time, I'd learn either or both of Russian & Chinese. By the way, I knew Steve Allen when he attended Shurz Hi-school in Chicago at the same time I attended Austin-Hi.

(Three days later on 3/15/79)

My letter to you started 3 days ago - am jumping from one thought to another as the phone rings, people come in, etc. Cannot avoid interruptions of business &/or thoughts. Tell me, do you drink & smoke? I do.

Strange - you say you saw my family. I still do NOT care whom or whatever you may have learned from them; not even if you were impressed! I have not inquired of any of them, and none have advised me that you appeared before them. I shall not mention it to any of them. The only one with whom I have any contact is Art, the youngest brother. A few years ago he started his custom of sending me a birthday card with an innocuous little blurb inside, and so I have followed suit. Again I say, strange, the kind of world & people we have nowdays. Absolutely NO loyalty & all the other virtues that formerly were so prevalent in everyday life among family members. Some people just came in so will have to postpone my rambling from one subject to another, perforce.

(March 19th as you can see I do not have the time to complete ideas & - thoughts while letter-writing; that's our life-style)

From your statements I am compelled to think you have no positive goals to shoot for; possibly you have to wait for certain developments to take place before you can decide. Just as I am now waiting for an insurance company lender to call me back as regards a client of mine who is intending to build a new casino in Reno & wants to know if I can obtain the loan money for him. My question to you: would it not be feasible for you to shoot for an associate professorship you'd enjoy along with augmenting your present income, whatever it may be? As I see it, there are just so many productive years in most everyone's life within which to build up a, or for, a Trust Fund for the future. Of course, everyone must also build for one's personal life as well.

Love, John

Chapter 36

"Things are getting awfully complicated, Renee." I shook my head, marveling at all that was happening.

"What's happened now?" she asked with a slight smile on her face. Poor Renee was always being told of the minute details in my on-going personal soap opera.

"I didn't tell you before because we've been so busy dealing with that other junk, but there have been several shifts taking place. About a month ago, Spens called."

"And?" she prompted.

"And he was fascinated by what I have learned. He's no longer mad at me for upsetting everyone." Renee smiled again. She had predicted that Spens would get caught up in the script once he had absorbed the information about being Jewish. "He added something. In 1956, he and Dad drove to Buffalo before going on to California. While he was there, my dad asked his cousin, Belle, to marry him."

"Belle? Isn't she the one who has remained Orthodox?"

"Yes! No wonder she didn't answer my letter."

"No wonder is right. But, Kate, you've missed one implication. Your father had gone to incredible lengths to hide his Jewish background. Why would he want to marry someone who obviously was Jewish?"

"Don't ask me. Like everything else about him, it doesn't make any sense. Anyway, next Spens tried to do the same thing I'm doing with my father, get to know him. But, our father sent him a vicious letter. Here's a copy that my father sent."

...

DUBOSE MORTGAGE COMPANY
Our Investments Will Earn You More Than Will
The Sweat Of Your Brow
April 17ᵗʰ, 1979

Spenser DuBose
--------- Street
San Francisco 941—

Dear Son Spenser:
In reply to your's of March 12ᵗʰ, "it certainly being a long time", remember, that you & you alone are responsible for it being so. If June [his wife, who was a nurse] had ignored you in Fair Oaks [when Spens was seven] when you came down with Scarlet Fever (as you have ignored us) you might have died or become a permanent cripple in one or several respects. Instead she cared for you, cooked special foods for you including 3, different kinds of soup, tended you with medicines and such, anytime of day or night. If June had told you to 'go to blazes' when you later on wound up with an infected eye (or other type) tooth while you lived in San Francisco [as a freshman in college] you would have 'loved' that. Instead, she made you come home, arranged an emergency appointment, then drove you to Orinda where our dentist took care of you, and then she paid for it. Afterward, brought you home and took care of you with special foods, etc., until you chose to leave.
When your illegitimate son was born that you & his mother had, who drove to San Francisco where you lived, purchased about $200. worth of baby clothes for him, then delivered same to you there?, - but us. That is, before you both palmed the baby off to some other people who wanted him? Do you want to be reminded of many, other kindnesses that were bestowed upon you before & after the abovementioned? Remember, I 'never palmed you off' after gaining custody of you at 5 years of age. You say that you are, "-unsure of what I am thinking of you". Why do you pretend to be stupid, when I know better? Your last visit to me at my office during the summer of 1974 - - upon leaving I informed you of my critical, back operation

scheduled in November & December of 1974. Since then, not one word of inquiry as to whether I made it or not, not one word or contact at all. While at U. C. Moffitt Hospital June stayed in my room, never leaving it for 3 weeks; even had another bed installed, and during the Christmas holiday season she decorated my room beautifully. Can you possibly, with propriety, extend to me or June any palatable, extenuating circumstance which was reason enough to ignore us for 4 ½ years?

Your sister Kate, she of the onion-thin-skin must have prevailed upon you to write to me. During all my younger years I felt that life's span is TOO short. Unless a person is convinced of that AND is imbued with the <u>virtue of humility</u>, memory can become heavily burdened with regret & remorse. Ten years ago this coming July [when my mother died] I pleaded with Kate then in Oakland, to come see me. Afterward, June also plead with her, to no avail. Kate refused!!! To date Kate & I have not met. Since then we have corresponded sporadically. She 'has' done extremely well scholastically; a Phi Beta Kappa, a PhD., has a respected position at Yale. But sorry to relate, happiness as yet has not been accomplished by or for her. You too, 'could have excelled' in your field. We all 'could' have had so wonderful a relationship – maybe still can (?). As the Mexicans say: "Quien sabe"? I have absolutely NO intention of propelling you into a 'guilt-trip', but if we do not learn from the past, anyone's future can become very bleak, indeed.

Best Regards,
Dad

JD/with C.C. to Kate

...

While Renee read the letter, I tried to figure out how to respond to it. The tone had made me furious. Once again, I wanted to smash him for hurting someone.

"Whew, that is bad," Renee commented when she had finished reading. "Why do you think he sent it to you?"

I shrugged in disgust. "Only someone crazy can understand a crazy person. I don't understand what he's doing. He obviously thought that I would approve of it. I don't. It's one of the worst pieces of nastiness that I've ever encountered."

"It's possible that there's something beyond mere approval-seeking going on." Renee stopped for a moment to gather her thoughts. "When you were a child, you were all bad and Spens was all good to him. His last few letters to you have indicated that he is beginning to like you and that he may also be 'losing it.' If so, then you may be becoming the all good child and Spens, out of necessity, is now becoming the all bad child."

"Ah, don't talk that way, Renee. I don't want him to think I'm all good when he doesn't even know me."

"That's a symptom of his illness, Kate. What you want and reality will have no impact on what he thinks."

"Yah." She was right, no doubt about it. But I didn't want life to be this way.

"Right now, his attitudes are very shaky towards both of you. If you do anything negative, he'll try to find a way to reject you."

"I know," I sighed. "All I want is for him to leave me out of his viciousness."

"Then write him," Renee suggested, "and tell him not to send copies of letters he sends to other people. Don't respond to the contents of the letter itself, or you will get right in the middle of his attack on Spens."

. . .

DUBOSE MORTGAGE COMPANY
Our Investments Will Earn You More Than Will
The Sweat Of Your Brow
May 15th, 1979

Dear Daughter Kate:
In reply to your's of April 22nd -
Not having the leisure (?) time available that you seem to have I have decided to not keep pace with your long narrations, as much as I have enjoyed that which you incorporated in them. I do not have the time & patience; neither do I choose to become more involved emotionally for fear the stress & strain may do me harm. On Aug. 16th, 1978 you wrote at length asking many questions & after its'

receipt, from day to day I found a few minutes to jot down answers to all, to the tune of seven (7) legal-size sheets of paper. I never sent you that long letter. Then on April 22nd, 1979 (your last letter) after its' receipt I wrote two (2) legal-size sheets of paper; am not sending that to you either. There are a number of reasons for these conclusions, prime of which that I did not in any way desire to hurt you then, now or ever.

Have never considered myself a 'square' but, for more than ten years you have addressed me as, "Dear John" & that's a lousy pill to swallow. When Spenser addressed his envelope to me recently he did not show the good taste to write "Mr.", though inside he did start out by saying, "Dear Dad". Wonder if he will answer my last to him (?).

Have no desire to even appear picayunish & yet, though men can & do infuriate audiences by answering questions with questions, you on the other hand are typically woman by your ambivalence and only answering questions or speaking of that which you decide to do, ignoring all else. <u>Ambivalence:</u> you decry my mention of matters past as that which you either do not remember or care about (When?), & yet in your last letter you inquire about my home life as a child. I feel that TOO much time is (& has been) spent by either &/or both of us being critical, rather than being spent building rapport. Therein lies stress & strain for which (additionally) I care not one whit.

Recently my fine wife May after sensing my displeasure & yes, my frustration, after reading a letter from you, suggested that I fly to your home, see you & your two daughters, attempt to reconcile matters between us. After considerable thought I decided against doing that. Though I can be & occasionally am a tough business man, I can be most gentle, usually am (AND courteous) practically always to everyone. From your manner to me I deduce that gentleness, except to your daughters, is something I could not find in you. Long, long ago I learned that humility is a necessary ingredient in one's daily living. You know its' meaning, but I doubt that it is an integral part of your being. NO, I will not travel to see you, much as I so strongly desired to meet with you over 10-years ago at your mother's funeral. Had planned on writing but a short note, but it is so easy for written words to be misinterpreted, fearing just that, I have once again been too talkative.

Love, Your Dad or Father, but no more Dear John.

. . .

I responded that I was going to be in California that summer and would like to see him. His answer to that was he would see me if, and only if, I called him 'Dad.'

Meanwhile I had written Autumn, Nat, Belle and Art that I was going to Atlanta in late July to leave Becky for the rest of the summer, and then I was going to Canton, Ohio, to talk with my grandmother Anna. Could they please send me her address? The first three didn't answer but Art sent me an incredible letter. It was rambling, disjointed, full of bitterness towards everyone except his wife. He ended by saying that he never again wanted to hear from me.

Chapter 37

Becky and I set out for Atlanta in high spirits. She was looking forward to a month visiting her father, sister and numerous friends. I was looking forward to spending good time with Carole, many friends, perhaps Autumn and definitely Anna. Becky had taped her favorite records, mainly the Beatles, for the trip and we set off: Becky, her two gerbils, her dog Chien and I to the tune of "Let It Be." Perhaps I should have.

We'd made that trip so many times, five in the previous four years, that we had developed a full ritual around it. The first stop is always Stateline Park off the Palisades Parkway. There we walk Chien, gaze down at the Hudson River and over at New York City, while gathering strength for the hectic pace of the New Jersey Turnpike. Six lanes of traffic each way, roaring trucks, ugly sights, ugly smells: all are a shock to our senses. Becky, lying on the back seat with her dog, always retreats into music. I always retreat to my thoughts, leaving behind about twenty percent of my mind to watch the traffic.

My mind was on the girls and me during the first day of this trip. Superficially their anger at, and rejection of, me had looked exactly like my behavior toward my father. There was a difference, however: I had stayed with my kids, refusing to give up on them. Just as I had struggled to reach the four-year-old and the eight-year-old inside of me, so too did I struggle to reach the two children who had come from me. I was there day after hurt-filled day, refusing to give up, trying hard not to respond with anger from my hurt, trying to introduce some fun into their lives when they were determined to be miserable. My persistence had worked: we were now through the time of anger together. Becky and I were relaxed with each other again. Carole and I had our problems still, but they were diminishing. We talked at least twice a week by phone, we could laugh together again, and I knew that she was eagerly awaiting our arrival the next day. I was proud of myself for having changed my family's pattern of child-rejecting parent and parent-rejecting child.

After returning to New Haven, I had planned to fly to San Francisco to see my stepfather Bill, my brother Spens and my father. One day in Atlanta with Carole and I changed my plans. She was the one with whom I would spend my entire vacation. It was difficult to disappoint Bill and Spens. I felt only relief when I left my father a message with his answering service.

I called Autumn after I had been in Atlanta for a few days. She refused to see me and said that she had sent me a letter which said that she no longer wished to have anything to do with me. As for Anna, she would like to help but couldn't. Last September her nursing home had lost its roof in a tornado. Anna was unhurt but she had been moved to another home in Canton. Autumn did not know the address. Either she was trying to discourage me or she had given me a very good clue as to how to find Anna.

After two wonderful weeks in Atlanta, Chien and I set off for Ohio. He had to come with me because Becky would be flying back to Connecticut in the fall rather than being driven. I did not want the bother of a dog on this portion of the trip, but it turned out that he was a great comfort to me.

It was 95 degrees, the humidity must have been eighty percent, and the sun shone brilliantly. Although I grew up in Detroit, I had lived for nine years in Atlanta and had learned to love those hot summer days. In New England I often longed to feel the weight of the sun on my skin. I was in high spirits, full of self-confidence. I would find Anna, my grandmother. I wasn't going to be beaten by all those who were trying to keep us apart.

I went through Tennessee and Kentucky that day and did not stop until the outskirts of Columbus, Ohio. By the time I found a motel that would accept a dog, it was almost midnight, pouring rain, and cold. Chien was more than tired of being in the car. He had been whining and pestering me for hours and finally had turned to howling as only a hound dog can. My head was spinning from fatigue and hunger, but sleep won out over food.

Six hours later I was back on the road. It was a drizzly, gray day. Columbus to Canton cannot be done by superhighway, so the drabness of the day was more than compensated for by the interesting small towns through which I passed. I was ahead of my schedule and drove leisurely, playing my harmonica for company and enjoying my first time in Amish country.

The road into Canton, which was a far bigger city than I had imagined, took me right past the office of the local paper. I stopped. I explained that I was looking for the name of a nursing home that had had its roof torn off by a tornado the previous fall. At first the woman at the information desk said that no tornado had ever touched down in Canton. Then she remembered that a home had had its roof blown off by high winds three years ago. She made a couple of calls, got the name of the home for me and gave me directions.

As I approached the home I became more and more excited by what I saw. Two blocks from it was the Jewish Community Center. One block further and I passed a synagogue. Nat had made it possible for Anna to stay among people who were familiar to her! I had found Anna, and it had been so easy. Excitedly I parked the car, gave Chien a quick walk then chained him to a tree.

As I entered the home I was shocked. With all my thinking about Anna and with all my planning, I had not stopped to think about what a nursing home was like. The door entered into a huge room where very old people sat around the periphery in all stages of dress. Most were in wheelchairs; some were strapped into them. A television blared, and a few people were staring at it motionlessly. A couple of people were talking, one man was crying to himself. Some people rocked back and forth, muttering to themselves. Near the door an old woman, tied into her wheelchair, stared vacantly at the ceiling and spoke loudly to herself in Yiddish. I stared at her in horror, wondering if she were the Anna I had come so far to see. Was she Anna, my grandmother? For the first time I thought about the reality of fifty years of hospitalization and called myself all kinds of a fool for making the trip.

As I stared at the old woman in horror, a nurse came up to me and said that it was not visiting hours. I asked to see the director. I walked down a long corridor, with every room filled with sick and dying old people. At the end of the corridor was another big room like the first and, beyond it, the director's office.

I briefly explained what had brought me there, and she said that Anna DuBose sounded familiar to her. She checked through the current patient list but Anna was not on it. Together we checked back to 1970, but Ann's name did not appear on any list. Since I wasn't sure whether she would be registered under the right name, I then checked all billing statements back to 1970 for Art's or Nat's address. Nothing. Finally I had to face the fact that Anna was not, and had not been, at that particular home. It was not going to be easy to find her after all.

Chien and I got back in the car, but I didn't know where to go or what to do. If only I could have reached Renee, she would have helped me. But she was on a two-month camping trip, somewhere in Western Canada.

I drove aimlessly for a couple of blocks, then stopped in a shopping center. I could call Peggy, maybe she would tell me Anna's address if I promised not to reveal that I'd learned it from her. No one answered the phone. As I passed the Jewish Community Center again, I swung into the parking lot. Chien ran joyfully from tree to tree, and I followed slowly along behind with tears streaming down my face. Anna was beginning to die for me once again.

At the same time, I realized just how foolish I had been to get excited. I had forgotten that Autumn had said the home had been hit by a tornado last September and had settled for a high wind three years previously. I had forgotten Autumn's description of the home in her first letter as a converted old house and had settled for a low modern building designed as a nursing home. I wasn't thinking well at all. I had let myself forget my original plan of attack: to find a motel room, get a map of the city and use a phone book to plot out locations of all the homes before visiting any. If I continued on as I had been doing, I was going to end up badly hurt by this search. I had to stop feeling and start thinking.

Then it occurred to me that rabbis visit nursing homes. More important, I remembered the name of a rabbi whom my Yiddish teacher had said lived in Canton and also spoke Yiddish. At the time I thought that I was lining up a translator; now I see that I badly needed someone to talk with, that he was the only person in the city to whom I had any link at all, and that I trusted him to be able to guess what I was going through simply because he was a rabbi. The last was magical thinking, but it turned out that he was able to understand.

I called him from the Center, and he instantly agreed to help me. He suggested that I visit three nursing homes with a large Jewish population that were within blocks of where I was. I was to call him as soon as I did that and found a motel room.

As I got back into the car, I felt ten times better. I had someone who knew the city willing to help me, and that made all the difference. I was no longer alone. Chien and I visited the homes, but Anna was not at any of them. Then we checked into a motel that believed me when I said that he was a quiet dog.

It was still early enough that Art would be at work, so I called Peggy. Art answered, and I asked for Pam. I'd have to wait until the next day before phoning Peggy again. At that point, I looked at the phone book and discovered to my horror that Canton had a total of 45 nursing homes. I had visited only four of them so far. Obviously, I could not visit all of the remaining homes. I had to change my plans. Besides, each home that I had visited had taken its toll in hope, discouragement and self-confidence. I was getting close to an overload already.

I called the remaining forty-one homes and did not find Anna. At that point I got angry. Anna was somewhere in that town, all of the homes had said that she was not there, which meant either that she was registered under a different name or that one of my uncles had instructed the home not to give out information. Only Art and Nat definitely knew her location. Nat, because he had never lied to me and because he had not yet told me that he wanted nothing more to do with me, was the one I called.

Nat and I talked for less than five minutes. Basically, he said that he would not help because my years of silence indicated that I did not care about other people and he distrusted my sudden interest in his family. Then he hung up on me.

I felt fury first, then hurt. I had been a child when my father was hospitalized, and it had been Nat's place to contact me. It was the lack of contact that had made me conclude that neither he nor Art cared about me. Now he was blocking me for what was, primarily, his failure. That was one of the old family patterns: blame the victim.

A couple of hours later, I called Rabbi Spero. "Rabbi Spero? This is Kate Slaboda again. I called all the nursing homes and did not find her," I said in defeat. "Tomorrow I'm going to try my uncle one last time. I'm not very hopeful. In fact, I'm also planning to leave for New Haven tomorrow. I don't think that there's anything more I can do here."

"It's such a tragedy," he said with real emotion in his voice. "What they have done to you is terribly unjust. There's no excuse. Perhaps they've hidden her because she knows something that they want kept a secret. Maybe she's been trying for years to get something said."

I had thought the same, once, but I had dismissed the thought in fear. That's how someone who was paranoid would think, and so I could not let myself come to that conclusion. His saying it flooded me with relief. "It could be. All I want is to see her and talk with her."

"Is she Jewish?"

"Yes, I'm sorry that I wasn't clear about that. Both of my father's parents were at one time."

"Is your father *frum*?"

His use of the Yiddish word was like a lance. Had I been raised as I should have been, I would know what he was saying. "I'm sorry, I don't understand what you're asking."

"Observant."

"No. He hides his Jewishness. I just found out last year that he was a Jew. He was Orthodox once, though."

"And your mother?"

"No."

"You?"

"Me? I'm wandering. I don't know what I am anymore."

"Do you want to be a Jew?"

Each of his questions was like a blow, hitting at my confusion. "I don't know," I answered with profound discouragement. "I need more time to think. It's been a very confusing year for me."

"Well, Kate, call if I can help. Be well." More than anything else, his human response to me kept me from shifting back to the set of attitudes that I'd had when I first began seeing Renee: there must be something terribly wrong about me for my family to treat me this way.

. . .

The next morning Chien was missing from the room even though the chain was still on the door. I called him four or five times with growing panic before he gave an answering whine. He had crawled under the bed and was stuck. I had to lift up the corner to set him free. He was so delighted at our reunion that he began barking wildly, dashing around the room in his excitement. When the manager called to pass on complaints from the rooms on either side, Chien began howling at the phone's ringing as he always does. Thus were we evicted from the Holiday Inn.

After paying the bill, Chien barking all the while at people passing through the lobby, we went in search of breakfast. Then I called Peggy from a pay phone in the Holiday Inn lobby. Throughout the conversation people passed by, others made calls from the phones on either side and Chien, who was feeling mellow after a hamburger with all the trimmings for breakfast, tried to make friends with each person. In his overly enthusiastic way he would lunge forward on the leash with no warning, nearly dragging me away from the phone each time.

We must have made a strange sight, and we did judging from all the people who stared at us. I do not understand why the manager did not kick us out again. By the end of the conversation, several people were openly standing around listening to my half. One old woman came up to me, patted my arm and said that she was sorry. As for me, I was so immersed in what I was hearing and saying that I did not care if someone found it strange to see me crying on the phone attached by a leash to a dog who wanted to kiss the world.

"Peggy? This is Kate DuBose. I'm in Canton, Ohio, trying to find Anna. I've contacted the forty-five homes that are listed in the phone

book, but I didn't find her. Please tell me where she is. I promise that
I won't tell anyone you told me. I'll keep it a secret." Even I could
hear the desperation in my voice.

Her voice came back at me with gentle tones. She understood. "I
think that you had better talk to Art about it, Kate. He's right here."

"Peggy, please," I begged. "I don't think that he will talk to me.
He certainly won't tell me where she is. I'll call you back sometime
when he's not there."

"No, Kate. He's sitting right beside me and he'll talk to you. Try
him."

There was no choice. "Okay."

By this time I was crying, and I cried throughout my nearly half
hour conversation with Art. He repeated Nat's arguments of the night
before that my years of no contact proved I did not care about them.
He went a step further, though, and said that he thought I was out to
find an inheritance. How could anyone think such things of me?

Art asked me why I wanted to see my grandmother. He knew that
I had, after all, had a lot of contact with my mother's parents. Wasn't
that enough? "I can't give you a rational reason, Art. All I know is
that, from the moment I learned that she was alive, I have wanted
to see her. Knowing my mother's parents has nothing to do with
knowing Anna. She's my grandmother and I want to see her."

At one point, Art started to rant and rave about his two brothers.
They had treated him terribly. Nat had fired him, he was in the
process of filing for unemployment. Every now and then I quietly
said that I was Kate, I was neither Nat nor John. Then: "Why should
I help you? You're not part of my family. I don't know you, I don't
trust you. Even if you were part of my family I wouldn't help you.
I've learned that family can't be trusted. All my family is horrible. I
hate them all for what they've done!"

"I'm Kate, Art. I am not Nat. I am not John. I want to see my
grandmother."

"She's suffered enough. I don't want you to make her suffer
more."

"She's my grandmother, Art. I wouldn't hurt her. I haven't even
planned to introduce myself because my existence would probably

confuse her. I want to see her, talk with her for an hour or so, and then leave forever. I'd just be a stranger drifting through her life."

"Did you see Autumn?"

"No. She refused to see me. I did talk with her once on the phone. She said that she didn't know Anna's address."

"Autumn was lying. She knows exactly where Anna is. Even if she had told you, it wouldn't have done any good. I wrote the home and told them to deny her existence to all inquiries. She's not in Canton, Ohio, Kate."

"I know, Art."

"She's in Canton, Illinois." He hung up before I could say anything.

Art had given me what I had asked for, and I was stunned by what he said. Autumn had lied to me in her first letter, all of them had let me take a long trip that they knew was useless, they had taken extreme precautions to make sure I would never find Anna, or Art had just lied to me. Someone had lied: either Autumn from the beginning or Art just now. Autumn's lie, if it were one, was a gratuitous lie which made no sense; she could have said nothing. Art's lie, if it were one, made more sense because I was pressuring him tremendously and it was a way for him to end it. I believed Art despite the implications.

I loaded Chien into the car and headed towards New Haven. I cried for at least a hundred miles as I mourned the loss of Anna and thought about what had been done to me. Nothing made sense in any way.

As the day and miles passed, the beauty of Pennsylvania began to penetrate. Chien and I had a picnic, then a short nap, by a small lake surrounded by mountains. When I awoke we played for a while before getting back on the road. As we entered New Jersey I decided to try to spend the night at the home of some friends who lived very close to the road I was on. I didn't want to be alone.

I stopped to call Penny and David, and they said I was more than welcome if I didn't mind the floor. Penny didn't explain the floor part, but I realized why when I entered their house. Sitting around the *Shabbes* table were their three children, the Vietnamese woman with her two children who lived with them, Penny's brother and his girl friend, and an Israeli couple with their two kids who were visiting for two weeks. Seven adults, seven children and three languages were more than enough to get my mind off myself. We ate, sang and talked for three or four hours, and it felt so good to be in that healing atmosphere after what I had just been through.

Awaiting me when I got home was Autumn's letter in which she responded to my request for Anna's address. It had a Buffalo post office stamp on it and the envelope had been folded in half. She had mailed the letter to her parents for their approval and they had sent it on to me. In it, she said that my quest for our family history had gone beyond reason. I had shown a total lack of compassion and respect. And she ended with the hope that I could someday make amends with myself. I didn't bother to respond.

After a couple of days I wrote Art a letter. He had, in that very strange conversation, acknowledged for the first time that Anna was alive. I had to respond to what must have been a very frightening experience for him. I was not ready to give up on him despite what had happened. As it turned out, however, there has been no further exchange between us. I had hoped for a new level of honesty from him but he didn't respond, and I became unable to try again with him. The hurt was too deep.

Chapter 38

There was still my father. He hadn't known about my trip to Ohio, presumably, and I still wanted to reach him. I wrote him a strange letter, flippant and self-mocking. I told him about going to Ohio, holding Chien and crying, throwing a pillow at the wall in total frustration after talking with Nat, what Art had said. I told him that I wouldn't give up on Anna; I would find her eventually, even if she were long dead by then. And then, for the first time, my father began to answer some of the questions I had been asking. His letter was filled with nonsense and lies, but it had some answers, finally.

. . .

DUBOSE MORTGAGE COMPANY
Our Investments Will Earn You More Than Will
The Sweat Of Your Brow
August 28, 1979

Dear Daughter Kate:
Yours of 8/8/79 received and I am in a quandary as to how to reply. My brother Nat once wrote to me while I was in a battle in Germany -- (and wed to your mother). He flippantly suggested one thing and another about German girls. I became so angry I wrote and cussed him out for being a damned fool. Then in 1957 while May and I lived in Fair Oaks he wrote something equally stupid to me over which I gave him hell once again. Since then I've not received one letter from him in over 20 years. From brother Art

244

I receive birthday and Christmas cards, but from neither have I heard one word about your UN-warranted visits or calls to them in Buffalo. Strange!

When a negro born black comes to realize that by an accident of birth he is considered inferior and is constantly, daily reminded of it, he becomes bitter, resentful and unable to cope with it, does what he can to rise above his immediate destiny. Once had a general contractor named Charles Dolce working for me and whenever I introduced him to a client the client would ask, "What kind of name is that", I'd reply, "Italian". Charles as I could see in his face, resented being classed as an Italian. Just as each baby in my opinion, is a single entity, he or she looking like nobody else but itself, so is each individual a single entity. Just because she or he is born to parents of any nationality and/or religion is no reason for the innocent child to also be so branded. It is up to each child to rise above anything and everything which is part of its natal environment! Said Charles probably experienced as a child being referred to as a dago, wop, spaghetti, etc. As a child I was ganged-up-on by others in a totally Catholic neighborhood, called a kike, Christ-killer, etc., had my nose broken in UN-fair fights, all to my mystification. Then there came a time when I decided to assert myself, fight back, became so proficient with my fists, my former assailants who never fought me singly, became more fearful of me, called me Duke with respect and caution. Fists were then known as dukes, and my persecution ceased entirely. In those days all Catholics were taught by parents and church that if anyone was anything other than Catholic, they were heathens, would never enter heaven. So before leaving home and afterward because of my attendance @ Methodist and other churches including Catholic, I never acknowledged or told what my mother had been blessed or cursed with being born to, religionwise. I could always see and hear prejudice in most everyone (even today but -- not at me), remember the horrible pogroms I read of in Russia where the streets ran with blood of innocents, the terrible happenings elsewhere in this world. All those years I vowed I would never subject any future child of mine to that same, horrible abuse. In return for my concerns I now have two children; Spenser as far as I know is not prejudiced against blacks, etc. -- you keep harping about Yiddish! I am so sick and disgusted with your discussion of it I almost wish you were never born.

Back around 1952 one of my brothers told me that my mother died in a resthome. Your efforts as described by you to find her, border on the ridiculous! I wonder: have you spent (or wasted) as much time on your mother's side of the family? Did your mother tell you while teaching you the facts of life that upon my first visit home from an Army Hospital in 1946, her uncle Guy and his wife threw a party for me which was attended by Guy and his wife, your mother's parents Bert and Nana, Avis and I. And during the evening Bert got a bit potched and though seeing me all broken up in so many ways, he made the stupid statement heard by all present. "Look, my sweet daughter Avis 'could' have married the doctor she worked for as a secretary but instead married John who will probably not be able to support her," and much MORE crap that really made my evening. Did your mother ever tell you what a lovely homecoming I had? Did you learn about her two brothers Chuck and Tom -- both nice guys, who were always taking my part? About Michael's father, a fine guy as well, an air force officer who never after their divorce acknowledged or supported Michael? That before the divorce once became so angry, he threw a dinnerplate at your mother, it broke causing the bad scar on her left arm? That Michael's father, Sonny Giodano's parents ran the biggest -- whorehouse in Niagara Falls before and after Michael's birth? Should you and I be prejudiced at Michael for that or for being Italian? Would not your former husband resent being called or thought of as a 'dumb polock'? Ethnic compulsion and discussion plus the constant referral to it from you or anyone else, be damned; I do not want to hear anymore from you about it! There are higher and mightier traits and goals to pursue in this world.

I sometimes suspicion that you and/or Spenser may be critical of me because you both have more college training than I have of my grammar, syntax or semantics. I had two years of Univ. of Michigan study in Flint, Michigan learning the basics of that which I now use in my business. To get back to your first paragraph from which I quote out of context, "- my (your) fear of you (meaning of me)."

What the hell kind of fear can you possibly have of me? One time and one time only, I moved in your direction intending to spank you for your ever-worsening habit of refusing to eat what your mother prepared for dinner and your constant and arrogant piddling with it. Your mother objected and I never did spank you though I felt you really deserved it. As to my erecting another barrier between us; never intended to, never will, unless you or anyone else shows intent to hurt me or my great wife May in anyway. Besides, if you can be so critical of me without my asking for it in word or deed, why are you so concerned? Now I ask you: what is your motivication, what are your priorities? Are they peace and rapport with me, answers to my comments or continued disregard of them? When you are sitting in a home with friends and one makes a statement to you, do you answer in kind or speak of something UN-related? Then why do you do otherwise in correspondence? Your refusal to comment on what I say indicates to me as being cheap, feminine guile and/or dishonesty. I'm in a business in which people MUST reveal, answer questions and pledge their collateral; if they lie or appear false I do not deal with them. Was it not Sigmund Freud who once asked, "What does a woman want?" I ask you, "What do you want? For a man such as I who has practically a weekly appointment with a different doctor for different ailments, do I need anymore stress and strain from you or anyone else? Life is complicated enough without constant upset from anyone, particularly from one's children. I say that you had better straighten up and start flying right, be more truthful to both me and yourself, more mundane, forget the past in my family, etc., forget your foolish fears, as only you can hurt yourself. Either that or let's sever this for all time.

Further re my mother -- long ago a cliché was born: Let sleeping dogs (or situations) lie. I can understand why Nat and Art were angry with you, and you must understand that as there are matters in all religions and/or bibles that must not be questioned, the same is true in private life. I too was once naive -- when a girl would tell me that she was sick I would stupidly ask, "From what?" - instead of asking instead if I could help her in any way.

As to meeting between this Christmas and New Year's -- that's out. For over 20 years past I close up a few days before

Christmas, return a few days after New Year's day, happy for the respite, from work and that we had prior to leaving put up our Christmas trees at home and office. This year was long ago arranged, as are next year as well. Your thinking processes stymie me. All this harangue about 'how I was injured' (But never once have I mentioned your back! Are you confusing me with Spens?) and no concern of 'how the injuries left me feeling', the nine-hour operation time, etc. Do you ever concern yourself with priorities? I am not throughout this trying to scold you -- just trying to fathom your style or method of thinking.

Long ago I believe you one time stated that you needed a father to turn to. In my opinion, every child no matter what its age, needs both a mother and father to turn to. And at thirty-five you are not too old to do so now. But as stated in this letter earlier, if your method of turning to me continues as it has up until now, we had both best sing that oldie, "Let me go lover."

I repeat that, in NOT any of the above is there any intention to hurt or scold you. All of us are born babies, have to crawl before we can walk, have to experience many hurts, frustrations, before we can learn. But if we refuse to learn the facts of life, how to love and give to others, then the Good Lord above has wasted His time and effort in creating us.

Learn something from this Kate, for your sake, for my sake, for God's sake, and you will be a much happier person.

All the Best to you, Your Father

Afterthought:

It is my belief that had I not left you and your mother and been permitted by her to properly teach you, you would NOT be divorced from Joe Slaboda today. I can remember a day long ago returning home from work and being told by your mother that I better spank Michael right away because he had sassed her all day long, been incorrigible and nasty. Foolishly, I took him down into the basement where we lived then and spanked him. Though I did not spank him hard, he screamed and hollered as if he were being murdered. Then afterward he climbed the stairs crying, went right to your mother who then cradled him, wiped his tears and further mollycoddled him while she glared at me. (I remember that day, too.

That was the day that you held him by his feet and bounced his head on the cement floor. I remember.) I hope the Marines made a man of him. Have you learned from them just where Michael is now?

JD

Chapter 39

After returning from Ohio I was a bit numb for a while, and I buried myself in my work as a way to avoid thinking. For the first time since my separation from my husband, research became fun again. As I began to enjoy it more, I thought about it more and thus came up with interesting experiments more frequently. They, of course, made the work even more fun. I was in a positive feedback loop that was a return to the old me, the pre-divorce me, for whom everyday in the lab was a new adventure.

As the Jewish High Holidays were approaching, however, I began to feel very much excluded from where I should be. By *Rosh Hashanah*, the Jewish New Year, I was miserable with longing. I wanted to participate but had no way. Even if I had, I wouldn't really belong. That night Penny, my friend from New Jersey, called. She said that she had an extra ticket for the *Yom Kippur* services and wanted to know if I'd like to join her. "Come, Kate, we'll show you some of your beginnings. We'll teach you what it means to be a Jew." I instantly agreed, although it meant a very long drive, and felt a great unwinding inside me, a release of tension that I had not known was there. I was at peace in a fundamental way; at least some Jews felt that I belonged with them.

I drove to New Jersey for *Yom Kippur* and had supper at Penny's and David's house. After supper we walked to the synagogue. My first surprise was how beautiful the service was. I had had no idea that most of it was chanting and group reading, despite my intensive study for over a year. My second surprise was at the chaos. No one was chanting or reading exactly in unison. Each seemed to be going at his own pace. Some people were just talking to the people next to them, ignoring what was going on. There was a constant flow of people in and out of the room. Kids were running up and down the aisles. Altogether it was a far cry from the decorous services that I had seen in churches, and I loved it. I couldn't follow what was going on and finally gave up, read the English translation of the service, and then realized that I was doing what everyone else was doing: going at my own pace.

As I drove back to New Haven late that night, I decided to go to work the next day rather than continue with observance of the holiday. It really wasn't mine, after all, and I would know no one at the Yale service. I didn't belong there.

I went to work. All the Jews were missing, which meant that the lab was nearly half empty. During the morning the feeling that I was not where I was supposed to be grew stronger and stronger. Without clearly deciding to do so, at eleven I stopped working and drove to where the Yale Reform service was being held. It was over for the morning. I went back to the lab and worked until the afternoon service was to start.

Just like the night before, I was surprised. The Reform service was in English. There was no beautiful chanting, and everyone read in perfect unison. It was nice to know what was going on but the beauty and sense of freedom of the previous night were missing. There was, however, another kind of beauty that I found in the words of the service. They were mirroring, in symbolic form, so many of the different feelings I had experienced in a year of trying to join my father and his family. I felt a sense of belonging with that room full of strangers simply because their words could have been my words had I been able to express myself.

. . .

"Come in and sit down, Kate," the rabbi said. Employed by Hillel, he had an office in one of the massive gray stone buildings forming the freshman quadrangle at Yale. Rabbi Arnold Jacob Wolf was a short, pudgy man with virtually no neck and a warm twinkle in his eye. He had a well-trimmed salt and pepper beard. When I had called to make the appointment, his secretary, sitting in the outer office, had not asked why I wanted to speak with him. Now, though, he did.

"I'd like to talk with you about the possibility of conversion," I shakily began. As soon as I said that, Rabbi Wolf literally jumped out of his chair and ran towards the open door connecting his office with his secretary's. He closed it. When he was seated again, he asked me to continue.

"I don't know what's involved. I don't know if I'd be accepted as a convert, but I need to explore the possibility." I could feel my heart pounding as I talked.

"Okay, Kate, before we go into that, could you answer a couple of questions?"

"Sure," I said. "I'll try at least," wondering with a bit of fear what was coming next.

Speaking slowly and gently, he began. "How long have you thought about conversion?"

"In some respects, I've been fighting against it nearly all my life," I answered with surprise at my words.

He smiled then as he asked, "And now you've grown tired of resisting?"

"Yes," I sighed. Where had this sense of heaviness come from?

"Can you tell me about it?"

"It's more complex than I've indicated so far, but since I was at most twelve, I've been aware that I identified with Jews." He nodded to keep me going. "When I was seven I asked one of my neighbors what the difference was between Jews and Christians. Her answer was that Jews were still waiting for the Messiah while Christians thought He had come already. It made me decide that Jews understood the world better than Christians."

"How?" he asked.

"People were still fighting and killing each other. If the Messiah had already come, that wouldn't have been going on. Anyway, ever since then I've considered, then rejected, conversion. The question kept coming up, and I kept pushing it away. No one ever said to me 'don't convert'. I kept saying it to myself, though."

"Why?"

I sighed deeply before answering. He was good, really good, at asking the right questions. "There was a sense that I did not have the right to intrude. That must sound pretty strange, I guess." Rabbi Wolf shook his head no. "Maybe I would be found unacceptable, and I didn't want to face another rejection. Also, I've read that rabbis have the obligation to discourage a potential convert on three separate occasions, and I didn't think that I could take it."

"Did you have much contact with Jews as a child?" he asked.

"When I was a child, none that I knew of. I grew up in a town, Royal Oak, Michigan, that was restricted. No Jews or blacks could live there. The Shrine of The Little Flower, where Father Coughlin preached his antisemitism and support of Hitler was there. I then moved to a different town and in high school all the Jews from the neighboring town sent their kids to my town's school. Since the Christian kids dropped out at sixteen, the last two grades of high school were about seventy percent Jewish. Also, since I was in all advanced placement courses, in almost all of my classes, except for gym I was the only non-Jew. I even joined the Jewish sorority."

Rabbi Wolf laughed then and shook his head. "And I bet that you ended up as valedictorian, too."

"How did you guess?" I asked in amazement.

"Jewish kids are pushed to excel. They often overachieve because of that. I have the feeling that you weren't pushed, which means that you had to be very, very good to stay up with that competition. . . . Why have you stopped fighting against converting now? You've resisted it for a long time, something must have happened to cause this change."

I looked closely at him, measuring his ability to hear the answer, measuring my ability to trust him enough to give it to him. He was a kind and good man. He might not understand, but he would be able to hear what I was saying. "I found out that my father was raised as an Orthodox Jew." When I said that, Rabbi Wolf looked as if he had been slapped in the face.

"And you never knew?"

"No."

"Never suspected?"

"No. I haven't seen him since I was twelve."

"But you grew up with him until then?"

"Until I was eight."

"And he never mentioned Judaism to you?"

"Never, not once."

"And you concluded that Jews were right about the Messiah," he stated almost to himself. I didn't answer. He took a deep breath, then asked me how I had learned that my father was an Orthodox Jew.

The story flowed from me then. Outwardly calm, I told him about the abuse, my divorce, my work with Renee, finding out the family secrets, everything. When I talked about what happened in Ohio and how I had felt, I noticed that he matter of factly reached up to wipe tears from his eyes. That he could enter my space enough to cry endeared him to me forever.

When my story was over, silence entered the room. I sat, waiting. Rabbi Wolf stared out the window. When he turned back to me, he spoke with extreme gentleness in his voice. "I hear all sorts of tales. Many students come to me about their families. Usually the problem in Jewish families is too much entanglement and in Christian families the problem is too much distance. Your family is atypical."

"Crazy."

"Yes, probably crazy. In Chicago in the 1930's it was hard to be a Jew, Kate. That's where and when I grew up. Most Jews tried very hard to assimilate, few actually hid whom they were, though."

"I've assumed that they moved to Buffalo in order to be able to hide."

"That's probably true. They always stayed by the water, though."

"What do you mean?"

"Ahah! You missed that," he said with a touch of glee. "Odessa, Chicago, Buffalo, Detroit - all those cities are port cities, Kate."

"You're right," I said with admiration. "I never realized that. What do you know? My family needs to be near the water." For unknown reasons, that was a charming thought to me.

Rabbi Wolf turned back to practicalities. "Will your daughters convert, too?"

"No, I wouldn't even suggest that to them. They're fifteen and thirteen. If they convert, it will have to be out of their own needs now.

They're too old simply to follow me. I'd like it, but it probably won't happen." For the first time since we began I could feel tears forming. "Which means, of course, that ultimately my father and his brothers will win. There will be no more Jews in the family. Thousands of years of tradition will cease. I will be the last Jew." Okay, I would be the last Jew, that would be my role from now on. They would win, but they would not win until I died. "Rabbi Wolf? Is it wrong for me to think about converting if one of my reasons is to block my father and his brothers from reaching their goal as long as I can?"

"It would be, Kate, if that were your only reason."

"It's not, honest, but it is one of them. There are quite a few others. One, I feel like I'm carrying on the life that was taken from Anna, my grandmother."

"Many Jews today feel as if they must live their lives also for those who perished in the Holocaust. It is a noble desire."

"Also, there's the thought of that chain of observance that stretches back to the beginning of the world. I must not let it be broken. If I'm the last one, I can't help that, but I will not let it be broken before the inevitable happens. I will do what I can, that's all I can do." He nodded his understanding, swallowing hard. "Look, I know a lot about Jews, but I know very little about Judaism. I feel very ignorant. I don't truly know if I have any belief at all. But I know that I am willing to study, to learn, to begin to observe, at least to a certain extent. I'm willing to try to find what the Jew has always found through study. If I do, I want to convert. If I don't, I won't. Is that enough to begin with?"

He smiled. "It's more than enough at the beginning. All beginnings are hard, but I will try to make it easy for you. I still have more questions, though." When I nodded my agreement, he continued. "Is it possible that conversion will put distance between you and your daughters? You don't need more than you have."

"I haven't thought about that possibility. Probably not. I've been doing so much changing lately that a little more change won't even be noticed."

"Please consider it."

"I will. Thanks."

"As I've listened to you talk, Kate, it was clear that you have read intensively. It is also clear that you have some romantic ideas that don't match reality. If you'd like, I will give you some books to read, and we can meet once a week to discuss your reactions. Would you like that?"

"Very much," I answered with a sense of relief. Now I had a guide, a teacher. "I would like that very much. I thank you."

"Also, every Thursday evening I study *Talmud* with some graduate and postdoctoral students. Would you like to join us?"

"But I don't read Hebrew."

"We work with a translation."

"Then, yes, I would like that. Yes."

After giving me directions to the apartment where he met with the students to study, we went into the outer office. Except for doorways and windows, the entire room was lined with filled bookshelves. For so many months I had been scrounging through libraries and bookstores, trying to find every book dealing with Jews and Judaism that existed. Here, spread before me, was the treasure I had been seeking. Selecting three thick books, he handed them to me with instructions to read them and make a list of questions before I came to see him next week. Staggering out under that load, I was feeling good, excited, but wondering what I had gotten myself into.

Chapter 40

I remained in therapy with Renee when she came back that fall, because I needed her help in dealing with my experiences during the summer while she had been away. Yet, I could feel that the time for us to end was approaching.

Dad and I wrote each other several times that fall. Just as during the previous spring, we began to irritate each other more and more. I stayed with the flippant tone instead of going back to my normal straightforward and open letters, because it was getting results. Within it, however, I complied with his every request, answered his every question and commented in detail on everything he wrote. I was aware that I was pressuring him very hard as the fall went on, and that there was some risk of crossing the line that would lead to his total withdrawal. I was willing to take that risk because I wanted answers, because I was tired of reigning in my personality to accommodate to his limitations and, as the fall progressed, because my need to have him in my life was decreasing as he disappointed me over and over. He simply was no longer worth the effort. Had Renee still been helping me with the letters to him, perhaps there would have been a different outcome, but I was determined to handle him by myself.

During that period I reached the end of my ability to tolerate separation from Carole. Nothing was worth the wrenching that all of us felt. Becky missed her father and sister, I was concerned about Joe's parenting of Carole, Carole was clearly unhappy. And so I made a decision: I would return to Atlanta the next summer whether or not

I could arrange a job in the interval, and I would stay until both girls finished high school. I loved my work, but it was not as important to me as my girls. Somehow, I would find a way to support us for the three years until Becky graduated from high school, and worry later about repairing my career.

I told my father about my decision, of course, and that led to the end of our correspondence in a way that I do not understand yet.

Chapter 41

"It's over, Renee. I cannot keep up a correspondence with him any more. I simply want him to go away. I am sick of his back, sick of his 'good wife May', sick of his irrelevancies - Sylvia Porter, Howard Cosell, for Pete's sake, and Doris Duke. Doesn't he know of her work to prevent child abuse? I'm sick of his pompous tone, sick of his lies, sick of his twistings and turnings to evade the truth, sick of him! He still equates love with violence. The man is not even human! He doesn't understand human relationships and feelings. He uses the words but with a hollowness, an emptiness that indicate he does not understand. He's a pretend person, not real. He doesn't even speak English! He speaks another language that uses English words, but the words have a different meaning in his language. Renee, please! Can I stop?"

After my tirade, I expected Renee to ask me what I was overreacting to. Thankfully, she didn't. "Sure, Kate. You don't have to go on with this. I've been waiting for you to give up on him."

"Mike and I used to call it 'calling uncle'. When things got too rough between us, when someone was close to an overload, saying 'uncle' was the signal to back off." (Where had that piece from so long ago come?)

"Did it work?"

"Always, Renee. Neither of us ever pushed the other over the line. Anyway, I want to call uncle now. Can I?"

Renee paused before answering. "Are you calling uncle or are you simply tired?"

"Tired, profoundly tired. When I go to the mail box and see his handwriting on an envelope, I feel heavy and slow. I sigh deeply before gathering the energy to open it and read yet another bunch of nonsense from him. I've got a lot better things to do with my life than to waste any more time on him."

"Okay, Kate, you are hereby released from the task." Renee smiled at me. "You know, though, that there are several things undone?"

"Like what?" I asked with some puzzlement.

"Like, you haven't seen him," she responded.

"I know. I don't want to."

"Fine, but how much of not wanting to is fear and how much is disgust?"

I was quiet for a moment while I checked my answer against my feelings. "There's some fear, yes. It's still there. When I read that he had been thinking of flying here last spring, it was like seeing my nightmare in print. That scared me. But my fear level is much, much lower than it used to be. I haven't been depressed since I got my child back. I've gained a lot from this exercise in futility." Renee smiled again at the use of my self-contradictory words. "I see him with adult eyes now, Renee, or at least with mostly adult eyes. I can predict how he will respond now. I was pretty sure that this last letter would be outrageous, for instance. If I were his therapist, I'd be delighted by the progress I've made with him. But I'm not. I'm his daughter, and I am appalled by what he is revealing to me." I shook my head in renewed disgust as I stared at the floor.

Renee's soft voice floated across the room to me. "There's something else, Kate. You've never confronted him about his physical abuse of you."

"Yah," I sighed. "I never brought it up, did I?"

"Nope."

"It would have interfered with trying to get information from him."

"Are you sure, Kate, that that is the only reason?"

I had to smile at her sharpness. She was damn good. Superb, even. "You caught me, Renee. I could do it today, right now, but there's no point. It would be a gratuitous act of hurtful behavior on my part. I don't want to live with the thought that, during my last contact with my father, I deliberately hurt him for no purpose but revenge. I'm not protecting him; I'm protecting myself."

"You still love him," she stated.

"Yes," I sighed again. "Yes, I love him. It makes no sense, but I do. Look, there were times, admittedly rare, but there were times when he acted like a good father." Renee raised one eyebrow in disbelief. "There were, Renee. When I was three and scared by thunder, he turned out all the lights in the house during a storm. He sat with me by the window and showed me how beautiful the sky was as the towering clouds were revealed in the flashes of light preceding the noise. I've loved thunder storms ever since. He gave me a beautiful present. When I was five I was badly hurt while playing with a friend. My father came to get me, and as he carried me home and put me to bed until the doctor arrived, no person could have been more caring, gentle and reassuring than he was. He really did care the Halloween I had mumps and could not join the other kids who were having so much fun. He did love me, I know it. The times of love between us were rare, but they did exist, and it has done me no good to deny them. They were there, along with the terror and hate, Renee."

"Okay, Kate, you've convinced me that adult you, Big You, loves him. There's just two more topics I want to raise. The first concerns that bathtub scene you remembered." *(the elephant's trunk walks up my stomach leaving sticky patches in a random patter.)* "We've never discussed it. Do you think that you were sexually abused, Kate?"

I thought in silence about what she asked, measuring my feelings against what I had learned about sexual abuse. "I honestly do not know, Renee." *(the elephant's trunk waves in front of my face)* "The memory is very intense." *(it hits me on the nose moves up toward my eye)* "'It', the thought of 'it' happening again terrified me at the time." *(it slides down my cheek leaving a trail of wetness)* "'It' was obviously sexual." *(it caresses my neck)* "But I have not one single memory other than what happened in the tub that day that suggests sexual abuse by him." *(i try to move my head but his legs clamp it tightly between them i hold my breath hoping it will go away instead of eating me it pushes hard under my chin and I can't breathe i gasp for air and the elephant's trunk dives into my mouth)*

"What about by others?"

"The only other memories I have is from when I was about five and about eight, and they concern my mother, not him." (Now we were going to have to go into them, dammit. I should have kept my mouth shut.)

"Okay, Kate, give with the information," Renee said in joking tones.

Half-laughing, I began. "When I was about five, during the summer, my mother made me go to bed one night without any clothes on." (*the bedroom door slowly opens and light from the bathroom draws him in silhouette he stands without moving i lay without breathing a cord of tension connects us each knows that the other is aware*) "I begged and pleaded to be allowed to wear my underpants, she insisted that it was hot and I would be more comfortable naked. She wouldn't let me pull up the sheet, so I had to wait until she turned out the light and closed the door. I was so scared, Renee, I felt so totally vulnerable." (*i hear him walking down the hall towards my room the knob turns, the door opens i hold my breath waiting to see if I will have to go away again*) "But that was also the time in my life that I was scared of the dark, convinced that an alligator lived under my bed and would eat any part of me that hung over the side, convinced that bad men lurked in my closet," (*peter and the wolf hair and teeth and growling he put my head between his legs and jammed it in my mouth*) "and would get me if I were uncovered." (*my mother walks into the room wearing her snowflake dress one hand holds her side the other covers her mouth she sits down and watches my father bounce up and down on me*) "So I don't think the memory tells me anything except that my mother was insensitive to my fears." (*stupid kid i am sick of your stories and your lies forget about the elephant's trunk i don't want to hear about it again*) "What's new about that?"

"Did you fall asleep eventually?"

"When my mother was going to bed, I called out to her and, again, pleaded for some pants. She gave them to me and I instantly went to sleep."

"What's the other memory?"

"Nothing much," I evaded. "Just another example of my mother's insensitivity." (*i see the cot it is an army cot from the second world war olive green*) Renee looked at me, not even bothering to ask.

"Okay. I know what you want. *(i see my father)* I was eight or so. It was just after my father was hospitalized." *(the elephant's trunk is going to eat me)* "I started wetting the bed at night and my clothes during the day. I was horribly embarrassed about it, of course, and I tried to hide it. Well, Mom found out and decided that there was something physically wrong with me. She insisted that she had to exam me." *(he has his shoes on)* "I was crying and begging, but she went ahead with it. I think that I felt as raped by her as any female could possibly feel." *(he put his thing in my poop-place and my pee-place)* "Nothing was wrong with me, of course, except that I was regressing in response to what I had just lived through. Those are the only memories I have, Renee."

(i am three someone from behind is lifting me from being on my back to standing on the floor i look down i am naked and blood is flowing down my legs more on the left than on the right an exasperated male voice my father's says i asked you and I asked you and you said I wasn't hurting you i do not respond a towel hip-high comes around both sides of my legs from the back and I am being wiped off)

"For whatever it means, Kate, you do not have the psychological profile of someone who was sexually abused."

"I know. I read the books to check it out. But the memory is so very intense of that day in the tub, Renee. I was happy, content, enjoying his care, and then I was terrified. There's a sense in the memory of fighting this time, not letting 'it' happen again. What do you think, was I sexually abused?"

Renee sighed. "I do not know, Kate. From what you have told me, your sexual behavior is not like someone's who was abused, you don't seem to have any sexual problems at all. You have no other memories that suggest sexual abuse. I'm sure that you were reacting to something specific and sexual, but I don't know what it was. If I had to say something, I would say 'no, you probably weren't abused sexually.' But that's only a guess."

(i feel a vise-like grip from behind on my neck my father stands behind me holding me with his left hand at my neck his right hand comes around on my chest caressing we are in the living room in Royal Oak I am maybe four maybe five more four than five the contrast between what his two hands are doing is too stark he propels

*me up the stairs with his left i can see each stair thirteen in all there
is no carpeting they are a blond, highly shellacked wood he forces me
down the hall into his bedroom he closes the door he undresses me i
do not do anything i stand rigid he undresses he lifts me onto the bed
and then he bounces on top of me until I cannot breathe when he is
through i come back from my walk get dressed and go outside)*

I had to smile as I proposed, "Since neither of us are sure, let's
give my father the benefit of the doubt on this one, Renee. I have one
label, physically abused, that's enough for me. Okay?"

She laughed in agreement before continuing. "Okay. But, Kate,
there may come a time when you begin to have new flashbacks that
you cannot understand. I am not entirely convinced about the sexual
abuse. If you begin having flashbacks again, contact me immediately.
Will you promise to do that?"

"I will, but I am also sure that I will never again have another
flashback. We've gone through them all. I feel it, deep down. I'm
okay, Renee."

"Yes, you are now. I have a question for you, a tough one. Your
father was crazy. Is that the cause of his abusive behavior?"

I almost had to shake my head from the stunning blow that she
had delivered. Boy, she was good today! "No. . . . I never thought
about it, but no. . . . That is not why he abused me. My mother wasn't
crazy, but she was abusive. Most crazy people are totally non-violent.
Maybe being crazy made him more violent, but basically he's a
violent person who also happens to be crazy. I can't excuse what he
did on the basis of his craziness. That would be a cop-out for me, it
would be accepting my mother's interpretation of what happened and
I won't do that. For the last year, his letters have been abusive, Renee.
I've taken it, ducked when I could, because I wanted information. But
he has continued to abuse me in every single letter, with no exception.
The letter he sent to Spens was a horrible example of his abusiveness.
No," I said, shaking my head in rejection of the idea, "his abuse of
me was not from his being insane."

"And you want to end his abuse, now?" Renee asked.

"Yes, forever."

Part III: Moving Toward Roots

Chapter 42

The *Talmud* study group was both a completely new experience for me and something quite familiar. I had never sat down with anyone and talked using the particular set of assumptions of this group: God exists and it is our job to discover the implications of His laws. At the same time, the method of *Talmud* study was identical to the process used in my graduate education and daily in the lab. I had long ago learned to think in the way this group functioned and felt at home immediately with them, even though their assumptions were not mine. For the purpose of discussion I could work from any coherent set of assumptions. Occasionally, though, I got so caught up in the discussion that I momentarily accepted the assumptions without doubt. When that happened once, I found myself feeling very angry at God for the way He had designed the world. I ended the anger only by reverting to skeptical me, who could laugh at my ability to get caught up in what I was doing to the point of forgetting myself.

. . .

"No! I don't want to talk about it. Leave me alone." Damn, Renee. For four long years she had been badgering me. Was she never going to stop?

"What's happening, Kate?" she asked, ever patient.

"Your question scared me. I don't want to deal with that subject. Every time we take a close look at something, my feelings change. Sometimes, I end up letting go completely. This time, I don't want my feelings to change, not in any way."

"Okay," she said in pacifying tones. "We don't have to. Would you like to discuss the weather? Why you don't believe in reincarnation? How about chromosomes? I've heard that you're an impassioned speaker when you talk about chromosomes."

"Don't give me any shit right now, Renee. Chromosomes are my specialty, and you'd have to pay me if I talked about them, just like I pay you when you're talking about your specialty."

Damn her! She was smiling, almost laughing, at me. "You're paying me right now to talk about my specialty. Why are you wasting your money? I thought you were broke and couldn't afford to waste even a penny."

"Come off it, will you? I just don't want to talk right now. It's my money; I can choose to waste it if I want."

"Yep, it's your choice. Okay, I'm tired and need a break, anyway." I looked up at Renee. Her eyes were twinkling and she had a big grin on her face. We burst out laughing simultaneously.

"Okay! I'm being a rebellious teenager again. Everyone has the right to regress occasionally. The reason that I don't want to talk about Judaism is that I don't know what I'm doing. I'm embarrassed."

Renee looked surprised. Almost always now, I knew what I was doing. "Do you know why you're embarrassed?"

"Yah."

"Do you want me to drag it out of you, or are you going to talk?"

Boy, she could be irritating at times! "Choices! You're always forcing me to make choices."

Patiently, she explained again. "As I've said so many times, in a way you are your choices, Kate. What you do reveals what you are and determines your feelings about yourself."

"I know, I know. But I'm also more than what I do. I'm also all those feelings that allow me or force me to make any particular choice."

"Yes, and I want to know this part of you that is making a choice about Judaism."

I shook my head in negation. "I'm not making any choice, I'm just exploring. I won't be able to understand why my father and his brothers rejected Judaism until I understand what it is. Also, I feel very uncomfortable talking about religion with you."

"Would it help if you knew my feelings about religion?" When I nodded 'yes', Renee continued. "Okay. I'm a Jew, and I'm very proud of it." Renee is a Jew, too? "Being a Jew is central to my identity. Since we learned about your family I've been trying to understand what it would be like to deny that part of myself. I couldn't do it, it would destroy me.

"Notice that I haven't said anything about religion yet. Being a Jew is much more than a set of religious beliefs and practices. It's a way of life, a set of laws of behavior that reveal our value system. Being a Jew is doing far more than it is believing."

"Since I was a young child I have believed that there is a force out there somewhere, that sees to it that the sun comes up each day, that the moon and stars shine, that the earth keeps spinning. God is a good name for that force. That force isn't going to make sure that I get a new pair of shoe laces if I need them, and it's not going to pat me on the head and tell me that I've done a good job. It is, though, going to keep the world going, and that's a big job."

Fascinated by what she had said so far, hoping to keep her talking, hoping that eventually I could find a way to ask some of my many questions, I asked, "What about the laws in Judaism?"

"According to tradition, they are the way the Jew repairs the universe. You see, it was perfect before God introduced man, an imperfect creature. The covenant between God and Jew is that God will keep the world going and the Jew will observe God's laws in order to restore perfection."

I was feeling defeated once again. "That's a very poetic way to look at life. It's charming, really. But it's not for me. Look, Renee, you believe in a force that keeps the world going, I believe in energy flow and statistics."

"What do you mean?"

"Well, you see an intelligent power and I see a process. Think of a sine wave flowing over time. The wave, energy, passes above and below the X-axis. When it's above, it's positive energy; when it's below, it's negative. Where it crosses the X-axis, at the node, the absolute amount of energy is zero. Can you make that picture in your head?"

When she nodded yes, I continued. "Okay, according to the latest work in astronomy, the universe did have a beginning. There was a point in time when there was no energy. I think that astronomers are simply measuring back to the node. I think that the reason why astronomers have postulated a beginning point in time is that they are looking at the node and they don't have the instruments that can measure the preceding energy in our universe, in the time before the node. And people who believe in God, you for instance, may just be looking at the time when there was zero energy as the beginning point, also, and postulating a beginner. "

This was getting terribly complicated for Renee, I knew, because her mind didn't work in pictures the way mine did. She had words, but no pictures; I had pictures, but no words. Sometimes it was almost a miracle that we were able to talk with each other. "Are you following me?" When she nodded again, I continued. "Now, from the time of the last node until the present life has arisen. I see stochastic processes in operation. Suppose you're at point A and could go three different ways. Each of these ways has a certain probability associated with it. Now suppose that once you select a path, the path again subdivides, again with a probability associated with each branch. In such a way, you could end up at a point or condition that had a very low total probability of occurrence associated with it when you were standing at point A. I think that such a process, a stochastic process, led to the evolution of the universe and life. The beginning of life could have had a very low initial probability, but at each branching point the probability of choosing a path that led to life might have been fairly high. Also, there may have been several different routes to life. Now, if you can think of life as organized, localized energy, we're almost there. Instead of the evolution of life, then, we have the evolution of a localization of energy."

Poor Renee. She was getting far more than she had asked for. "When I think of life, that's pretty much what I see: a concentration of energy. More and more the findings in genetics tell me that life is one. To me, organisms and species are just convenient ways to subdivide the energy that is life."

"So I'm back to energy. If the laws of thermodynamics hold, and they have so far, the existence of a concentration of energy suggests a universe finite in time. But as I said already, what is measured as a beginning may just be a node. If it is, then time can be infinite and a stochastic process can account for life. That leads to the fourth law of thermodynamics which I postulated in my Ph.D. comprehensive exam: given an infinite amount of time, the highly improbable has a high probability of occurrence. And thus our universe and us exist."

Wow! That had come out sounding more rational than I would have guessed. It was a pretty good explanation. "What I've just said may not make sense to you, though. It's hard to translate the moving pictures I see into words. I see swirling clouds of probability, which probably says nothing to you. I see a beginning that may be a node and an end that may be a node. I have to break the rules of science to come up with a prime mover."

Very gently, Renee interrupted me. "Kate, some people call energy God or life God."

"I can't, Renee. First, life is just organized energy. Second, organized energy is a localization in time and space due to an outcome of a stochastic process that had a high probability of occurrence in infinite time."

"You've been telling me what you think. How do you feel about what you think, Kate?"

"Ah, Renee," I said with real sadness, "that conclusion leaves me feeling as if the universe is dissolving and slipping through my spread fingers. The beginning and end are process, which has no characteristic except the ability to make itself manifest. It's a lot, and nothing, on which to hold."

"Non-anchored?" she guessed.

"In a way. It certainly increases my sense of aloneness in the universe."

"How?"

"My problem is that I've chucked my old identity, which was destructive, and I need to find a way to orient myself in time and space. The way I want to go is to return to what once was in my family before everything went so bad. That way, Judaism, is blocked off to me by my view of the world."

"I don't see how."

"Well, it's obvious to me. To become a Jew now, I'd have to convert. Conversion is a religious act requiring belief in God. I believe in energy flow and stochastic processes. I'm too well-trained as a scientist to become a Jew."

Renee smiled at me with what looked like fondness. "I think that if you asked a rabbi what constitutes a good Jew, he would say that a good Jew is one who observes the Law. He wouldn't mention belief at all."

"Really?" Maybe there was a way out of my predicament after all.

"Take my word for it, Kate. I've been a Jew longer than you have." We both had to laugh at that.

"Okay, Renee, I will the next time I meet one."

"Now can we please go back to my original question to you? What are you doing about Judaism?"

"I've been meeting with a rabbi once a week. He and I talk about what I've been reading." I was feeling a little sheepish. "Also, I study *Talmud* with a group once a week."

"And how long has this been going on?" Renee asked with a tinge of exasperation.

"Nearly two months," I answered meekly.

"Do you enjoy it?" That was a surprise question!

"Yes, very much. It doesn't make any sense for me to enjoy it, but I do."

"Why doesn't it make any sense?"

"I don't believe in God, remember? What am I doing studying a non-existent God's laws? It's totally irrational."

"Yes, it is, and you've been enjoying it very much."

"Yes, that's my problem. How can I possibly enjoy something that makes no sense? It's like I've got two parts: I'm a totally logical scientist and I'm a totally illogical *Talmud* student. The parts don't fit together." My embarrassment was causing my cheeks to flame red.

"They will," Renee reassured. "You're learning how to let a little irrationality into your life for the first time. Did you really expect to change a lifetime habit overnight?" I shook my head no, not so much because I hadn't expected it, but because that would be a dumb expectation had I thought about it. "Besides, Kate, I'm willing to bet that you are very logical in your *Talmud* study, which requires logic above all. Do you really think that your *Talmud* study is irrational? Some of the greatest thinkers in the world have studied *Talmud*. Were they being irrational?"

"No," I defended myself, "but they were brought up within the system. I wasn't. It's artificial for me."

"Not if you're thinking about conversion. Are you?"

"Sort of," I admitted.

"And so you're sort of seeing how it feels to be a Jew? I don't see anything irrational in that. If you were to convert without a prior investigation, now that would be irrational."

I wanted to laugh and let go of the topic, but I had one more important question. "But why am I thinking about conversion? That's what doesn't make sense."

"Sure it does. You could construct a very tight argument to justify what you're doing. It would be an argument based on emotional experiences and needs. Kate, your feelings are as real as this table here. It's okay to take them into account in your actions. It's when you don't that you get into trouble, in fact. But what bothers me about what you're doing is that you haven't told me about it before. If I hadn't asked, would you have continued in secret, reading about Judaism at night under your covers with a flashlight, in the same way that you read as a child?"

"No, I'm not reading under my covers again. Do I have to tell you everything that I'm doing and why? Can't I have a little bit of privacy? I'm really getting tired of this."

"Whoa, Kate! You're sounding scared again. By now you know darn well that not wanting to talk about something is an indication that it's connected to your childhood experiences. Why don't you think about that until I see you next week?"

Chapter 43

Eventually I began going to the Friday night service at Hillel. At first it was very confusing, and I could not follow the group for more than two minutes without getting lost. There is never enough time to complete one section before going onto the next in a Jewish service. Because it was all new to me, I had too much to absorb to handle everything even if there had been enough time allotted to each section. Week after week I had the frustrating experience of reading about the same one third of each section before skipping ahead to the next in order to stay somewhere close to where everyone else was. Week after week, I eventually gave up trying to remain in synchrony with the rest and sat back and either read at my own pace or just enjoyed the atmosphere.

I never missed a meeting with Rabbi Wolf; the times with him were, in some ways, the best that I had each week. Our talks ranged over the centuries, from Abraham coming down out of the mountains, to the emperor of Japan asking him from what point Jews counted time. From the beginning, of course. In the *Talmud* it says that whoever teaches *Talmud* to someone is like a father to that person. Rabbi Wolf, my teacher, became like a father to me. He taught me the Law, but he taught me more than the Law. He taught me new ways of seeing the world, just as Renee had done before him. During my last months in New Haven, I was confused and undecided about what Judaism meant to me, but the support of the two of them allowed me to explore it with eagerness and joy.

My discussions with the rabbi and with the *Talmud* group, my experiences on Shabbes, at times it all seemed very strange to me. I wondered often about what I was doing. I didn't know where it was leading, but I was not pressing myself to come to any conclusions. I was simply learning and considering. At some point I would know what would be best for me, and then it would be time to act.

What made it possible for me to continue doing whatever it was that I was doing was the traditional Jewish emphasis on behavior. Thoughts and feelings do not truly matter in Judaism; only the behavior of a person counts. A good Jew is one who obeys the Law. If I had to wait until I believed in Judaism, I would never get to the point where I could even begin to explore conversion. Conversion is a religious act, requiring belief; but belief, like feelings, comes from behavior. And so I acted and waited with curiosity to see what my behavior would do to my feelings and belief.

. . .

"Imagine, if you can, a gigantic white oval-shaped structure. Its surface is highly polished, with a depth to the whiteness that seems to go on forever. And the whiteness has pinks and blues and other soft colors in it if you look closely. As you approach it, you see a small opening, one just big enough to allow entry. You enter and first perceive only darkness. As your eyes adjust, however, infinitely far away, towards the top, you see flashes of light, beautiful colored light. It appears to come from many mobile-like structures. And as the mobiles slowly revolve, you hear the gentle tinkle of bells. Almost you don't hear and you don't see because the lights and sounds are so fragile and delicate.

"I call this my egg, Renee. To reach it I need only to close my eyes, and I'm enveloped by a sense of wonder and gentle awe. My egg is always with me, just inside, an eye blink away. It's so incredibly beautiful that I would like to invite the entire world inside to rest in the peacefulness. My egg, my beautiful egg, offers calm and quiet and a sense of joy. When the world outside is spinning in confusion and noise and rushing, I can go into my egg and feel a child's primary delight at beauty. It's a beauty beyond understanding but always there." It felt so very good to share my egg with Renee. Without her I never would have reached it.

When she spoke, her tone was as soft and as gentle as mine had been. "It sounds as if you're pregnant, Kate."

"Maybe I am. If so, it's not with child."

"When did you first notice your egg?"

"I don't know exactly. A couple of months ago, maybe. I know that I should have told you about it before." Renee nodded yes and I smiled at my old habit of secret-keeping. Maybe I would never learn. "But I had to keep it as just mine for a while. I was afraid that it would go away if we talked about it."

"What is your egg, Kate?"

"I'm not sure, Renee. It may be a new level of peace inside me. It may be Judaism. I'm not sure. Sometimes I think that it's love."

"What kind of love?" Always with the questions, that one. Well, her questions had taken me very far from the beginning.

"For my child, the world. Who knows?"

"Does it scare you at all?"

Oops, she guessed. "At first it did, " I admitted. "It's rather crazy to have a gigantic egg inside you, isn't it? Do you know anyone else in the world who has this kind of internal retreat, filled with beauty?"

"Many people," Renee reassured. "Most aren't as acutely aware of it as you are, most can't see it as vividly or describe it so graphically, but many people carry peace around with them like you're doing."

"Do you?"

"Sometimes, yes. I can't see mine, though, because I don't think and feel in pictures like you. I just feel it, I guess. It's knowing who I am, being pleased with myself, knowing that I'm doing what's right, loving myself. And so much more, of course."

"Do you suppose that my egg will stay with me from now on?" I asked with concern for it.

"I can't tell, Kate. You know that I'm not good at fortune telling." We smiled at each other with fondness, her for my consistent asking for reassurance, me for her consistent refusal to predict. "I would think, though, that it will stay with you as long as your child feels secure and protected by you."

"It's like an added, unexpected, beauty bonus that I got just for reaching that child. It wouldn't be there if I hadn't done it. All these years that I've lived without my egg when it could have been mine, Renee!"

"Are you angry?"

"No," I said, shaking my head. "I'm just terribly sad that I have missed so much that is beautiful in life. I could have had it all along, maybe. Maybe if my parents hadn't been so bad at being parents, maybe I could have had it with me from the beginning."

"Or maybe something that beautiful could only have been yours by going through all the hurt and pain that have been yours. Maybe it's your reward for your struggles. There's no way to know, Kate."

"I know, Renee, I know. Maybe, even, it was a gift from you which you couldn't see but I could. Maybe it's just love that you gave me, and in the giving it grew to fill up all available space inside me because love given generates love in return."

"Like rising bread will fill up all space?"

"Sort of." I looked across the room at Renee and felt the full force of all the time and patience and understanding and, yes, love that she had been giving to me for over three years now. How could I ever possibly repay her? The weight of my debt to her, the sheer hopelessness of repayment, pulled down at me and, again, I felt acute sadness.

"What's wrong, Kate?"

I sighed. "Nothing. I'm just feeling sad."

"About what?"

"It's going to sound crazy." She waited, not saying anything, giving me the time to feel the pressure of the growing silence and to feel my need to talk. "It's like this. I was looking at you, remembering, and I could feel everything that you have given to me. I can't possibly repay my debt to you. There's no price that could be put on what you've given to me. And so I was feeling inadequate and grateful and very privileged and a bit overwhelmed by the hopelessness of my situation."

Renee spoke slowly, staring intensely at me. "Can your girls ever repay you for all that you have given them?"

"No, but I don't expect them to. It was my job to give, theirs to take what they needed. Someday they will give to their children in the way that I have given to them. That will be their repayment to me."

"Love flows down the generations?"

"Yes. It's the uninterrupted flow of love and caring which keeps people human."

"Is our situation so very different, Kate? True, it's been a lateral flow of love in our case, but you are going to take what I've given to you and pass it both horizontally and vertically. And you're going to receive it from others in the same way, just as you always have. That's my repayment, Kate."

Chapter 44

Christmas Day, 1979. Two years ago exactly, I had been fighting off a waking nightmare. One year ago, I was going through the motions of celebration for my children and trying to figure out who I was. This year was going to be different. The girls were with their father again this year and I was free to spend the day as I wanted for the first time in my life.

I slept until nearly noon, took Chien for an hour's walk through the snow, then settled in front of the roaring fireplace with a good book. Not until late afternoon did I actually realize that it was Christmas.

As early dusk settled in, I pulled out the phone book that I had received from the telephone company the day before. It was for the small town of Canton, Illinois. Pulling out my stationery, I began writing Anna letter after letter. The home where she was would deny her existence if called but they would also give her any mail that came for her. I wrote her at each of the nursing homes listed in the phone book.

Dear Bobe [Grandmother],
 I hope this reaches you. I have been trying to find you for a very long time. Everything is fine with me except that I need to hear from you. Please write.
Kate

The message was unimportant, I could have written anything. If she got my letter she would be confused at anything in it. I didn't expect her to answer or to write. I expected to get all but one letter back, and the missing one would tell me where she was.

The letters started coming back marked "Not here," "Not a patient," "Return to sender." I checked off each home as the letters arrived. Then on Friday a letter came back marked "Expired -- return to sender." She had died sometime since last August when I had been in Ohio. I had found her, but I was just a bit too late. From the moment that I had learned she was alive, I knew that I was racing time. I lost.

Anna died for the third time on Friday. She had been dead for thirty-four years for me. She came alive for a little over a year, she died briefly when I was in Ohio, and then she died for the third time on Friday evening.

She never knew of my existence even though our time on earth overlapped for thirty-six years. She was never told about me. I, in turn, will never know how she looked, how tall she was, what her voice was like. I will never know now what could bring a smile or a frown to her face. Never will I have the experience of seeing her for a moment in someone else.

I went to the Hillel *Shabbes* service, asked the rabbi about the Law, and he said that I could say *Kaddish* for her. At the beginning of the service I sat in the back row crying quietly and filled with anger. My family had successfully kept Anna and me apart. None had had the decency to tell me of her death. I would show them; I would do for Anna what none of them could do. I would say *Kaddish* for her because, no matter how she ended, it must have been important to her at her beginning. I would say *Kaddish* for her because, by saying *Kaddish*, I would be accepting what my family had so shamefully hidden. *Kaddish* would be my revenge.

Then I remembered the Law: a person must rejoice on Shabbes. Even mourning must be suspended. All around me people were singing with joy, and it was my obligation to join them. As I reviewed the last year and a half, I began to sing also.

I stood at the proper time and began the ancient hymn of praise. Never had I felt connected with the past quite as much as I did then. I don't know who the people from my past were, but they survived long enough to raise children, who survived long enough to raise children who . . . my existence is proof that I am part of a chain of survivors that extends back to the beginnings of life on earth. I am proud of them all, and thankful. Without them, I would not be. The efforts of all who came before me to survive obligate me to continue to survive for as long as I can. They did not know that I would exist one day, but if they had, they would have wanted me to live for as long and as well as I can. I am of them, and I will do my best to ensure their wishes.

I said *Kaddish* for Anna and for me. Because I had needed nine other people in order to say it, I had gone to a place of joy with tears in my eyes. I ended up singing.

. . .

"She's dead, Renee, she's dead! On Sunday I called the home where she had been, and a nurse told me that she died about two months ago. She fell and broke her hip about the time I was in Ohio looking for her. She never recovered." I watched Renee through my tears, hoping for a word of magic that would take the hurt away.

"And now you're mourning."

"God, yes, I'm mourning! I wanted to see her so badly, I tried so hard. I'll never see her now. I'll never hear her voice now. It's too late, she's dead. My goddamn family has won. They beat me. The bastards managed to keep Anna and me apart long enough for her to die. They didn't have to do it, they could have let me see her. I wouldn't have hurt her. I just wanted to look at her, to hear her talk, to know that the woman in front of me was my grandmother. Is that asking so very much of life, to see your own grandmother? It didn't have to be this way, the bastards made it this way."

"No, Kate, it's not asking too much. And, yes, Kate, they made it be this way. They couldn't let you see her."

"But why?" I pleaded, as if Renee could tell me.

She sighed heavily as she answered, "Neither of us will probably ever know why. 'Why' lies in the long ago, Kate. It's buried under their hurt that is so strong that it blocked them from responding to your cries of help. They couldn't do it, Kate, or they would have."

"Yah," I said with deep bitterness, "and I had to pay the price for their hurt." I looked out the window, not seeing, tears pouring down. God, how I hurt. Anna, my grandmother Anna, was dead.

"May I tell you a story, Kate?" Renee asked with gentleness.

"I guess so."

"When Ken, Dawn and I were on that camping trip last summer, we drove through the western part of Canada. It was heavily forested. One night we set up camp after dark." God, why was she bothering me with irrelevancies now? "I awoke very early, at sunrise, and walked by myself through the woods. After a little bit, I came to a tremendously large field that stretched on and on. It was filled with brilliant red flowers." As Renee talked in an hypnotic fashion, I could feel myself calming down. The tears still flowed, but the anger and sense of outrage were beginning to diminish. "I had never seen such a flower before. It was small and delicate. The carpet of red was one of the most beautiful sights I had ever seen. We had a flower identification book with us, and later that morning I looked it up in it. The book said that this flower was the first plant to grow after a forest fire. So what I had seen was an area that had been burned very recently. It had been the site of a tremendous fire. Trees had been destroyed, animals had been killed there. The destruction was recent and it must have been terrifying."

Renee stopped talking. It was clear that her story was over, but I couldn't see the point of it in the first place. Puzzled, I said, "And?"

"Kate, something very beautiful can come out of what you are experiencing, in the same way that a raging forest fire gave rise to the carpet of red flowers. Your hurt and pain and disappointment can be the basis of something entirely new, something so beautiful that it will take peoples' breath away when they see it. You can use what you are feeling to make that beautiful thing, if you want to."

I looked at Renee, feeling her words, not knowing what to say. Anna, my grandmother Anna, was dead. This time she was dead for good. A two year search for her had ended in failure. I remembered my surprise and joy upon learning that she was alive. I had learned her language so that I could speak with her. I had been so foolishly sure that I would find her in Canton, Ohio, and I had been so devastated when Art told me that Autumn had lied to me. I had set off on an adventure into my family's past, and I had found Anna, my child, my egg and Judaism. Anna was gone, but I still had my child. My egg glowed inside me, a work of wonder, and I had found a home in Judaism. I was a Jew, no one could ever take that away from me again. Carole was waiting for my return to Atlanta, and soon I would be there, helping her to grow into the beautiful person that she could be. Becky would be with me. Spens was a part of my family again. Maybe Mike would be again someday.

So many wonderful changes had happened in my life. I had struggled, been terrified at times, bursting with hurt, hurting so badly that I was nothing but hurt at times. Without Renee I could not have done it, but without my own courage I could not have done it either. There had always been a core of health in me, a basic goodness, a still, small voice that had fought on my side at the worst of times, and I had trusted blindly in its existence even when I had no reason to suspect its existence.

Anna was dead. My search for her had given me my self, and I could take that self now and use it. I could use it in my work, in my play; I could use it to reach other people. I could use it in love. I could be a point in the tangled web of relationships from which, and hopefully to which, flowed love, caring, nurturing and giving. Anna, Renee and I had made all of this beauty possible. Still crying softly, I went over to Renee and held her for a long while. Comfort and peace enveloped me, and my egg glowed brilliantly inside me.

Part IV: Reprise

Chapter 45

Peter and the Wolf, hair and teeth and growling. He put my head between his legs and jammed it in my mouth. The elephant's trunk walks up my stomach and leaves sticky patches everywhere. The cot, I see the cot jumping out at me. There's no where to hide, Sis, just forget it, don't remember it, it didn't happen. Where do I go when I go away? White, all I can see is white. The elephant's trunk waves in front of my face. It hits me on the nose, moves up toward my eye, slides down my cheek, leaves a trail of wetness. It caresses my neck. I hold my breath, hoping against hope that it will go away instead of eating me. I try to move my head from side to side, but my head is clamped tightly between his legs. It pushes hard on my neck. I gasp for air and the elephant's trunk dives into my mouth, down, down, tearing me apart. My egg is broken.

Chapter 46

I delay. I do not want to write what needs to be written next. I would just as soon leave this part untold. No one needs to hear it. Yet, the still, small voice that has kept me going since childhood says that I must continue now. It is important to tell all.

. . .

In 1985, while I was stopped at a red light, a car ran into mine, tearing some back muscles, breaking four vertebrae, and herniating four disks. When I had X-rays of my neck and back for the first time in my life, the doctor looked at them and asked, "What happened to you as a child? You have all sorts of indications of broken bones, and your back looks as if you are at least 30 years older than you are." I was so stunned by his question that I almost did not hear the rest of our conversation because of the images of my parents beating me, throwing me, hurting me, that were streaming through my brain. Their acts were actually engraved in my bones.

Immediately after the accident, I began to have flashbacks of sexual abuse by both of my parents, and the peace I had achieved while working with Renee was shattered by them. The flashbacks continued for several years, during which time I slipped into the classification of a chronic pain patient. Finally, the flashbacks broke through into awareness, and I learned for the first time of my sexual abuse. My mother had used the business end of an enema bag, and my father had used what Nature gave him. With that awareness, most of the physical pain ended. It returns at odd moments and at times when either my stress is too great or I have done something physical that I should not have. Even a sneeze or prolonged headache can trigger the muscle spasms and pain, though. I now have eleven herniated disks and a scoliosis that makes my back look like a bowtie on X-ray, so pain is always lurking even when I am feeling good and stress is very low.

At the time I was working with Renee, I was incapable of bringing the flashbacks of sexual abuse into awareness. Most of those memories were stored as body memories, rather than as verbal or visual memories, because I had dissociated (gone for walks by the ocean) during the times of sexual abuse. Also, I was extremely young when the sexual abuse was at its worst and could not put words to the events then. I needed the simultaneous stimuli of touch and pain to bring the memories forth, which gradually occurred during physical therapy after the accident. If I had not had the experience of extreme pain coupled with touch, I may never have known about the sexual abuse in my childhood.

Once again I went to see Renee, and she strongly urged me to get back into treatment to have help dealing with the memories. I remember so clearly sitting next to her on the couch, her arm around me. We had been talking for an hour or so. "Katie," she said, "you can handle this, too. You can get to the bottom of the damage, remember the bad, replace it with good. You can do it, Katie, I know that you can. You already know how to do it from me. Now you can take that learning and use it to heal yourself. It's going to be tough, but you can do it."

Renee was in New Haven and I was in Atlanta, so I found a therapist who was skilled at dealing with post-traumatic stress disorder (PTSD). Her eventual diagnosis was a relief to me because I had come to suspect it: I had multiple personality disorder. It took thirteen years of hard, painful work to convert the remaining eighty-seven parts into the whole that is me today. Renee and I, in all our work together, had managed to fuse only two parts, the four-year-old and the eight-year-old kids.

What about my egg? Somehow, the therapist and I managed to do the impossible: we put Humpty Dumpty back together again. I do not know how we did it. That time is a blur to me, a period of my life that evokes shudders when I try to remember. All the bright spots stick out like mountain tops in a fog, like driving through the Smokey Mountains early on a summer morning: times of laughter with my children, the graduation of each of them from college, Becky's marriage, the births of my grandchildren, the purchase of a small place on an island off the coast of Charleston so that I could walk the beach in reality, the publication of textbook after textbook, celebration of *Shabbes* and the Jewish holidays with close friends, watching my grandchildren play T-ball and soccer, simple pleasures from interacting with people whom I love, all those times are islands of brightness surrounded by fog and mist. I had many students, I loved, I laughed, I cried, I clung to my dog when things got really bad, and the therapist and I rebuilt that egg. It is as beautiful as it was when I was working with Renee. It glows with soft lights, pinks, and blues, and yellows, and other soft colors, magical music is in the background, almost not to be heard but definitely there. I can see it when I close my eyes, and sometimes when they are open, too. It is right inside, a place to go when the world gets to be too much, a place of renewal, a place of love.

Epilogue

All the work with Renee was thirty years ago. I returned to Atlanta in 1980. Carole immediately moved in with me, and both girls stayed with me until they went to college. Once more we became a family, and we remain close today. Carole is an accountant who now has her own farm and numerous animals. She also has a small side business that holds animal shows monthly, and sometimes Becky helps her with it. Becky managed a many-horse stable and worked for a veterinarian. Next, she sold veterinary products and was extremely successful. Then, she married a wonderful man and had two even more wonderful children, a boy and a girl. Becky and her husband are married for life, and she is ever-so-much better as a wife and a mother than I was. I teach genetics in a local university and have published nine textbooks, along with many other works, mostly scientific. I converted to Judaism in 1981 with Rabbi Wolf, who by then had a congregation in Chicago. I had to do it again in 1984, when the local Hillel rabbi explained to me that I was not a real convert until I had been in the *Mikvah*, or ritual bath.

In 1981, I met Spens in San Francisco, and then we drove to Sacramento and met my father in a Red Roof Inn restaurant. I was not scared. As the evening went on, I saw my father for the first time with adult eyes, just as Renee had wanted for me. I saw that he was a man to whom façade was all. I saw a man with no depth to his personality. I saw what so many years of lying did: it eliminated all but the superficial. Several times during the evening he tried to check

291

A Still, Small Voice

on how much I remembered from so long ago, including the bath tub scene. I pretended not to have any memories, which both pleased and emboldened him to check more and more. Thus, I confirmed many of my memories.

I think he thought he had escaped scott free, with no memories by me of what he had done, and that was okay with me. When we parted he said, "If I have harmed you in any way, I hope that you will forgive me." That "*If* I have harmed" caused a flash of internal anger but I did not want to live with the fact that, during my last encounter with my father, I ended it on an angry note. My decision protected me, not him. So, I quietly replied, "I understand." I did, too. I understood that he was so lost as to who he was that he could never acknowledge what he had done. I also understood that my fear was over and my anger was hurting only me. I turned away from him and had no further contact with him.

In 1993, Mike called me. He, too, became a part of my family from that point on, and the world felt right once again for the first time since Spens went to live with our father. My two brothers were back in my life.

Our father died in 1994 after a series of strokes. While he was in a nursing home in Sacramento, two women tried to get him released into their care. That was during a time when a ring of gypsy women in Sacramento were getting old, dying men to change their wills to give all their possessions to them. The TV program *60 Minutes* had recently run a story about them that I had seen. I was called by the nursing home, which was wondering if they could release him to the women. At that time, my father was paralyzed, could not talk, and was being fed by intravenous tube. When I said no and that the nursing home should call the police to report an attempted kidnapping, the women took off and were not heard from again. I doubt if they even knew him.

Our father died several days later. Spens and Mike were the only two at the funeral, which they had conducted by a rabbi. I did not attend. When it was over, Mike called and sang, "Ding, dong, the witch is dead!" He sent me pictures of our father in his casket as proof.

In going through his papers afterwards, Spens found the citations that proved he had been injured, but just not as he had always said. Later, I found much more information online. He was not a tank commander. He was a mortar platoon leader, which I think might be more dangerous and require more courage than riding in a tank. Instead of being blown out of his tank, he received a minor wound on his nose from an artillery fragment on December 23rd, 1944. That is how he received the Purple Heart. His platoon was almost overrun several times by German soldiers from December 17th through the 23rd. That was along the Belgium-German border in St. Vith, in the Battle of the Bulge. For his actions during that battle, he received a bronze star on January 11th, 1945. He disappears from the army records after January 11th and I do not know how he received his back injuries. My mother lied about the jeep accident in Georgia and perhaps the nurse who was supposedly with him. Why? That is just another unknown piled up on the heap of unknowns. He lied about his role during the war and definitely about his severe back injuries, for which he did not receive a Purple Heart. Why? Perhaps he did steal a jeep and ran into a tree after pulling out of the Battle of the Bulge, but in Belgium or France not in Georgia. All I know is that he was with General Patton, and the best information I can get about his experiences because he is dead is to watch the movie *Patton*.

A year and a half after all became one and my life became internally peaceful for the first time, my stomach ruptured as I took the first bite of supper at my friends' house. After surgery and tests the diagnosis was stage IV lymphoma. Although the cancer is in my stomach, it is not stomach cancer. It is a cancer of the type caused by the bacteria that results in ulcers, even though testing showed that I had never had contact with that bacterium. It was carefully explained to me before chemotherapy began that my cancer had been around for twenty to twenty-five or even more years. It could be controlled, but it could never be eliminated because it was so slow-growing. It has been four years since I had chemotherapy.

My brothers were actually more damaged as adults than I was, perhaps because they were male and felt they could not ask for help as adults, perhaps because they did not dream, as I did, of something else than what was, perhaps because I have always wanted to understand everything and they did not share that with me, or perhaps because I saw that change was possible at eight, during my father's commitment hearing, and they never did. Each was at least as bright as I but that did not protect them. In turn that suggests that my intelligence, *per se*, is not what protected me, either.

All I know for sure is that I held onto those pieces and fragments into which I was broken until I found people who could help me fuse myself together. Psychotherapy, both with Renee and the woman who followed, was much worse than chemotherapy. Even I find that statement to be extreme, yet I know it is true. Without the psychotherapy, however, I could not have endured the entire surreal experience of stomach rupture, diagnosing it myself instantly and telling my friends to get me to the hospital immediately, surgery, being told I had stage IV cancer, and having chemotherapy while I continued to teach. Without psychotherapy I would have experienced what happened to Mike when he had successful surgery for prostate cancer and required no additional monitoring at all. He fell into the pieces that he had become so long ago and reached the point where he literally could not even move, totally destroying what little he had built of a life.

I was lucky enough to have the ability to make cherished friends (one dates back to when I was four, others to when I was eleven), to be able to distinguish good and helping people from those who are not, to have the wisdom to hold onto some people and let go of others, and to be able to act on my desire to belong to a community, composed of Jews and non-Jews, that would shelter me in times that became tough. When I was in the hospital, for instance, friends took chewing treats to my dog where she was boarding. Others took her out for an afternoon run in the woods with their dogs. When I was just out of the hospital, many friends fed me. When I continued teaching during chemotherapy, one friend made my supper every night. That allowed me to expend my last ounce of energy on walking my beloved Labrador retriever in the woods every day instead of cooking. On days I could not summon that last ounce of energy to walk my dog, others did. I found this community not by chance and not by active seeking, but largely through the grace of one woman who had been more damaged by abuse than I. I thank her as I thank all of my community for their support and help.

Acknowledgements

I thank Maureen MacLaughlin for her superb editing job.

Many people, so very many, have helped me learn that, despite appearances, there is much good in our world. Some do not know of their role, others remain nameless even to me, but a partial list of those who helped must include the following: Addie, Aimee, Aldine, Arnold, Avi, Barbara, Betty, Carole, Chrissy, Cindy, Colleen, Con, Chrissy, Danny, David, David, Debby, Deborah, Emmanuel, Eycke, Jack, Janet, Janet, Jessie, Ken, Kathy, Kelly, Kermit, Marty, Mary, Mel, Miriam, Monica, Myla, Paula, Penny, Peter, Rick, Sadie, Sam, Sandi, Stan, Susan, Ursula, and Wes. Without Renee Rocklin, though, none of it would have happened.

Taken June, 1947, at the farm of Tom, the author's uncle and the brother of Avis. From left to right, top: Nana, the author's grandmother, age 51; Emily, the author's great-grandmother, age 76; Avis, the author's mother, age 28. Bottom: the author, age 3 ½. The crease in the photo was made by Avis when she folded it and placed it in her album, with the author hidden from view.

The author's paternal great grandfather, Samuel Bozman, at age 6 in 1891. The photo was taken in Odessa, Russia.

John, the author's father, age 33. Approximately 1943.

Mike, the author's older brother, age 3 ½-4; Avis, the author's mother, age 25. Approximately 1943.

Chuck, the author's uncle and the brother of Avis, age 25. Approximately 1943.

Both photos taken October 22, 1944, at the house of Bert and Nana, the author's grandparents. Avis, the author's mother, age 26; the author, age 8 months.

On the back in Avis's handwriting: the author "refused to behave for this one."

On the back in Avis's handwriting: the author "raised ---- in this one. My posture is horrible due to her struggles, sorry, Sweet."

Both photos taken December, 1944, during the Battle of the Bulge, at the house on Westmoreland.

The author, age 10 months; Mike, age 4 ½; Bing, the family dog.

Mike, the author's brother, age 4 ½; Bing, the family dog; Avis, the author's mother, age 25; the author, age 10 months.

At the house on Westmoreland. The author, age 20-22 months.1945.

At the house on Westmoreland. The author, age 28-30 months. 1946.

Taken in 1946, at the house on Westmoreland. The author, age 3.

Taken in June, 1947, at the farm of Tom, the author's uncle and the brother of Avis, the author's mother. Blackie, the family dog; Mike, the author's brother, age 8; Jean, the author's aunt and Chuck's wife, age unknown; the author, age 3 ½.

Both photos taken in 1950, at the house on Alexander, in Royal Oak, Michigan.

From left to right: Mike, the author's brother, age 11; Avis, the author's mother, age 31; the author, age 6; Spens, the author's brother, age approximately 18 months.

Mike, the author's brother, age 11; the author, age 6; John, the author's father, age 40.

At the Veteran's Administration, in downtown Detroit. Spens, age 4; the author, age, 7. 1951.

At the house on Alexander. Spens, the author's brother, age 4; the author, age 7; Mike, the author's brother, age, 12. Late 1951.

Photo taken in 1954, while on a day trip to a Walled Lake with the author's father. The author, age 10; Mike, the author's brother, age 14 ½; Spens, the author's brother, age 6.

Photo taken in 1962, for graduation. The author, age 17.

Renee Rocklin at approximately the time the author was working with her (1976-1980).

At the South Carolina coast where the author has a condo. The author, age 46; Jessie, the author's yellow Labrador retriever. 1990.

The author in South Carolina, approximately 1994.

Printed in Great Britain
by Amazon